Preaching Romans from Here

Preaching Romans from Here

Diverse Voices Engage Paul's Most Famous Letter

Edited by
Lisa M. Bowens
Scot McKnight
and Joseph B. Modica

CASCADE *Books* · Eugene, Oregon

Cascade Books
An Imprint of Wipf and Stock Publishers
199 W. 8th Ave., Suite 3
Eugene, OR 97401

www.wipfandstock.com

PAPERBACK ISBN: 978-1-7252-5817-4
HARDCOVER ISBN: 978-1-7252-5818-1
EBOOK ISBN: 978-1-7252-5819-8

Cataloguing-in-Publication data:

Names: Bowens, Lisa M., editor. | McKnight, Scot, editor. | Modica, Joseph B., editor.

Title: Preaching Romans from here : diverse voices engage Paul's most famous letter / Edited by Lisa Bowens, Scot McKnight, and Joseph B. Modica.

Description: Eugene, OR: Cascade Books, 2023 | Includes bibliographical references and index.

Identifiers: ISBN 978-1-7252-5817-4 (paperback) | ISBN 978-1-7252-5818-1 (hardcover) | ISBN 978-1-7252-5819-8 (ebook)

Subjects: LCSH: Bible. Romans—Criticism, interpretation, etc. | Bible. Romans—Sermons.

Classification: BS2665.52 P80 2023 (print) | BS2665.52 (ebook)

VERSION NUMBER 12/18/23

To my family (Bowens and McKoy) for your steadfast examples
of what it means to live a life of faith and encouragement
in the midst of a groaning creation (Romans 8:22).

For my student-pastors (McKnight) who yearn to preach Romans in
a way that makes sense to the gospel's calling for multiethnic, diverse
churches where the grace of God flourishes in the power of the Spirit.

To my grandchildren (Modica): Olivia , Joseph, and
Emmett—thanks for giving me the hope, joy, and peace
in believing the good news is for all (Romans 15:13).

Contents

Acknowledgments

We are grateful for the many contributors to this volume—who have now become "friends." They showed us the value of understanding Paul's letter from diverse perspectives. We are also grateful for their perseverance while navigating the challenges of the COVID-19 pandemic (our project began in March 2019). They were a joy to travel with on this project.

Many thanks to our editor Michael Thomson for his vision, encouragement, and patience with this project. We are also thankful to Rodney Clapp for his editorial acumen and to Rachel Saunders and others at *Wipf & Stock* for bringing this volume across the finish line.

Contributors

Efrain Agosto is Bennett Boskey Distinguished Visiting Professor in Latina/o Studies at Williams College.

Raymond Aldred is director of the Indigenous studies program at the Vancouver School of Theology.

Eric D. Barreto is Frederick and Margaret L. Weyerhaeuser Associate Professor of New Testament at Princeton Theological Seminary.

Lisa M. Bowens is associate professor of New Testament at Princeton Theological Seminary.

Raymond Chang is president of the Asian American Christian Collaborative and the Executive Director of the TENx10 Collaboration at Fuller Theological Seminary.

Carlos A. Corro is lead pastor of Imago Church and the executive director of Reflectors Consulting.

T. Christopher Hoklotubbe is director of graduate studies of NAIITS: An Indigenous Learning Community and assistant professor of classics at Cornell College.

Melanie A. Howard is associate professor and program director of biblical and theological studies at Fresno Pacific University.

Cheryl Bridges Johns is visiting professor and director of the Global Pentecostal House of Study at United Theological Seminary.

Regina Langley is an independent scholar based in Pennington, New Jersey.

Te-Li Lau is associate professor of New Testament at Trinity Evangelical Divinity School.

Sung Uk Lim is associate dean and associate professor of New Testament at Yonsei University.

Gerald C. Liu is the Emerging Faith Communities Cultivator at the Great Plains Annual Conference of the United Methodist Church.

Scot McKnight is professor of New Testament at Northern Seminary.

Joseph B. Modica is university chaplain and associate professor of biblical studies at Eastern University.

Jinwook Oh is visiting professor in the department of social work, Sejong Cyber University.

Amy Peeler is the Kenneth T. Wessner Chair of Biblical Studies at Wheaton College.

Brian Robinson is an independent scholar based in Media, Pennsylvania.

David Rudolph is director of Messianic Jewish Studies and professor of New Testament and Jewish studies at The King's University.

Sze-kar Wan is professor of New Testament at the Perkins School of Theology, Southern Methodist University.

Eric Lewis Williams is assistant professor of theology and black church studies at Duke Divinity School.

Joel Willitts is professor of biblical and theological studies at North Park University.

H. Daniel Zacharias is associate dean at Acadia Divinity College.

Introduction

Lisa M. Bowens, Scot McKnight, *and* Joseph B. Modica

1. Why This Volume? (Joseph B. Modica)

This introduction begins with an uncommon *mea culpa*. In a previous volume, *Preaching Romans: Four Perspectives,*[1] the editors (McKnight and Modica), with a keen insight from Scot's wife, Kris, realized that the volume was lacking diversity, especially among the sermon contributors.[2] After pondering Kris's astute observation, we (McKnight and Modica) decided to correct this deficit. What is presented here is that correction.

Truth be told: the editor of our first volume took a position with another publisher. He was very interested in this new project. We then brought along an essential person to be one of the editors (Bowens), who had just published a landmark volume on African American readings of the apostle Paul.[3] Her ingenuity, leadership, and collaboration have been indispensable. So there you have it: a second volume on reading the apostle Paul's Letter to the Romans.

This volume is structured with seven main essays highlighting various perspectives—racial and ethnic as well as topical—on reading Romans. This time we tried to be as inclusive as possible. A question inevitably is: Could there have been other perspectives represented?

1. McKnight and Modica, eds. *Preaching Romans.*

2. There was nothing wrong with what was submitted, it just needed more intentional diversity.

3. Bowens, *African American Readings of Paul.*

Undoubtedly, so perhaps we'll offer another *mea culpa* here; yet we still believe this volume fills a necessary lacuna and will serve well the academy and church.

Each essay also has accompanying sermons demonstrating the perspective described. Often it is in preaching that one can clearly hear how a perspective influences an interpretation. We hope that you'll read (and reread) these essays and sermons with the hopes of understanding Paul's message anew for us today.

2. The Importance of Social Location (Lisa M. Bowens)

It has been an honor working with Scot McKnight and Joseph B. Modica on this volume, which lifts up the significance of diverse voices for interpreting Romans. These diverse voices illustrate the value of space and place for biblical interpretation. In the introduction to *True to Our Native Land*, the first African American New Testament commentary, the editors write, "Space matters. Where we come from and who we are influence how we read the Bible and how we translate it theologically so that it becomes meaningful and effective in our lives."[4] This statement underscores the fact that the space we inhabit influences the questions we bring to the text, the questions we allow the text to bring to us, the themes we lift up in the text, and the particular characteristics we recognize in the text in our preaching and teaching. Space and place shape how we see and interpret Scripture and at the same time Scripture shapes our own space and place. For example, in the invitation letter sent by the editors to the contributors, we commented that Romans is the most influential New Testament book for Christian theology in the history of the church. In his essay, Raymond C. Aldred records how he responded when he first read this assertion. He writes, "I remember thinking, 'Maybe where you're from, but not around here!'"[5] Writing from a North American Indigenous perspective, Aldred demonstrates that many Indigenous peoples see the gospel as one great story and rather than viewing Romans as a theological treatise, they see Romans as testimony and witness to Jesus's presence with the Indigenous populations. Hence, reading Romans from his Indigenous space opens up interpretive possibilities for those that do not

4. Blount et al., eds., *True to Our Native Land*.

5. See the essay by Aldred in this volume.

inhabit that space but are now invited to listen to, hear, and learn from one who does inhabit such a space. Aldred's essay is only one of the many powerful compositions within this monograph.

It is important to note that these interpreters are not articulating *the* Asian American perspective, *the* Latino/a/x perspective, *the* Indigenous perspective, and so forth. We recognize that within each of the perspectives presented here, diversity exists. That being said, readers of this volume will see that in the following pages these interpreters preach Romans from their particular space and the spaces of their respective communities. In doing so, they help us to expand our own inhabited spaces by enabling us to see the text with new eyes and hear truths within the text that we may not have heard otherwise. The communities represented in this volume speak to the value of their inhabited spaces and at the same time speak to the inhabited space of all Christian believers. From the beginning of the early church, God called believers to inhabit a diverse space, a space created by the outpouring of the Holy Spirit upon women and men from various nations around the world (Acts 2:4–12). The unfortunate reality is that the church has often failed to live fully into this diverse space due to its complicity in racism, sexism, and oppression. Yet the wooing of the Spirit relentlessly beckons the church to live out its divine identity even in the midst of current intense societal divisions that often demand and mandate our allegiance. *Preaching Romans from Here*, however, bears witness to the greater allegiance God calls believers to re-member and em-body, that is, both the diversity and unity of the people of God: "So we, who are many, are one body in Christ, and individually we are members one of another" (Rom 12:5).

3. Can There Be Unity in Diverse Readings of Romans? (Scot McKnight)

In a recent scan of more than a dozen books of sermons on my shelf from a diverse group of preachers, and the names need not be mentioned to save my own skin, I found almost no sermons on Romans. There was not one sermon on Romans 5–8 in these books. I was taken aback, if not stunned. I wondered if it was the case that mostly white evangelical men like to preach from Romans. I don't have an answer to that question, but I do know from experience the evangelical preachers love Romans and Paul and Galatians (if they are in a hurry). Which does answer that question somewhat.

What we have in this collection of sermons challenges both the absence of sermons about Romans for many and the one-sidedness of the white evangelical's obsession with the categories of Pauline soteriology. This is an obsession that can avoid the social dynamics and implications of Paul's theology, not least of Romans, which in chapters 14 and 15 does more than its share of upsetting some tables in early house church divisions over who's got the best approach to the table life. These sermons as individual sermons and as a collection challenge the standard absence and also show the inadequacy of too many sermons on Romans. The implications of the theology of Romans collide with much of American society, and these sermons will contribute to that collision.

The essays and sermons in *Preaching Romans from Here* clearly locate Romans in a specific context, and as such the voices in this volume speak words that will prove discomforting for some preachers of Romans. They will challenge social injustice and racism and classism and sexism. But something will come to the surface more than once: these writings will use the very text used by others but this time around they will subvert the dominant readings and sermons about Romans.

Over the years I have read deeply in Pauline studies and that means in Romans scholarship. The tensions between the Reformation and the new perspectives are noticeable, as is tension also between the apocalyptic approach and the Paul within Judaism theory. What I have been fundamentally surprised by is that when it comes to Romans 5–8 the categories all these proponents use are not only the same (Spirit, flesh, sin, grace), since if you are doing Romans you have to do it on Romans' terms, but they are understood in very similar categories. One might search then for unity between Pauline studies today by concentrating conversations on Romans 5–8. Paul would jump up and start clapping if we did so because those chapters are designed to bring together the weak and the strong in the house churches in Rome.

The unity one finds in the major terms of Romans will, however, by subtle shiftings of meaning turn many a sermon and many a reading of Paul inside out. For that we can be thankful to those willing to show us their cards in these essays and sermons.

Reading and Preaching Romans in the Puerto Rican Diaspora

Eric D. Barreto

Locating Romans is a critical step in preaching the letter's vision of a God whose promises are true, whose grace transforms the world, whose love knows no end, whose justice sets all things right. Here, I do not mean primarily finding the particular locations of the communities in Rome that first heard Paul's letter read aloud. Nor do I mean in the first place foregrounding the historical and cultural realities of life under the Roman Empire, as scholars can best reconstruct them. These are important locations of Romans for the preacher and the exegete alike. Here, however, I am referring to the location of the contemporary readers of Romans. Those locations—richly diverse and powerfully pluriform—are a vital resource for faithful, prophetic proclamation of Paul's letter.

Romans has clearly not suffered from scholarly or homiletical neglect. This very volume will certainly join an ever-growing section of a seminary or a preacher's library. If anything, however, its *occasional* theologizing has tended to be *universalized*. Paul's particular concerns with specific communities whose members Paul explicitly names and whose stories he seems to know and whose hopes and fears he allows to shape his writing, have attained in the reading of many a universality that seeks to transcend social location. For some, that universality—this sense that the content and vision of the first readers of Romans escapes the particularities of any one place or time—is the very theological heart of the letter. That is, the power of Romans for some preachers comes from its transcending of any one moment or location. In preaching Romans, therefore, many seek to find a kernel of theological insight so persuasive and powerful that it escapes the particularities of our moment and even the moment of the letter's earliest reception.

This essay proposes, alongside many other scholars but especially minoritized readers of Paul's letters, that the very particularity of the reading locations of those communities we have been called to serve are at the very heartbeat of our proclamation of Romans. The aim of the preacher of Romans is thus not to extract universal theological insight but to dwell with this text's particularity alongside and interlaced with the particularities of a specific community today. Moreover, paying attention to diverse and different communities and trusting that God's voice will speak through the particularities of their interpretation is not a homiletical problem for the preacher to solve but the very site where the Spirit might imbue our preaching with a wider grace than we may have first imagined.

In the case of this essay, I draw my attention to the island of Puerto Rico, the place that has shaped me into the person and follower of Jesus I am today.[1] Struggling under the weight of colonial rule for generations, the people of Puerto Rico and its diaspora bear within their bodies stories of courage, persistence, and faithfulness. In that way, the narrative about God's faithfulness that Paul weaves in Romans finds a vibrant home among the stories of Puerto Ricans in a way that illuminates vividly the homiletical import of Romans, not just to fellow Puerto Ricans but any who seek in Romans a word from God today. In short, I propose that this Latinx community's reading of Romans is valuable for all kinds of communities.[2] In communities largely shielded from the deleterious effects of colonial rule, it may even prove necessary.

---

1. See also Agosto, "Islands, Borders, and Migration." Here, Agosto makes a compelling case that Puerto Rico's status as "a contested space—a border—one now being crossed by thousands of departing Islanders" creates privileged exegetical space to make sense of "the border and sea crossings of the ancient migrant worker, the Apostle Paul" (151).

2. To be clear, what I propose is a—not the—Latinx and/or Puerto Rican reading of Romans. Latinx communities are diverse and complex in a way that belies the seeming simplicity of the terms used to label Latin American-descended communities; the theologies of these communities are equally diverse and complex. See Aponte and de la Torre, *Introducing Latinx Theologies,* and Valentín, *Mapping Public Theology,* 5–37. In addition, though the number of Latinx biblical scholars remains alarmingly low, our contributions to the study of the Bible is extensive. See, e.g., Agosto, "Hermeneutics"; Hidalgo, *Latina/o/x Studies and Biblical Studies*; Lozada, *Toward a Latino/a Biblical Interpretation*; and Segovia, *Decolonizing Biblical Studies.* See also González, *Santa Biblia,* and Lozada and Segovia, eds., *Latino/a Theology and the Bible.* For an introduction

Reading from Puerto Rico and the Puerto Rican Diaspora

When Hurricane María reached the shores of Puerto Rico, the storm devastated the island. Estimates by George Washington University's Milken Institute of Public Health pinned the number of dead at nearly three thousand.[3] The storm was devastating, but its effects were also an echo, a revelation of the vicissitudes of the United States's colonial rule that had dominated Puerto Rico for more than one hundred years. A more significant outlining of Puerto Rican history and culture is beyond the scope of this essay, yet I do want to spend some time here setting the context of a reading of Romans from Puerto Rico and the Puerto Rican diaspora.[4] That is, I will provide only an initial sense of these contexts in order to invite readers from other social locations to begin to imagine the richness this one island and its diverse people might invite in the reading of Romans. I will do so with a particular focus on how the winds and rains of a hurricane revealed the colonial realities that mark life in Puerto Rico and the Puerto Rican diaspora alike.

We can mark the beginning of the history of the United States's role in Puerto Rico in the wake of the end of the Spanish American War, when control over Puerto Rico shifted from Spain to the United States in 1898 as a spoil for the victor of the conflict. In 1918, Puerto Ricans were granted citizenship in the United States even as the political imagination of the United States sought to create a space for Puerto Rico that was neither statehood nor a colony. And thus a number of legislative and judicial decisions has continually sought to define the undefinable and to deny the undeniable: the reality that a colony exists within the bounds of the United States. Economic policies have fractured industry and agriculture alike on the island over the last one hundred years. All this political and economic neglect has resulted in a financial crisis in recent years in Puerto Rico.

And thus all along the way the mass migrations of Puerto Ricans to cities across the United States have reshaped those cities but also Puerto Rico itself. The extractive realities of colonial rule apply not just to physical resources and labor but to the people who leave home, seeking

---

to preaching in Latinx contexts, along with several sample sermons, see González and Jiménez, eds., *Púlpito*.

3. Milken Institute of Public Health, *Project Report*.

4. For a brief and readable introduction to Puerto Rican history and culture, see Duany, *Puerto Rico*. See also Barreto, "Puerto Ricans."

something beyond the colonial restrictions imposed on Puerto Rico. For several generations, significant numbers of Puerto Ricans have moved from the island, first to the northeast United States and cities like Chicago, and more recently to Florida. More Puerto Ricans today live in the mainland United States than on the island itself.[5] And the effects of Hurricane María only accelerated these trends. The Puerto Rican diaspora calls many cities in the United States mainland home.

So, when Hurricane María arrived on the southeastern coast of Puerto Rico on September 20, 2017, the devastation the storm left behind was not just a natural disaster but the remnant of a political and colonial sabotage. In the end, Puerto Rican stories and identities are tied to the experience of being colonial objects, to be sure, but that is not the entirety of the story Puerto Ricans tell. Puerto Ricans have also discerned ways to be subjects of a narrative about persistence and bravery in a particular place, an island that nurtured flourishing life even as an outside force sought to suffocate the breath of a people via colonial force.

My interpretation of Romans confesses that these experiences of coloniality illuminate preaching of a text written to a community living at the very heart of the Roman Empire. Paul and the communities he seeks to shape also find themselves wrestling with the realities of colonial rule. Living, belonging, and believing at the very cartographical heartbeat of the Roman Empire, they all would have been shaped in clear and subtle ways by the empire's conquests, propagandizing, and the social and urban environment Rome crafted. The experiences of colonial life in Rome and San Juan are not identical, of course, but that's not the exegetical or homiletical argument I hope to pose. Instead, contemporary experience will illuminate exegetical and theological insights into the Letter to the Romans that other contexts will not make clear in the same way.

Themes in Latinx Theology

Let's also turn to another key ingredient in this approach to reading and preaching Paul that can be found in the rich, diverse contributions of Latinx theology more broadly. Related to and influenced by Latin American theologies and especially liberation theologies, Latinx theology

5. The United States Census Bureau reports a population of just over three million inhabitants of Puerto Rico in 2019 (see their QuickFacts chart) while The Center for Puerto Rican Studies at Hunter College estimates that nearly six million Puerto Ricans lived on the mainland in 2019. See their "Puerto Ricans in the United States at 2019."

centers the lives and faith-filled experiences of Latin American descendants living in the United States and Canada. Latinx theology is complex, encompassing a diverse set of communities tracing ancestry and historical experiences to an equally diverse set of countries and communities in Latin America. What holds these various theological approaches together is a conviction about and commitment to discerning God's presence in and among Latinx peoples and communities. Here, I highlight four particularly helpful insights that emerge in Latinx theologies.

Teologia en conjunto

In many Latinx theologies, community, communal discernment, partnership, and allyship are distinct spaces for God's activity. Such theologizing is a collaborative, communal, collective effort more than the strivings of disparate individuals. This conviction and approach is named "*teologia en conjunto*." Such a theological approach foregrounds how dependent all Christians are on one another, on the witness others bear, on the ways communities together deliberate the shape of God's grace. Such an approach assumes that theological insight can emerge not just from gifted, traditionally educated theologians but from everyday folks learning, living, and loving in ways not often acknowledged by academies and even churches.

Thus, reading and preaching Romans from a Latinx perspective calls for us to engage a *community* of readers together discerning the shape of God's faithfulness according to Paul's letter. This would mean, of course, pondering the composition and shape of the communities who first heard Paul's letter read, by, for instance, paying close attention to the litany of names with which Romans closes.[6] Instead of seeing these names as detachable from the theological heart of the letter, they represent the first readers of a letter likely shared orally by Phoebe. It is their stories, questions, hopes, and fears that sparked Paul's composition of Romans and thus our preaching of Romans must return to an historical and even imaginative re-creation of their lives and faithfulness.

And yet an approach to *teologia en conjunto* would also extend necessarily to those of us who continue to read these letters in diverse contexts today. *Teologia en conjunto* suggests that the fullness of God's voice we might hear in the interpretation and preaching of Romans

6. See Gaventa, *When in Romans*, 6–14.

cannot be found in a univocal, homogeneous interpretive space. Instead, the witness of Latinx communities, our pluriform experiences of colonial rule, our stories of the promises and costs of migration are not detachable components of interpretation that we must sacrifice in order to attain purportedly objective exegesis, but a powerful venue for the Spirit's activity, a clarifying path by which God can make God's voice that much more evident.

Reading in Context

Second, Latinx theologies have emphasized the contextuality of all biblical interpretation and every theological approach. Latinx theologies embrace the particularities of culture and perspective as attributes—not deficits—in biblical interpretation and theology alike. The rich contexts from which we read and theologize are therefore not mere impediments on the way to universal biblical and theological claims for all peoples at all times but the very path by which the Spirit makes possible a diversity of faithful interpretations.

Latinx biblical interpretation in this mode deems "objective" biblical interpretation impossible but also undesirable. Too often, biblical interpretation claiming to be objective and free from bias only masks the particularities of the interpreter; that masking can function perniciously by occluding biases that sustain colonial imagination and preclude the gospel's promise of resurrection life. Thus, a Latinx reading of Romans would take seriously the contextuality of every reader, every reading, every proclamation. A diversity of approaches and interpretations is therefore also not a problem to lament but the very interplay that allows for God to speak in many languages, in many contexts, to many peoples. Moreover, the contextuality of every reading does not call for us to retreat to our own ethnic, theological, and ideological enclaves since a single reading will prove impossible to discern. Instead, the plurification of reading approaches calls for us to be lovingly curious about the ways communities other than our own read and interpret and preach. The aim in discerning the contextuality of all readings is not the siloing of interpretation but the encouragement of curious listening to the witness other communities bear, not so that we can claim—or worse own—the readings of others or merely appropriate them for our own contexts, but to appreciate the diverse ways God has spoken in other communities and to wonder how God might well be teaching us something about God's grace in the words and languages and contexts of a community not our own.

Lo cotidiano

The first two theological insights lead to a vital third, an insight I think is the very drive-wheel of many Latinx theologies. Latina theologians and mujerista theologians like Ada María Isasi-Díaz contend that robust theological insight can be found in the everyday lives of those most marginalized by the structures of the world.[7] Isasi-Díaz turns especially to Latina women laboring in often invisible though indispensable ways: tending hotel rooms and offices, caring for the children of the wealthy, cooking and cleaning in the kitchens of fine restaurants. *Lo cotidiano* suggests that there is significant theological value in turning away from centering academia and pulpits in our search for theological insight and instead focusing attention on the faithful lives and transformative perspectives of those laboring on the underside of history.

A God in Solidarity with and Who Liberates the Afflicted and Oppressed

All these approaches to the nature of interpretation and community culminate and are rooted in a confession about God's power to liberate and God's commitment to the poor, the afflicted, the marginalized. In this way, the influence of Latin American liberation theology on Latinx theology is evident. That is, even as I focused above on sketching how Latinx theologies tend to imagine how we read, proclaim, discern, and preach in *community*, that communal effort is intimately connected to a *God* who draws near to those who yearn for justice and a world turned upside down.[8]

What we have to understand is that whether in the case of the churches of Rome to which Paul wrote, the contemporary Latinx

---

7. My own work and preaching has been particularly shaped by Isasi-Díaz, *Mujerista Theology*.

8. As Tamez, *Amnesty of Grace*, 114, contends, "But God did not [free the human being and condemn sin at the same time] from outside the world of God's creatures. God did it through human beings in order that they too might participate with authority in the liberating event."

communities who wrestle under the weight of colonizing forces, or the communities to which any of us is called to preach, these communities and their belonging together were not and are not mere vessels for Paul's important ideas. They were not and are not just temporary homes for Paul's universal, lofty ideas. These ancient communities themselves were Paul's best ideas; better, these communities are manifestations of God's own goodness and grace. The shape of these communities and their theological shaping are not incidental to Paul's letter; they are utterly necessary if we hope to understand Paul and his letters two thousand years hence. God speaks through Romans not by setting our doctrine right so much as setting our lives back into place, a place God created for us, a home where God's gifts are most tangible. And that home is the place where we worship, the place where we eat, the place where we lament and rejoice, the place where we belong. That home has been carved out by God for us. That home is belonging.

In the case of Romans, the focus on a God who saves, liberates, and transforms the world is a most necessary homiletical aid among those preachers who tend to turn to Romans in search of a sense of *our* salvation more than *God's* righteousness, *our* deliverance more than *God's* activity of liberation. Instead, a Latinx approach would point to the way God's liberation and the transformation of a community's life are intimately tied one to another and thus both are simply indispensable in the preaching of good news according to Paul's Letter to the Romans.

Turning to Romans

With these contextual pieces in place, we can turn to Romans and wonder what distinctive preaching perspective communities in Puerto Rico and the Puerto Rican diaspora might bring to the pulpit and how those perspectives might just illuminate how other communities need to hear God's word in Romans anew and afresh. In short, these preaching approaches draw communities to the immediacy of the crises we face and how God draws near to those who suffer precisely and graciously in those moments when all seems lost.

Sin and Death and the Full Shape of Salvation

In Romans 6:11, Paul exhorts, "So you also must consider yourselves dead to sin and alive to God in Christ Jesus." Dead to sin and alive to God in Christ Jesus? There are days when that confession seems easier to voice than others. When death is not stalking our communities in the twin forms of pandemic and racism, police violence and anti-black prejudice, destructive storms and the legacies of colonial neglect, it may seem more possible to confess confidently with Paul that we are dead to sin and alive to God in Christ Jesus. But when sin entangles every aspect of our everyday lives, when racism and sexism and homophobia and colonial imaginations worm their way into every corner of this world, it may prove that much more difficult to proclaim along with Paul that I am, that we are dead to sin. How then might we proclaim that we are indeed and truly and wholly dead to sin?

Perhaps we have to move carefully here so that we can connect this ancient confession and the realities of the world today. Paul is describing not the world as it is, the world he saw with his own eyes. After all, he lived in a world where empires reigned and spilled blood, a world of hunger and want, a world of disease and plague. Even more, I wonder if Paul is describing not even the world as it could be, some placid dream, some intoxicating promise that lets us float on the high of a heavenly destiny while we suffer in the moment. So also, our preaching of this text ought not invite our communities to naïveté or an empty dream. No, Paul is describing the world as God is making it, the world God is crafting right here and right now and forever. Paul's declaration that we are dead to sin is a way to collapse the future of God's promises and the present of our realities, a way to know and feel and be the resurrection people Jesus has already made us to be.

As I noted earlier, I worry that too many Christians and especially too many preachers see the letters of Paul as a pile of confessions, a litany of doctrines, a list of things we believe on a checklist. In the church where I grew up, Paul was often a favorite source for all our deepest convictions. Paul's letters leapt out from a distant culture, time, and place with the freshness of the moment because they were letters written directly to us, to address every question of doctrine, every inquiry about dogma. The letters were distillations of what we believed. The letters were carriers of Paul's thinking, injected directly into my mind so that I too might know the mind of Christ.

But what if we realized that Paul's letters were not the careful, organized thoughts of the theologian as much as the anguished, desperate storytelling of a preacher at the cusp of a world being turned upside
down? What if Paul was writing theology not for the calm of everyday
life? What if Paul's letters are not really the contemplation of deep and
high insight? What if Paul was telling a story for the end of days, a story
to make sense of a world seeming to be crumbling that much more with
every unjust day that passed?

That is, what if we read Romans not in the calm of a privileged
community but in the eye of a hurricane, the aftermath of generations
of political neglect, the grief of the space between the world as it is and
the world God has promised? When the world seems to be falling apart,
when communities are frayed, when nations shake, that is when we most
need Paul's letters, not as an escape into some ethereal imagination about
doctrine and thinking the right things but as a pathway into the soil of
everyday life, the cries of the harmed, the lament of the dying, the theological insight of *lo cotidiano*.

Death is dead. Sin is dead. This is what Paul urges us to confess, not
because Paul is naive, not because Paul is closing his eyes and stopping
his ears to the pain of his neighbors, to the realities of his own life in an
empire that would take his life. This is a bold proposition in this moment
in history. We declare that death is dead not because we will pretend that
all lives matter. Not because we will refuse to face squarely an upside-
down world. Not because we will neglect the more than 600,000 of our
neighbors who have died as I am writing in the United States during the
pandemic, too many of them alone. Not because too many tend to see in
the desperate journey of migrants at the border a problem to keep away
rather than a community in need of succor and hospitality.

No, we will confess that death is dead and sin is dead when we live
"Black Lives Matter." We will confess that death is dead and sin is dead
when we confess that the systemic, sinful tentacles of racism and colonialism and homophobia are coursing through our veins but that those
logics have died at the cross of Christ. Those ways of structuring the
world have no power over us because death is dead and so is sin.

And notice that the death of death comes at a high cost. It is not
some easy and magical exchange. The "in Christ" at the end of 6:11 carries a great deal of weight. It is Jesus's death that makes death die. It is
Jesus's death at the hands of the empire that crumbles the throne room
of Caesar. Jesus dies as we roar approvingly at the foot of the cross that

empire is keeping us safe by terrorizing someone else. It is Jesus's death that liberates us from the false promise of prosperity on the backs of those who suffer.

The death of Jesus clarifies who we are but also whom God has made us to be. Death, it turns out, is clarifying. When we gaze into the eyes of those dying under the weight of empire and fear, when we hear someone breathing their last, when we are witnesses as someone calls out to their mother, we run directly into the clarifying power of death, the way death exposes our frailty and brokenness and injustice.

But death is dead. Romans 6:10 reads, "The death he died, he died to sin, once for all; but the life he lives, he lives to God." Death had one shot and missed. Death came for the king, and death missed. But Jesus's life, his life is so much more than empire's failed attempt to kill him. His life is abundant and free, full of grace and love and transformation and, yes, the judgement that sets the world right.

And his life is now ours. As Romans 6:5 reminds us, "For if we have been united with him in a death like his, we will certainly be united with him in a resurrection like his." The life of the one delivered by Christ is one liberated from the sting of death and the shackles of sin. Of course, it's one thing to say this aloud; it's a whole other matter to live as if what we confess is actually true.

If death is dead, then a pandemic that deals death in ways that show us how deeply imbedded racist structures are in every aspect of life is a call to action towards life. If death is dead, then the death of people of color whether because of pandemic or racism or colonizing neglect is not just an accident of history but a call to a different world. If death is dead, then the cries of African American neighbors are not just another protest but a holy demand that death stay dead. If death is dead, then protest is not just a way to signal our holiness but a way to align our hopes and our lives with those who cannot breathe.

Dead to sin and alive to God in Christ Jesus? There are days when that confession seems easier to voice than others. But there are no days when that confession is no less true. There are no days when that confession does not bear upon us as we leave this place to enter a world God has already made new. As Elsa Tamez has written, "However, the justified person cannot forgive the condemnatory logic of the system that excludes. Instead, on the contrary, the justified person continually struggles against that logic. The system that excludes comes under the wrath of God, and God has condemned that system to death."[9]

The End of Romans 8 and the End(s) of Imperial Violence

In the verses leading up to Romans 8:26–30, Paul reflects on suffering, concluding that the suffering we now experience, the afflictions we now feel, are echoed across all creation. When we suffer, creation moans. When we hurt, creation groans. Our grief is not a silent cry before a God who has shut God's ears. Our grief is not a hidden loss from which God turns. Instead, our grief is a wordless echo that rings throughout all of creation. Our losses are evoked with sighs deeper, clearer, that much more tangible than whatever words we might utter.

Suffering, Paul says, is a cosmic reality interwoven with innumerable personal realities. This grief I feel, this suffering I experience, redounds in the breadth of God's creation. Also, Paul suggests, suffering is a communal exercise in this way as our cries echo throughout creation. Yes, suffering is communal and cosmic but so too is the redemption God is already enacting and will bring to completion one day. The redemption Paul narrates bursts through the confines of any one individual life or even human life as that redemption brings all of creation into alignment with God's creative, graceful, just purposes.

And so we wait for now. We await the redemption of our bodies in hope, in expectation, but also in prophetic demand. That is, the kind of waiting Paul narrates here is neither passive nor patient. The kind of waiting Paul describes is demanding in its prophetic stance. The world ought not be this way. The world ought not be pockmarked by death and violence. The good creation ought not be burdened by loss and grief. God's creation ought not be mired in sin and injustice. Even the rocks echo our prophetic supplications. Even the nonhuman animals join the chorus of grief. The very air trembles as we together await the fulfillment of creation's purposes.

It is in light of that hope that Paul declares the intercessory power of the Spirit. The intercessory power of the Spirit is not an anesthetic to dull our pain nor a simple promissory note that says things will be better one day nor a mere fantasy into which we can escape, if but for a moment, the cruelties and indignities of world bent around sin and injustice. Instead,

---

9. Tamez, *Amnesty of Grace*, 164.

the intercessory power of the Spirit is prophetic. This kind of hope—the kind of hope Paul narrates as chapter 8 closes but also the kind of hope which the marginalized articulate and live—is hard-won in the trenches of life. This hope won't be satisfied to have pain softened or dismissed. This hope screams that pain into the depths of creation. This hope calls out to God who has promised to set the world free. This hope calls out to a God whose grace is abundant. And here's a truth we as preachers must acknowledge. All the ways we seek to understand, to explain, to detail these realities fall short. Even Paul here falls short because words are not up to the task of describing the pain of suffering creation echoes and the hope of deliverance God has promised.

There is another piece of context that is vital here. Here Paul declares what we know. But just a few verses earlier, Paul reminded us what we do not know. "Likewise the Spirit helps us in our weakness; for we do not know how to pray as we ought, but that very Spirit intercedes with sighs too deep for words." What if the space between "we don't know" and "we know" is where Paul is calling us to imagine ourselves living and moving and having our being? What if God's promise fills the space between what we don't know and what we know? What if God's promise is that space between the Spirit's intercession and our confidence in God's grace? And what if when we seek to fill that ineffable space with every word we can muster, every understanding we think we have built, every bit of clarity we have constructed, we miss the still silence of God filling out every hope we have, hearing every bit of suffering we have born, healing every wound, drying every tear?

Conclusion

Romans was an occasional letter. Paul's proclaiming of the gospel therein responded to a moment in his own life and that of those gathered in Rome, some of whom he names explicitly in chapter 16. Similarly, our preaching of this oft-read—but often harmfully deployed—letter must seek its own occasional approach. Preaching this letter requires us to know something about antiquity, of course, but also to listen carefully to the stories about grace and hope, grief and loss our neighbors are weaving all around us. After all, when we stop heeding these stories, communities of faith can easily turn in upon themselves, not noticing the ways our assumptions about God's grace have been misshapen by sin and injustice. The possibilities of how we might preach Romans are manifold, vivid, and transformative. Part of the task of the preacher seeking those possibilities is not just a close study of the words Paul once wrote but how those ancient words flourish in new ways among those most trodden underfoot by the empires still stalking the oppressed.

Sermon

God's Delight in Unlikely
Meztizo Community

Romans 2:10–11, 12:1–2

Carlos Corro

*But glory and honor and peace for everyone who does good, the
Jew first and also the Greek. For God shows no partiality.*

—ROMANS 2:10–11 (NRSV)

*Do not be conformed to this world, but be transformed by the
renewing of your minds, so that you may discern what is the
will of God—what is good and acceptable and perfect.*

—ROMANS 12:1–2 (NRSV)

I AM HUMBLED AND privileged for the opportunity to serve as a contributor to *Preaching Romans from Here,* specifically from a Latinx perspective. Latinx preaching provides the following two unique contributions for the edification of all students in homiletics and hermeneutics: First, Latinx preaching makes an exhaustive emphasis on the correlation between the social location of the Bible and the social location of Latinx people. Second, the Latinx pulpit preaches a subversive eschatology. Furthermore, this subversive eschatology serves as a tangible hermeneutic preached uniquely through the Latinx context, due to the nature of US Latinx congregations being multilingual and multicultural. Moreover, the congregational diversity of US Latinx congregations to which Hispanic[1] pastors preach is a tangible example of the church that the apostle Paul addresses in the Epistle to the Romans, a mix of people and cultures becoming one new people in Christ. This congregational diversity in turn serves the wider church and all students of homiletics to learn from the unique Latinx preaching context and style, because whenever the church finds ways to live multiculturally and multilingually, that serves as a subversive sign of the future that all Christians, regardless of cultural background, proclaim: namely, our shared hope together in Christ, striving to continually reflect the kingdom of God as we live out the New Testament vision of new creation.

The serious study of Latinx homiletics and hermeneutics is urgently pertinent to the current theological training of preaching ministers. Furthermore, Latinx preaching demands the attention of theological trainers here and now especially in light of recent Pew Research studies and current US census statistics. Both studies affirm the reality that Latinx people are indeed the fastest growing demographic in the US. "As of 2020 the U.S. Hispanic population reached a record 60.6 million in 2019, up 930,000 over the previous year and up from 50.7 million in 2010, according to newly released U.S. Census Bureau population estimates."[2] In 2021 there are approximately sixty million Latinx people in the United States and that number is likely to increase as the twenty-first century continues. Based on current Pew Research studies, "Between 2010 and 2019, the Latinx share of the total U.S. population increased from 16% to 18%. Latinos accounted for about half (52%) of all U.S. population growth over this period. They are the country's second largest racial or ethnic group, behind white non-Hispanics."[3]

This staggering increase in the Latinx population has made this culture the largest minority group in the United States as of 2019, which is

---

1. In this chapter I will be referring to Latinx and Hispanic interchangeably. Latinx is a person of Latin American origin or descent (used as a gender-neutral or nonbinary alternative to Latino or Latina). Hispanic is a Spanish-speaking person with Latin American descent.

2. United States Census Bureau, "65 And Older Population Grows Rapidly."

3. Noe-Bustamante et al., "U.S. Hispanic Population Surpassed 60 Million."

thirty-one years faster than 2015 Pew Research and 2010 US census data estimates that had the Latinx population reaching 50 million by 2050.

Moreover, the wave of Hispanic immigration from various countries in Latin America has also played a significant role in the current US Hispanic religious landscape. Many of these newly immigrated people from countries such as Honduras, Guatemala, and El Salvador are coming to the US already as Christians. Upon their arrival and through their settlement into a new country, some of the first needs they seek to fulfill are their spiritual and religious needs. Thus, both the internal growth of the US Latinx population and the current trends of immigrants from Latin America have direct correlations to the steady growth of US Latinx churches. I believe it is due time to learn from this current movement of Christianities. Furthermore, it is this firm belief that has led me to engage the topic of Latinx homiletics and hermeneutics. I have specifically chosen to focus on the Latinx perspective for this chapter, because these currently growing US Latinx worshipping communities are being ministered to, molded by, and spiritually shaped by the preaching that is done in their churches.

In Romans, we find that God creates an unlikely community. God sees two communities and makes them into one new community. In fact, the apostle Paul throughout the New Testament refers to the people of God as a new humanity, where Jews and Greeks, two different cultural groups, come together and make one new group, a new people.

Two unique communities becoming one new ethnicity is inherent to the lived experience of Latinx people, who are composed primarily of persons who identify as Meztizo, meaning people who are of European and indigenous American descent. The ancient church in Rome had both Jews and Greeks, richer and poorer, as well as a variety of social statuses and ethnicities. The church in Rome was spiritually Meztizo. Furthermore, the Roman Empire did not know what to do with the Christians in Rome. It was indeed the Romans who came up with the idea to refer to early Jesus followers as Christians. This new title was not meant to be a new religious category but in many ways it served as the end of categories to describe the unlikely community of Jews, Greeks, and everything in between together in the pursuit and worship of the living Lord Jesus Christ.

The church community in Romans was made up of people who probably would not be friends of their own accord. They would have probably passed each other by in the marketplace or previously would have been invisible to one another. However, now because of Jesus they are a new community together. Not just one culture assimilating to another culture but they are indeed a third culture, a gospel-centered Christlike culture. God bringing two groups together and making one new group at the church in Rome serves as a witness of the power of the gospel to establish hope through restored relationships. As a part of the family of God, we are called to proactively lean into the ministry of reconciliation (2 Cor 5:18) as a people who would not ordinarily belong together, now unified through the power of the Holy Spirit. Moreover, the church in Rome that Paul addresses is, as Lesslie Newbigin describes, a living witness and a viable hermeneutic of the gospel.[4]

Romans 2 and 12 point to a story of reconciliation where two different people groups are learning more about God when they go deeper with one another. Romans 12:2 invites us to not conform to the patterns of this world. Furthermore, we are called not only to reject "worldly" things out there, but to go a step further, to break out of the shell of complacent, cultural Christianities and to let go of the religious-club insiders and outsiders mentality and instead join a greater narrative about God, specifically a God who shows no favoritism.

> But glory and honor and peace for everyone who does good, the
> Jew first and also the Greek. For God shows no partiality. (Rom
> 2:10–11 NRSV)

God showing no partiality means that because of the power of the gospel, there are no ethnic, geographical, or cultural barriers any longer in the way of anyone to experience new life with God. Neither is there a people group that is somehow inherently closer to God or further from God. Now because of the grace of God, we are all on common ground. As God's people, we can become more open to God's presence and experience deeper intimacy with God when we engage in living out the gospel as an unlikely community.

The story of God using an unlikely community for his purposes and glory in Romans, continues even today in my ministry as the lead pastor of Imago Church, in Visalia, California. The vision that God has placed on our hearts for Imago Church is that together we may live and serve as a gospel-centered, multicultural community where hope is built through restored relationships with God and with one another. Our mission stems from this vision; God has formed Imago Church to be a church that is good news to the city, not just to ourselves; we are blessed to be a blessing.

---

4. Newbigin, *Gospel in a Pluralistic Society*, 227.

We are a church that reflects the city and its rich multicultural diversity. And we are a church that seeks to connect the city so that people who would not ordinarily belong together can gather around the worship of Jesus. Perhaps instinctively, as human beings, we typically, for perhaps sociological or tribal reasons, tend to gather with people who we look, think, and act like. At Imago Church, we make a deliberate and intentional effort for our congregation to reflect and serve the community in which we live and reside, as the community that it is, not as we would manufacture the community to be.

Perhaps the most important contribution that Latinx preaching provides for the wider theological, homiletical, and general Christian community is the subversive eschatology that serves as an ongoing narrative throughout the preaching done in US Latinx congregations. The unique multicultural and multilingual US Latinx worshipping communities gathered around the proclamation of the gospel serve as a tangible sign to the world and to the entire Christian family that God is indeed creating a new humanity that is united in faith and diverse in the expressions of that faith. The God that US Latinx pastors preach about is a God that brings beauty out of chaos, even such chaos as five hundred years of colonization, genocide, isolation, and the marginalization of being made to feel like strangers in a familiar land. Indeed, even that chaos is no match for the redemptive power of the God who chooses to speak to gathered worshipping communities through the glorious and mysterious witness of preaching.

Sermon

Baptized into Newness of Life in the Face of Evil

EFRAIN AGOSTO

Sermon Preached for Greenwood Baptist Church
Brooklyn, New York
Virtual Worship Service
Sunday, June 21, 2020

Text: Romans 6:1b–11

Should we continue in sin in order that grace may abound? By
no means! How can we who died to sin go on living in it? Do
you not know that all of us who have been baptized into Christ
Jesus were baptized into his death? Therefore, we have been buried with him by baptism into death, so that, just as Christ was
raised from the dead by the glory of the Father, so we too might
walk in the newness of life. For if we have been united with him
in a death like his, we will certainly be united with him in a
resurrection like his.

We know that our old self was crucified with him so that the
body of sin might be destroyed, and we might no longer be

enslaved to sin. For whoever has died is freed from sin. But if we have died with Christ, we believe that we will also live with him. We know that Christ, being raised from the dead, will never die again; death no longer has dominion over him. The death he died, he died to sin, once for all; but the life he lives, he lives to God. So you also must consider yourselves dead to sin and alive to God in Christ Jesus.

Introduction: "Grace Abounds"

In the days of the apostle Paul, some folks thought they had it all together. "Grace abounds, so let us just enjoy life and not worry about much. God will take care of everything." Perhaps some thought that with the Roman Imperial Order in charge, all would be well? Or, alternatively, the belief in the soon return of Christ meant for some that just action in their earthly lives was not necessary. The apostle Paul himself may have engendered such theologies of what we would call today "pie in the sky."

Yes, if we fast-forward to 2020, this is a *Kairos* moment we are living today, where all is being challenged—systems, policing, race relations, presidencies. This is especially a moment in which the reality that Black Lives Matter is being put forward and perhaps finally more supported, even though we have been reminded again and again for a long time that such is the case. Black Lives Matter.

Indeed, we have been challenged before, and should have been, but perhaps until this critical juncture in our history, too many folks have been living their lives oblivious to the lives of others, oblivious even though we were reminded time and again. Reminded, again and again, sadly, with police killings over recent years, including, let me say some of their names, Eric Garner, Michael Brown, Tamir Rice, Freddie Gray, Sandra Bland, Philando Castile, Breonna Taylor, George Floyd, Rayshard Brooks, and those killed by vigilante "wannabe" police, including Trayvon Martin and Ahmaud Arbery. And so, so many others, too many, sadly, for me to name in this brief sermon.

However, we can ask ourselves, "How could you not be concerned with such a pattern of malicious, brutal killings by those in power for so long?" These are just the recent names. Can you imagine, just as an example, how many enslaved persons in the two years after the Emancipation Proclamation in 1863, died at the hands of their enslavers, as a matter, for them—the slave masters—of business as usual, during the time it took for word to finally get to Texas on June 19, 1865—Juneteenth? Indeed, those masters might have been going to church every Sunday singing God's praises and hearing sermons about "let grace abound"! But sin is insidious, writes Paul in this passage, Romans 6:1–11, one of the lectionary texts for this Sunday, June 21, 2020.

Continue in Sin?

The challenge of the text is about continuing in sin, even after the miraculous offer of transformation made possible through the life, death, and resurrection of Jesus the Christ. And, yet, writes Paul, in effect, we still deal in death, in sin, in systemic sin, including, we must add, the sin of systemic racism. No doubt people, as individuals, try not to be racist against Black and Brown bodies, but it is the insidious system of oppression—policing, health and economic inequities—that is the racist reality of this nation historically and currently; it still rears its head. I read on Friday the governor of Florida blames the upsurge of coronavirus cases in his state on Latinx seasonal farm workers who are too clumped together in housing and work. Well, who is to blame for that? The farmworkers themselves? Or their employers, or, for sure, the governor himself for his government's slow response to the agriculture industries that called for help early and often in the pandemic in his state? This is the insidiousness of systemic sin, where those impacted most by racism, health inequities, and unfair labor practices are blamed for their plight. "Grace abounds; never mind sin, therefore," they say. But, yet, asks Paul, "how can we who died to sin go on living with it?"

Many in the US might have an understanding of sin and evil that goes something like, "I am trying hard as an individual, I am not perfect, I'm doing my best to live in grace." Yet, too many of those same folks might turn around and support systems and policies that perpetuate overarching, not just personalized, systemic evil, including injustice and racism. It is not just about you and me, although we certainly can and must do better to eradicate that sin from our being and listen to those voices that can help us and show us how. But how can we "do better" individually—let "grace abound" in our lives—and *then* turn around and support the systems, policies, policing, politicians, elected officials, school systems, economic systems and practices that perpetuate inequalities against Black and Brown bodies? If indeed we are "buried with Christ and resurrected into new life," which we affirm publicly in our water baptism, then we must speak out and demand change *and* be the source of change. That is why the marching and the protests must continue. And the young people are leading the way. They are showing us how to walk, literally, into the newness of life, even though there is danger in doing so, including the danger of contracting this horrific virus during those crowded marches, God forbid—not to mention police and political violence against those very same marchers for justice. But march we must. Because for grace to truly abound, sin must be truly eradicated.

United in Death and New Life

In my living room at home hangs a painting by my son Joel Agosto, a professional illustrator, which pictures Mary and child as persons of color. She is sitting on a park bench with her deceased son's body draped on her lap. It is a stunning image of the death of Jesus of Nazareth, at the hands of cruel imperialists. This death had deep meaning for early Christ believers, so much so that they proclaimed an embodied new life, a resurrected Christ, and symbolized it through entry in baptismal waters, as Paul describes in this Romans passage. Early believers, and now us today, rose from those waters, into a new life of commitment to love, do justice, and practice relentless care for one another, including the poor and oppressed. How can we celebrate the grace of God in making this new life possible for us in Christ, asks Paul in this passage, and not demand as well that sin be eradicated so that grace and love might abound? Sin, we know, includes the insidious, violent, ongoing evil of racism. For grace to truly abound we must act to do away with the vestiges of sin everywhere. If that means defunding police so that social services and pastoral care might abound, then so be it. If that means electing officials who will work to redistribute wealth through fair tax policies so that all may have a living wage and all may have not just adequate but excellent healthcare, then let grace abound. If it means reforming our educational system so that kids—including Black and Brown kids—don't get left behind and I don't mean in just grades but in knowledge and power and skills and commitments to be the best they can be—then so be it. Let grace abound!

Certain things have to die for such a world to be a reality. Commitments to party and tradition must be under scrutiny. Let grace abound! Where party and policy perpetuate sin, they must be challenged and replaced. Let grace abound. Where notions of white supremacy—quiet and insidious though they might be in some corners, and yet in others loud and clear and violent—those notions of white superiority, must be challenged, called out and eradicated. No one holds a corner on truth. No one is better than anyone else because of their race, color, or creed. We are all made equal in the eyes of God. Such are the truths this country has espoused since its beginnings, yet at the same time the molders and holders of those truths enslaved fellow human beings because of the color of their skin. And even when the law changed the reality of enslavement, the law looked for ways to keep that enslavement by race in play. And later when persons from the Southern Hemisphere traveled here to partake of the so-called American Dream, they too were treated less than human. Indeed, most recently they and their children have been confined for months and months in cages on the border. What American Dream? The one that enslaves, the one that cages Black and Brown bodies? Perhaps we should exclaim like Paul does here in Romans 6—"What then are we to say? Should we continue in sin that grace may abound? By no means!" "No way!," he might have written were he around today. Not that kind of "grace"! We cannot be oblivious to sin and say we are living in grace! As Paul writes in his first-century way, "our old self" must be "crucified" with Christ "so that the body of sin might be destroyed" (Rom 6:6).

Conclusion: Let Grace Abound!

As James Cone has reminded us, Jesus of Nazareth was lynched for challenging injustices. The bodies of Black lives, including the four latest—Ahmaud Arbery, Breonna Taylor, George Floyd, and Rayshard Brooks—were also lynched—indeed before our very eyes on video. Their cries call out to us. "I can't breathe," pleaded George Floyd, a father, whose child cannot have him by her side on Father's Day, nor can the children of Rayshard Brooks. How many more fathers, mothers, brothers, sisters, children need to be crucified for that insidious sin to be eradicated? The news of the end of slavery finally came to Texas on Juneteenth 1865, yet why are Black and Brown bodies still being enslaved and murdered as direct outcomes of the sin of racism, this insidious evil that the cross of Christ and the crushed neck of George Floyd has meant to destroy once and for all. Yet not just once, not for all, not yet. So, we march on. But how many more lives need to be crucified and lynched?

"Whoever has died is freed from sin," writes Paul. Shall we live like freed persons and fight against the sin of racism that still enslaves? Paul continues, "We know that Christ, being raised from the dead, will never die again; death will no longer have dominion over him" (6:9). When will that be true in our day and age? When will grace truly abound and powers and principalities in our day, official or not, not deal in death? If grace abounds, why do even people of faith, who believe in the efficacy of the death of Christ for themselves, and get baptized in that belief to show their solidarity with Christ and his sacrifice, yet still, whether consciously or not, still deal in the systems that dole out death to Black and Brown bodies today? The time, the propitious time, the kairos moment to act, as *Sojourners* editor Jim Wallis wrote recently, has come upon us. Ahmaud Arbery, Breonna Taylor, and George Floyd, in particular, have called us to that moment, a time when things have come to a critical juncture. Shall we pay attention and do something faithful, graceful, and concrete?

The death Christ died, writes Paul, "he died to sin, once for all." Shall we honor the untimely, unnecessary, tragic, and brutal deaths of Ahmaud, Breonna, George, and Rayshard and all too many others, by saying "enough is enough"? Perhaps, this time we can make a difference and make it endure. We must consider ourselves—now—once and for all—dead to sin—the sin of systemic racism and all the systems, policies, and people that perpetuate it. And, as Paul concludes this paragraph, we can then be "alive to God," the God of love, mercy, and justice.

I agree with how Karl Barth, writing one hundred years ago about this text in Romans 6, concluded his analysis: "We actually encounter the impossible possibility of completely exposing the falsity of the reality of 'our' life and of stretching out towards the reality of our life in God."[1] Shall we stretch now more than ever—now is the time—and practice the love of God with all and for all so that grace might abound and sin not? Let us live therefore into the newness of life that our baptism calls us to do. No doubt we have our work cut out for us. But the voices of the dearly departed—Ahmaud, Breonna, George, Rayshard—call out to us to be truly in Christ and let grace abound. Let the church say, "Amen!"

---

1. Barth, *Epistle to the Romans*, 207.

Looking Back to Move Forward

African American Voices from the Past Engaging Romans

LISA A. BOWENS

Introduction

AFRICAN AMERICANS HAVE BEEN interpreting the Bible for centuries, for Scripture has been central to their resistance of white supremacy, racism, and enslavement. Historically, they utilized Scripture in their essays, public speeches, autobiographies, sermons, conversion experiences, and petitions, thereby indicating the importance of Scripture's voice for their own voices.[1] Paul's Epistle to the Romans played a valuable role in black articulations for freedom, justice, and equality. This essay will provide snapshots of black historical interpretative trajectories of Romans aimed toward black liberation by exploring briefly three African American interpreters, Lemuel Haynes, Zilpha Elaw, and Martin Luther King Jr. It will conclude with some ways forward for today's preaching moments.

---

1. The body of literature regarding African American biblical interpretation is vast and growing. Some important starting points are Blount et al., eds., *True to Our Native Land*; Bowens, *African American Readings of Paul*; Callahan, *Talking Book*; Copher, *Black Biblical Studies*; Felder, ed., *Stony the Road We Trod*; Powery and Sadler, *Genesis of Liberation*; Weems, *Just a Sister Away*. Portions of this essay appear in, draw upon, and build on earlier discussions in Bowens, *African American Readings of Paul,* and "Liberating Paul."

Historical Contexts

In order to understand blacks' use of Romans (and other Scripture for that matter) in their arguments for freedom and equality, one needs to take a brief inventory of the historical contexts in which these authors found themselves. From this nation's founding, the notion of white supremacy permeated every arena of American life—religious, social, political, and economical. In terms of the religious sphere, white supremacist interpretations of the Bible proliferated. For example, whites interpreted the Ham narrative in Genesis 9:18–27 as scriptural justification for enslavement of African Americans. For them, this passage sanctioned the idea that God approved slavery and ordained it specifically for blacks. Whites also read the story of Cain and Abel as a narrative that endorsed black enslavement. On this reading, the mark that God placed upon Cain as punishment for killing Abel was the mark of black skin.

Such readings of these Old Testament passages cohered with how whites read and preached Paul's words, "Slaves, obey your masters" (Eph 6:5; Col 3:22). As seen throughout the autobiographies of the enslaved, white preachers constantly proclaimed these words from Paul to the enslaved as an attempt to make them believe that God created them for enslavement only and that their salvation rested upon obeying their enslavers. Josiah Priest, a proslavery activist, encapsulates the beliefs of the time: "As to the intrinsic superiority of a white complexion over that of black, there is no question; for by the common consent of all ages among men, and even of God himself in heaven, there has been bestowed on white the most honorable distinction. White has become the emblem of moral purity and truth, not only on earth, but in eternity also."[2] Later on in the same essay, he writes, "Black, in all ages, has been the sign of every hateful thing."[3] Such views permeated the body politic, including those in political leadership, such as Thomas Jefferson, who wrote, "I advance it therefore as a suspicion only, that the blacks, whether originally a distinct race, or made distinct by time and circumstances, are inferior to the whites in the endowments both of body and mind."[4]

These horrific views were present not only in the South but permeated the North as well. In his article, "Negrophobia in Northern Proslavery and Antislavery Thought," Eugene Berwanger documents the

---

2. Priest, *Slavery*, 136.

3. Priest, *Slavery*, 138.

4. Jefferson, *Notes*, 153.

prevalent notion of black inferiority among both pro- and antislavery Northern activists. Berwanger writes that "as early as 1827 the *Ohio State Journal* spoke for many Northerners by declaring, 'we will never consent to see the two races placed on a footing of perfect equality,' and as late as 1860 the *Illinois State Register* continued in the same tone: 'Negroes have no voice whatever in [this nation's] political affairs. . . . They are an inferior race, and must remain so, politically forever."[5] For many whites this deep-seated belief in black inferiority, not black humanity, undergirded the rejection of the expansion of slavery into new territory in the West. In 1857, the people in Oregon voted to prohibit both slavery *and* free blacks from entering the territory. In referring to this vote, the editor of the *Oregon Weekly Times* wrote, "Oregon is a land for the white man, refusing the toleration of negroes in our midst as slaves, we rightly and for yet stronger reasons, prohibit them from coming among us as free negro vagabonds."[6] Thus, rejection of the expansion of slavery was not because whites necessarily believed in equality of African Americans, but rather they did not want blacks in their midst, enslaved or free. The aforementioned litany of white supremacist statements provides a glimpse into the prevailing sentiments of the time.

It is no wonder then that the nation's laws codified these views. In 1787, the US Constitution declared an enslaved African to count as three-fifths of a person. In 1850, the Fugitive Slave Act made it a crime to assist African Americans who absconded from enslavement, and in 1857, the Dred Scott decision stated that blacks, whether enslaved or free, were not and could not be citizens of the United States. They were property with no rights in federal court. In addition, the *Plessy v. Ferguson* decision in 1896 sustained the constitutionality of racial segregation under the "separate but equal" policy. This decision wreaked havoc upon blacks in the South and manifested in Jim Crow laws that permeated every arena of life.

In light of all of this history, how did African Americans employ Christianity and the Bible, particularly Paul and his Letter to the Romans, to speak out against slavery, racism, segregation, and white supremacy? The following black interpreters demonstrate how some of them went about such monumental tasks.

---

5. Berwanger, "Negrophobia," 272.

6. Berwanger, "Negrophobia," 272.

"Inspired Penman": Lemuel Haynes

Lemuel Haynes (1753–1833), an early black pastor and exegete, was the "first black to be ordained by any religious organization in America."[7] He served in the Continental Army and fought in the Revolutionary War. In his essay "Liberty Further Extended," written around the year of 1776, Haynes argues that the liberty Americans fought for from Britain should extend to blacks. In his treatise, he takes on the common views of his day, including the white supremacist interpretation of Genesis 9:18–27. Haynes argues against whites' use of the Ham passage to justify black enslavement, writing, "Whethear the Negros are of Canaans posterity or not, perhaps is not known by any mortal under Heaven."[8] He goes on to say "Our glorious hygh priest hath visably appear'd in the flesh, and hath Establish'd a more glorious Oeconomy . . . It is plain Beyond all Doubt, that at the comeing of Christ, this curse that was upon Canaan, was taken off."[9] Important to Haynes's critique is the unlikelihood of knowing the identity of Canaan's descendants.[10] Here, he also echoes Paul's words in Galatians 3:13, where the apostle states, "Christ has redeemed us from the curse of the law, being made a curse for us: for it is written, Cursed is everyone that hangeth on a tree." According to Haynes, even if blacks were descendants of Canaan, Christ's advent removes the so-called curse. Christ's coming refutes this white supremacist interpretation of the Ham narrative and delegitimizes this purported "scriptural basis" for enslavement of African Americans. Haynes declared "there is Not the Least precept, or practise, in the Sacred Scriptures, that constitutes a Black man a Slave, any more than a white one."[11] No Scripture sanctions black enslavement.

Haynes also opposed the prevalent notion among whites that the slave trade was an act of divine providence and a blessing to blacks because it "civilized" and "Christianized" them. Rehearsing the argument, he writes, "But I shall take notice of one argument more which these Slave-traders use, and it is this, viz. that those Negros that are Emigrated into these colonies are brought out of a Land of Darkness under the meridian Light of the Gospel; and so it is a great Blessing instead of a Curs. But I would ask, who is this that Darkneth counsel By words with

---

7. MacLam, "Introduction," xxi.

8. Haynes, "Liberty," 24. See also Saillant, "Origins," 236–50.

9. Haynes, "Liberty," 25.

10. Saillant, "Origins," 238.

11. Haynes, "Liberty," 19.

out knoledg?"[12] The question Haynes raises here comes from the book
of Job. Out of a whirlwind God queries Job in response to Job's speech
in previous chapters. Taking up God's whirlwind speech to Job, Haynes
exposes those who use the "slavery as a blessing" argument as people
void of knowledge and he fires off a whirlwind of citations from Romans
to refute this preposterous notion. "Let us attend to the great apostle
Speaking to us in Rom 3:8 where he reproves some slanderers who told
it as a maxim preached by the apostles that they said Let us Do Evil that
Good may come, whose Damnation the *inspired penman* pronounces
with an Emphasis to Be Just. And again in Chap. 6 vers 1. where By way
of interagation he asks, Shall we continue in Sin that grace may abound?
The answer is obvious, God forbid."[13] By marshalling these texts from
Romans, Haynes asserts that, similar to Paul, whom he calls the inspired
penman, who dealt with people exclaiming, "Let us do evil so that good
may come," proslavery advocates commit evil in the slave trade in order
to bring about some supposed "good" (civilizing Africans and causing
them to become Christians).[14] The slaveholders' stance, however, is un-
tenable. As Paul rejected those in his audience who held such views, so
too does Haynes. Employing Paul's words, Haynes boldly calls the slave
trade evil, not good, sin, not a blessing. Like the inspired penman before
him, Haynes rebukes his audience for their adherence to sin and informs
them that damnation lies in their future unless they repent.

Haynes again takes up Romans in the latter part of the essay to
critique Americans who fight for their own liberty and despise tyranny
from Britain and yet inflict upon blacks the very things they do not want
inflicted upon themselves. He writes, "Thou therefore which teacheth
another, teachest thou not thy self? thou that preachest a man Should not
Steal, Dost thou Steal? thou that sayest, a man Should not Commit adultery, Dost thou Commit adultery? thou that abhoreth idols, Dost thou
Commit Sacrilege? thou that makest thy Best of the law, through Breaking the Law Dishonnerest thou God?"[15] Haynes warns white Americans
of the danger of falling into "that class *the inspir'd pen-man* Speaks of"
here in Romans 2:21. Utilizing Romans, Haynes unmasks the double
standard of white Americans who yell "justice and liberty for all" but

12. Haynes, "Liberty," 26.

13. Haynes, "Liberty," 26.

14. Haynes, "Liberty," 26.

15. Haynes, "Liberty," 29.

do not include African Americans in the "all." Their hypocrisy speaks volumes. Haynes refuses to allow whites to paint enslavement as a divine institution or as a benefit to blacks. Like the inspired penman before him, who dared to speak out against those who would distort the gospel for their own aims, Haynes is the inspired penman of his day refuting those who utilize the slave trade for their own "Carnal avarice." He does not let slaveholders off the hook, but in contradistinction to their views, declares that slavery and the slave trade was "vile and atrocious, as well as the most inhuman."[16]

Zilpha Elaw, Phoebe, and the Holy Prophetic Spirit

Zilpha Elaw (1790?–1846?) was an early black woman preacher, one of the few black women during her time to proclaim the gospel. She faced severe opposition from women and men because of her gender and race. Despite such opposition, however, Elaw persevered, carrying the gospel throughout the United States and internationally. In her riveting auto-biography, Elaw chronicles her conversion, her call to preach, and her many preaching tours. She fills her narrative with mystical happenings in which she experiences supernatural encounters with God. In one such encounter at a camp meeting, Elaw writes, "I became so overpowered with the presence of God, that I sank down upon the ground, and laid there for a considerable time; and while I was thus prostrate on the earth, my spirit seemed to ascend up into the clear circle of the sun's disc; and surrounded and engulphed in the glorious effulgence of his rays, I distinctly heard a voice speak unto me, which said, 'Now thou art sanctified; and I will show thee what thou must do.'"[17] Further on she writes,

> Before the meeting at this camp closed, it was revealed to me by the Holy Spirit, that like another *Phoebe* [Rom 16:1], or the matrons of the apostolic societies, I must employ myself in visiting families, and in speaking personally to the members thereof, of the salvation and eternal interests of their souls, visit the sick, and attend upon other of the errands and services of the Lord; which I afterwards cheerfully did, not confining my visits to the poor only, but extending them to the rich also, and even to those

16. Haynes, "Liberty," 20.
17. Elaw, *Memoirs*, 66.

who sit in high places in the state; and the Lord was with me in
the work to own and bless my labours.[18]

While there are a number of important elements in this description of Elaw's experience, for our present purposes her alignment with
Phoebe is significant. Here Elaw sees part of her call as similar to that of
Phoebe whom Paul calls a minister in Romans 16:1. Just as God called
Phoebe to do the work of the church, God calls Elaw also to go forth and
carry the gospel declaring to people "salvation and eternal interests of
their souls." Elaw recognizes the ministerial leadership of Phoebe and
applies it to her own circumstances.

Later on in her autobiography, Elaw takes up the figure of Phoebe
again, this time to refute those who, citing Paul's statement about women
remaining silent, argue against Elaw's call to preach. Elaw responds to
such interpretations, stating: "St. Paul himself attests that *Phoebe* was a
servant or deaconess of the Church at Cenchrea; and as such was em-
ployed by the Church to manage some of their affairs; and it was strange
indeed, if she was required to receive the commissions of the church in
mute silence, and not allowed to utter a syllable before them."[19] For Elaw,
the fact that Paul calls Phoebe a *deaconess* of the church indicates that
"some quality of leadership is connoted by the term."[20] Elaw understands
that Phoebe had a role of proclamation in the church and was not silent.
She asserts, then, that as Phoebe was not silent, neither will she be silent,
despite those who would try to mute her voice.[21]

---

18. Elaw, *Memoirs*, 67.

19. Elaw, *Memoirs*, 124.

20. Gaventa, *When*, 10. The Greek term for deacon is διάκονος and Paul uses it
to describe himself as well. Jewett, *Romans*, notes, "Although earlier commentators
interpret the term διάκονος as a subordinate role, it now appears more likely that she
[Phoebe] functioned as the leader of the congregation" (944).

21. A number of scholars believe that Paul's recommendation of Phoebe in Romans 16:1 demonstrates that she is the carrier of the letter to the Roman congregations
and as such is the person who reads the letter to them. On these points, see the discussion in Jewett, *Romans*, 941–48. Gaventa, *When*, insightfully observes, "It seems clear
that Paul commends Phoebe because she carries the letter . . . This letter—the one that
stands first in the Pauline canon, the one over which an ocean of ink has been spilled,
over which countless theological battles have been waged (and are still being waged),
on the perilous rocks of which exegetical careers have been made and lost—this letter
was delivered by a woman. There is an irony in that detail that is perhaps best appreci-
ated when you consider that the history of Pauline interpretation (to our knowledge)
has been an overwhelmingly male endeavor" (12). On the topic of Phoebe reading
the letter, she writes, "Almost inevitably, Phoebe shaped the hearing of the letter by

To support her stance further, Elaw lists other women Paul refers to in Romans 16. She states,

> Paul wished every assistance to be given to those women who laboured with him in the Gospel. Tryphena laboured with Tryphosa in the Lord; mention is made of the services of many of the sisters of Nereus, of the mother of Rufus, many others are also very respectfully referred to by St. Paul. The prophet Joel predicted that God would pour His Spirit on His handmaids, and that they should prophecy [sic] as well as His servants; and this prophecy, Peter, on the day of Pentecost, asserted was fulfilled [Acts 2:16–18]; and if so, the Christian dispensation has for its main feature the inspirations of the *holy prophetic Spirit*, descending on the handmaids as well as on the servants of God; and thus qualifying both for the conversion of men, and spread of the Gospel. Priscilla took upon herself the work of a teacher, when, in conjunction with her husband Aquila, she expounded to Apollos the way of God more perfectly . . .[22]

Along with naming other women who labored with Paul, Elaw recalls Joel's prophecy and its fulfillment in Acts through the outpouring of the Spirit on males and females. Pentecost demonstrates that the "*holy prophetic Spirit*" qualifies both women and men for the "spread of the Gospel," as indicated by the litany of female names in the final chapter of the letter. The appearance of a number of women in Romans 16 illustrates that women played major roles in proclaiming the gospel in the early church and Elaw sees herself as continuing that prophetic tradition.

Elaw's autobiography countered the erroneous views of the time. Many whites did not believe blacks had souls and therefore could not experience conversion. Such views were an extension of beliefs that blacks were less than human and created for enslavement. Yet black autobiographies like Elaw's asserted that African Americans were human, did have souls, experienced conversion, and had divine encounters with God that affirmed their humanity and their dignity as human beings created in the image of God. For black women these divine encounters demonstrated

---

the way she read it, whether she rushed through some passages, lingered over others, paused to allow the words to sink in, or stopped to add an explanatory note at various points. Phoebe had a role in interpreting the letter" (14). Although Elaw did not have the privilege of modern biblical scholarship, her interpretive instincts regarding Phoebe's vocal presence in the early church was spot on.

22. Elaw, *Memoirs*, 124. For more on Zilpha Elaw see Pierce, *Hell without Fires,* and Smith, "'Unbossed.'"

that they had value and worth and that God called them too as partners in the divine proclamation of the gospel. These divine encounters were religious experiences that had political and social implications because these supernatural events empowered black women like Elaw to claim their positions as women in ministry in public spaces and places. Their voices mattered. Their lives mattered.

Martin Luther King Jr. and Marching to the Soulsaving Music of Eternity

In a variety of his speeches and sermons Martin Luther King Jr., preacher, pastor, and renown civil rights leader, employs Romans to speak out against segregation and the racist policies of the nation. We will discuss only a few instances here. In his sermon "Transformed Nonconformist" King uses as his text Romans 12:2—"Be not conformed to this world: but be ye transformed by the renewing of your mind"—to declare to his audience the importance of not conforming to the racist structures of the world. God calls believers to be nonconformists. While recognizing that "'Do not conform' is difficult advice in a generation when crowd pressures have unconsciously conditioned our minds and feet to move to the rhythmic drumbeat of the status quo,"[23] King nevertheless reminds Christians that God calls believers to do the difficult task. Believers are "commanded to live differently and according to a higher loyalty"[24] because they exist in two worlds simultaneously—"the world of time and the world of eternity."[25] Because Christians live in two worlds at the same time their allegiance should never be to an earthly idea or custom, which is timebound, but to God and God's kingdom of love, the world of eternity.[26]

King chastises the church because of its capitulation to slavery, segregation, exploitation of the poor, and its support of war. Instead of being leaders who oppose these ills, the church blesses and sanctions such actions. Part of this acquiescence to the status quo derives from church leaders who value the "cult of conformity." Leaders are more concerned with showmanship, maintaining large church membership, and making

23. King, *Strength*, 11.
24. King, *Strength*, 12.
25. King, *Strength*, 12.
26. King, *Strength*, 12.

their members comfortable than with preaching the truth. King asks pointedly, "Have we ministers of Jesus Christ sacrificed truth on the altar of self-interest and, like Pilate, yielded our convictions to the demands of the crowd?"[27]

King admonishes the church to reclaim its call to nonconformity. In order to do this, Christians need to recapture the movement of the early believers who did not conform to the world but were in many respects nonconformists. These Christ followers "refused to shape their witness according to the mundane patterns of the world" and they "sacrificed fame, fortune, and life itself."[28] Because they stood for the truth of the gospel, their witness changed the world. King writes that although "quantitatively small, they were qualitatively giants. Their powerful gospel put an end to such barbaric evils as infanticide and bloody gladiatorial contests. Finally, they captured the Roman Empire for Jesus Christ."[29] The church's reclamation of nonconformity, however, will have consequences. To refuse to conform means that one will suffer. King acknowledges the pain of this suffering in his own life. "Honesty impels me to admit that transformed nonconformity, which is always costly and never altogether comfortable, may mean walking through the valley of the shadow of suffering, losing a job, or having a six-year-old daughter ask, 'Daddy, why do you have to go to jail so much?'"[30] Despite the suffering believers may encounter for resisting conformity, the outcomes of a more just society and a church that reflects the kingdom of God are worth it, for truth must triumph.

King proclaims that the church must never become comfortable with segregation, discrimination, sectarianism, militarism, physical violence, religious bigotry, and economic policies that "deprive men of work and food."[31] He closes this powerful essay with a series of clarion calls to the churches of his day. "We must make a choice. Will we continue to march to the drumbeat of conformity and respectability, or will we, listening to the beat of a more distant drum, move to its echoing sounds? Will we march only to the music of time, or will we, risking criticism and abuse, *march to the soulsaving music of eternity*?"[32] Utilizing the lan-

27. King, *Strength*, 16.

28. King, *Strength*, 16.

29. King, *Strength*, 16.

30. King, *Strength*, 19.

31. King, *Strength*, 18.

32. King, *Strength*, 20.

guage of Romans 12:2, King urges the church to embrace transformed nonconformity, an existence that reflects eternity, not temporality. Although King addresses the audiences of his day in this essay, his words still resonate for our own time and place.

Conclusions

The murder of George Floyd, an African American man, in the summer of 2020 in the midst of a global pandemic revealed to many the reality of systemic racism, the ongoing nature of white supremacy, and the police brutality that many African Americans continue to face. George Floyd laid on the ground under an officer's knee for nine minutes and twenty-nine seconds, calling out for his dead mother and begging to be allowed to breathe.[33] The pandemic of racism appeared in plain sight for millions to witness. For many African Americans watching, his murder evoked the lynchings and murders of so many blacks by whites throughout the centuries, such as Emmett Till, Medgar Evers, James Chaney, the four little girls killed in the bombing of Birmingham's 16th Street Baptist Church, the nine killed at Charleston's Mother Emmanuel African Methodist Episcopal Church, and countless others. Floyd's murder happened during a time of other senseless murders of black people, such as Breonna Taylor, Ahmaud Arbery, and Elijah McClain. The trauma for African Americans of witnessing repeated killings of unarmed black people cannot be overstated. For many, these murders demonstrate the ongoing blatant disregard for black life. Such frequent occurrences, along with a repeated lack of holding those accountable who do such acts, reflect the voices like Josiah Priest, the *Ohio State Journal*, and the *Illinois State Register*, cited earlier in the essay, voices that espoused black inferiority to whites and blacks as noncitizens of the United States. The residues of the past remain with us. How can African Americans preach Romans from this place of trauma, pain, and bloodshed? Haynes, Elaw, and King show us some ways forward.

New Testament scholar Emerson Powery once wrote, "Fundamental to any black approach to any biblical text are the notions of liberation, resistance, and survival. These issues are derived from the history

---

33. For awhile the initial length of time was stated as eight minutes and forty-six seconds. However, during the trial of Derek Chauvin, the police officer who placed his knee on George Floyd's neck, it was demonstrated that the timing was actually longer, nine minutes and twenty-nine seconds.

of black experience worldwide."[34] As seen throughout our brief analysis above, liberation, resistance, and survival permeate the interpretive approaches of Haynes, Elaw, and King in their use of Romans. They resist racist interpretations of Scripture, false ideologies like white and male supremacy, the hypocritical nature of American rhetoric and behavior, and they denounce the church's complicity in the sins of racism, slavery, and segregation. Indeed, they call for the liberation of black people— their bodies, minds, spirits, and voices. This liberation extends to the political, social, economic, and religious spheres. Their resistance and call for liberation aims at black survival in the midst of a world focused on black destruction.

Underlying the notions of liberation, resistance, and survival is the theme of African American empowerment and agency. These interpreters "seized hermeneutical control" of Romans, employing Paul's letter to speak out against injustice and oppression.[35] They also seized hermeneutical control of the narration of African American experiences and rejected white people's narration of those experiences. The oppressor can neither tell the oppressed how to resist the oppressor nor can the oppressor tell the oppressed that their oppression really is a blessing. For example, Haynes refused to allow slaveholders' narrative of slavery as a blessing to blacks to remain unchallenged. King refused to allow white segregationists to narrate the lives of blacks under segregation as beneficial for African Americans and the way God intends the races to exist. Moreover, Elaw rejected those who would impose upon women the narrative of silence from Paul's letters, when in fact Paul himself speaks respectfully about women like Phoebe who labored with him in the gospel. Elaw contended that these women could not have been silent co-laborers. Consequently, neither she nor other women preachers should be silent.

Elaw's focus on the historical context of women in ministry with Paul lifts up another important element of some black interpretative approaches to Scripture, which is the importance of Scripture's historical contexts for certain black articulations of liberation.[36] For Elaw, Pentecost in Acts and Paul's litany of acknowledgment in Romans 16 of a number

34. Powery, "African," 327.

35. Braxton, *No Longer*, 12.

36. I use the language of "some" and "certain" here to denote that African American biblical interpretation is not monolithic. African Americans have different approaches to the interpretive enterprise. See footnote 1 for important starting places regarding these approaches.

of women signified women's prominence in the early church. Elaw connects these contexts to her own preaching context. Likewise, Haynes links Paul's audiences in Romans who teach one thing but do another and who cry out "Let us do evil so that good may come" to his own audiences, who share similar troubling characteristics. In a similar vein, King takes up Paul's admonition of nonconformity to the Roman congregation to speak to his hearers of the same need. King sees the courage of the early church in following this call as one that the people in his time should emulate. Not being conformed to the world and being transformed by the renewing of one's mind was not just a spiritual reality but a social and political one as well, and includes rejecting society's racist practices and ways of being in the world. What these interpreters demonstrate is that many black interpreters read the text through their experiences but they also allow the text to read their experiences. As such, historical contexts of Scripture play important roles in arguing against anti-black ideologies.[37]

Racism is the "combination of racial privilege, prejudice, plus power. Racism requires that one racial group possesses the power to impose its racial prejudices on another group; it can make the other racial group be treated as inferior."[38] As demonstrated in this essay, these interpreters lived in a time when racism was prevalent and they spoke out against white privilege, prejudice, and power. Elaw spoke out against both racism and sexism. All of them lived in a time of pain, trauma, oppression, and bloodshed, and yet they proclaimed a liberative gospel in their time and place, rejecting the lie of white supremacy and denouncing the hypocrisy of the nation and the church. Their voices beckon African Americans to do the same and to continue the struggle. Indeed, their voices urge *all* believers of every race to participate in the struggle for equality for all people and, to use the words of King, "march to the soulsaving music of eternity."

Today, racism persists. People still perceive black and brown folks as threats, criminals, dangerous, and inferior. Racial profiling, mass incarceration, unequal access to health care, racial disparities in education, and the unrelenting attempts to make it harder for people of color to vote reveal that the lie of white supremacy endures and, like a virus, mutates into various forms. Hence, we share with Haynes, Elaw, and King the place of pain, trauma, racism, sexism, and bloodshed. Yet, from this

37. For a particular contemporary example of this approach see McCaulley, *Reading While Black*, especially his interpretation of Romans 13, its historical contexts, and the implications for a "New Testament theology of policing" (29).

38. Daniels, "Transcending," 139.

place, do we dare to continue their legacy of proclamation in the midst of all of the challenges of the twenty-first century? History lives in our bones and refuses to be silenced.

Sermon

A Whole Lot of Groaning Going On!
An African American Reading of Romans 8:22–26

ERIC LEWIS WILLIAMS

Likewise the Spirit also helps in our weaknesses. For we do not know
what we should pray for as we ought, but the Spirit Himself makes
intercession for us with groanings which cannot be uttered. Now He
who searches the hearts knows what the mind of the Spirit is, because
He makes intercession for the saints according to the will of God.

—*ROMANS 8:26–27 (KJV)*

ALONGSIDE THE MILLIONS OF blessed memories of growing up with my
siblings in our childhood home and community, perhaps the fondest
memories of my childhood and adolescent years were the memories of
events that took place in my family's church, Westside Church of God in
Christ. Now, I grew up in an African American Pentecostal church and
it would be safe to say that in the worship life of my faith community
there was never really a dull moment. From the dynamism of the music,
the intensity of the preaching, the profusion of our assembly's praise,
to the chaotic beauty of the religious dancing, the sacred drama that
unfolded each week in our congregation could rival that of the theaters
of ancient Greece!

Of all of the treasured memories of my community's worship life, perhaps the single liturgical gesture that intrigued me most was my community's practice of prayer. From beginning to end, our worship services were heavily punctuated with the prayers of the faithful. Prayers of invocation, illumination, healing, salvation, mercy, and deliverance, were uttered humbly, yet boldly, before God's throne of grace. These petitions were chanted, intoned, embodied, and quite often offered through silent tears.

During seasons of communal prayer, I remember, as a child, that I often sensed that we stood in the very presence of God and that by some miracle God saw us, God heard our petitions, and in some special way, God spoke back to the saints who waited before God in prayer. I sensed that God was present, praying with us and praying through us. And that through this mode of address we participated in a practice that was at once, both ancient and new. Far beyond mere recitation of human words, the prayers of my community were embodied, guttural, visceral, and musical. During our seasons of prayer, it was as though the ether changed, and we were transported into the very presence of the living God.

It was much later in life that I would learn through my studies of history that the groanings I heard echoed in the prayers of my elders were part of a much longer and larger tradition. For since the earliest days of the involuntary presence of Africans in America, the emancipatory yearnings of my enslaved forebears were offered to God in earnest. They longed for deliverance from the bowels of the hell of the institution of slavery.

Though commodified and marked for death from the very beginning, my enslaved ancestors cried out to God for deliverance from not only the slavery of sin but also from the sin of the bondage of American slavery. These prayers, often fully embodied, would extend well beyond the limits of human speech. Even the great emancipator Frederick Douglass once recounted that he prayed for freedom for twenty years and his deliverance never came "until . . . [he] prayed with his feet!" Friends, sometimes the words of our emancipatory yearnings are inadequate. And sometimes the complexity of the dimensions of our oppression often leave us not knowing what to pray for at all! And like the prayers for deliverance that the enslaved abolitionist prayed with his feet, we join the apostle in the text that is before us, reflecting on the power of prayer at the very limits of human speech.

In this arresting passage, we find St. Paul, an embattled apostle, teaching the Roman Christians a valuable lesson about the Holy Spirit's ministry in seasons of despair and grief. Now the reason I refer to St. Paul as an embattled apostle is because generally, wherever we locate him in Scripture, he seems to be engaged in some form of conflict. He is either imprisoned, challenging Roman governance, opposing Jewish law and customs, or confronting newly formed Christian churches regarding their lapses in community norms. In fact, even before his conversion, he demonstrates this contentiousness and irascibility while arresting and persecuting the followers of Jesus. And so the apostle was what we might consider to be edgy and intense, irritable, and defensive, always brandishing his credentials as an apostle of the risen Lord. As you may remember, he always seeks to defend his claim to apostolicity as one born "out of due season."

Edgy and irritable though he may have been, what we must remember about Paul is that this same apostle had been granted by God access to great heights of spiritual ecstasy. He had been blinded by the light of God on a Damascus road. He testified of having literally seen the risen Lord. He experienced a foretaste of the glory of the world to come, and he had been caught up to the third heaven and had heard things that were too wonderful for him to know. Yet in our text, we find him again on this terrestrial plane, in this vale of sorrows, bearing witness to the believer's need for the Spirit's help within the context of human suffering and infirmity.

But who would make a better witness to the aid of the Spirit in human weakness than the apostle Paul? If anyone is a prime candidate for understanding the workings of the Spirit under the weight of human suffering, surely it would be him. For since his dramatic conversion near Damascus, for Paul, suffering had become a most faithful companion. Even after his conversion, he suffered rejection and scorn, for many of those to whom God sent him did not believe he had been born again. At critical junctures of his ministry when he needed a shoulder to lean on, he was deserted by his closest friends. He endured threats of assassination, suffered assault and castigation. He was shipwrecked on an island near Malta, and was bitten by a venomous serpent. By grace he was unharmed and shook the snake into an open fire. He at times struggled to finance the work of God. What is more, he suffered in his physical body, and he asked God to remove whatever ailed him, only to be told that God's grace was sufficient to carry him through. As one who waited before God for the fullness of redemption, the multiplicity of sufferings he endured as a believer caused him to groan inwardly. What he experienced in his body and spirit is the utterance that we might consider the first groan, for in the words of Paul, "all that will live godly in Christ Jesus shall suffer persecution" (2 Tim 3:12 KJV).

Not only does the human creature groan in our text, but, says Paul, nature itself shares in the groanings of the partially emancipated children of God. For like those of us created in the very image of God, creation yearns to experience the freedom that God has ordained. Creation anticipates, as it were, on tiptoes its participation in the glorious liberty of the children of God.

While all nature and the human creature groan and yearn for deliverance from the weight of sin, there is a third groan, to which Paul refers in verse 26. Unlike the first and second groan, the third groan comes from the very Spirit of God. This groan, though it originates beyond us, passes through us to God, for we know not what to pray for as we ought, but the Spirit that knows the mind of God prays through us. This groan is a groan that helps our infirmities when we pray. Given the reality of our current situation, when we survey the weariness of our world, it appears that the *cosmos* is turning back to *chaos*. And because that which is chaotic threatens to upend God's ethereal design, we need the cooing of the dove that fluttered over primal chaos on the morning of creation, inseminating and enabling it to respond to God's creative word, "Let there be!"

In this historic moment of global polarization we need a third groan of the Spirit that will reorient us from a path of death and destruction to a way of life and love. We need a third groan that will give us the strength we need to stand against multivalent forms of oppression that threaten to undo the social and spiritual fabrics of our culture. We need a third groan that will free us from preoccupation with our own self-interest. My brothers and sisters, when we take time to listen to the sufferings of the world, there is a whole lot of groaning going on. We live amidst a cacophony of groanings. Our world has been groaning under so much suffering. We need the Spirit to help our global infirmities. We have groaned under injustice. We have groaned under COVID-19. Our people have groaned under the heavy knee of law enforcement. We have groaned under state-sanctioned violence committed against black and brown bodies. We have groaned under the pernicious exacerbation of distress caused by climate change. We have groaned under the weight of pollution and human, ecological devastation. And what we need now is the third groan of the Spirit that will transform and transport us to the mind and design of God.

Come Holy Spirit and hear our cries; and pity our every groan. Breathe on us. Pray through us. Groan in us. For you have the power to help our infirmities. In the name of the Father, the name of the Son, and of the Holy Spirit. Amen.

Sermon

Separated, but Loved

Romans 8:35–39

R E G I N A D. L A N G L E Y

MANY OF US CAN remember the first time we sang "Jesus Loves Me."
Probably in a Sunday school class or walking to the altar for children's
meditation. As we rose from our seats and listened to the music, we sang
the first verse and refrain:

> Jesus loves me this I know
> For the Bible tells me so;
> Little ones to him belong,
> They are weak but he is strong.
> Yes, Jesus loves me!
> Yes, Jesus loves me!
> Yes, Jesus loves me!
> The Bible tells me so.

Just reading the words can take us back to the memory of our childhood worship experience. Totally oblivious to the happenings in the
world, there was giggling, whispering, and sharing stories that embar-
rassed many parents as children sat at the altar listening to the story of
Jesus's love. It would be many years before many of us learned or appreci-
ated the words and lyrics of all four verses.

"Jesus Loves Me" was written in 1859, but not as a song. The lyrics first appeared as a poem in a novel. Instead of singing the lyrics, the

words were spoken as a comforting poem to a dying child. Imagine: a song countless have sang for generations in observance of Jesus's redemptive love was first spoken as an expression of grief, a lament.

When Paul asked in Romans 8:35, "Who will separate us from the love of Christ?" he was not asking a question in a vacuum. Having experienced every type of suffering he mentions in this text—hardship, distress, persecution, famine, nakedness, peril, and sword—Paul was a "man of sorrows and acquainted with grief" (Isa 53:3). He was beaten, stoned, imprisoned, shipwrecked, and bitten by a snake. Paul knew heartache, anguish, pain, and misery. And, he knew lament.

Speaking to a community that is hurting, Paul assures this congregation that God's presence in Christ means victory over all their suffering.

But, for some people it is difficult to be assured of God's love in the face of so much suffering. How can one focus on God's love when they feel persecuted and criminalized because of the color of their skin? Every day there are stories of African Americans who are asked to leave spaces because they look "suspicious." There are stories of African Americans who have had law enforcement called because they were walking on the sidewalk, sleeping in the lobby of their dormitory, waiting for friends in a coffee shop, asking a person to leash their dog, sitting on a bench in the park, jogging down the street, or laughing and enjoying a ride on a train. This is only a short list of the violations people believe African Americans commit "living while Black."

Since their arrival on the shores of the Americas, persons of African descent have confronted the anguish of not being loved. Seen as second-class citizens, they were denied their basic human rights and dignity. Beaten until blood ran from their veins, limbs severed as they attempted escape, families separated on the auction block, worked from daylight to darkness, they lamented their situation as they cried out to a foreign god—a god they did not know, a god given to them by white preachers, in white churches, who instructed them "to obey their masters with fear and trembling, in singleness of heart, as you obey Christ" (Col 3:22). Under the midnight skies, they probably pondered: Who is this god that allows such atrocities to happen to us?

But, then, they separated themselves and went to the hush harbors to hear sermons and express a time when there would be an exodus from slavery and a road to freedom. As they sang and lamented in the words of the nineteenth-century spiritual:

Over my head
I hear music in the air
Over my head
I hear music in the air
There must be a God somewhere.

A civil rights leader, educator, and founder of the music group Sweet Honey in the Rock, Bernice Johnson Reagon changed the words to:

Over my head
I see freedom in the air
Over my head
I see freedom in the air
There must be a God somewhere.

In *Spirit Speech: Lament and Celebration in Preaching*, Rev. Dr. Luke Powery of Duke Divinity School contends that preaching is a powerful expression of lament. The slaves in those hush harbors shared their stories of mourning, grief, affliction, and loss. Their coming together validated their shared struggles. Taking great care to go undetected, knowing they could lose their lives if discovered, they cried out under the dark skies, knowing and believing a change would come. But, if "lament is a prayer in pain that leads to trust," as Mark Vroegop states in his blog post, "The Danger of Neglecting Lament in the Local Church," how can African Americans' lamenting lead to trust in a country steeped in systemic racism and brutality?

When National Public Radio aired *Being Black in America*, African Americans described their terror, rage, and fatigue regarding the killings that are all too familiar around the country. Jason Ellington of Union, New Jersey, stated, "I feel helpless. Utterly helpless." Nicholas Gibbs of Spring, Texas, is concerned about his two sons growing up Black. "To be Black in America, you have to endure white supremacy. You have to fear the police. To be American, you have the luxury of saying, 'They should have complied!' To be Black in America, you have to hope someone recorded your compliance because you may no longer be around to defend yourself."

The words of Rev. Carol Thomas Cissel of State College, Pennsylvania, communicate the persistent struggle of many African Americans who are "weary of living in a constant state of anxiety and fear." But, Paul says, "As it written, for your sake we are being killed all day long; we are accounted as sheep to be slaughtered." But, Paul also tells the persons who are questioning God's love for them, in trying times, that they are "more than conquerors through him who loved us."

Paul is speaking in past tense—who "loved" us. He is speaking of a love that has already happened. Because he knew of the undying love Christ had for him, he asked "Who can separate US?" When Paul states, "For I am convinced that neither death, nor life, nor angels, nor rulers, nor things present, nor things to come, nor powers, nor height, nor depth, nor anything else in all creation, will be able to separate us from the love of God in Christ Jesus our Lord," he was making a declaration of the security of God's love for all humanity, regardless. Whether facing danger, restrictions, locked in or locked out, persecuted, afflicted, or lamenting, nothing can sever God's love for us. NOTHING. NO THING can separate us from Jesus's love.

Many of us view God's love the way we see our love for one another. It is a love that says, "If you love me, I will love you. If you do something for me, I will do something for you." But, Christ's love for us is unconditional. God proves his love for us in that while we were sinners Christ died for us (Rom 8:8). We cannot separate ourselves from the love of Christ no matter how hard we try. There is nothing in the spiritual realm, not angels or rulers. Not demonic powers.

Although we may feel separated from God's love due to the hardships of life, Paul reminds us that while feeling separated, we are still loved.

The site of slave markets and auction blocks was a terrifying place for enslaved families. Testifying to their fear, pain, and horror, families were well aware how quickly they could be separated, children from parents and couples from one another. Forced to leave their families and go work on other plantations, sometimes in other states, many attempted escapes once they reached their new locations. Capturing the cruelty of family separation, many considered suicide. Nothing could prepare them for the trauma of the experience. In a 1938 interview, a witness to the slave auction recalled, "People was always dying from a broken heart."

Mothers never stopped looking for their children; children looked for their parents; fathers placed advertisements for lost sons; sisters looked for sisters; husbands searched for wives; and wives sought ways to find their husbands. Although they had been separated, sometimes for years, they still loved them, expressing undying love for them.

That is the love Jesus has for us. No matter where we go, no matter what happens to us, no matter how stressed we are in life, no matter what hardships we experience, God's love is always there. Nothing can separate us from it.

"I speak to you Gentiles . . ."

Asian Americans as Liminal Gentiles

Sze-kar Wan

ETHNIC TERMS AND CATEGORIES abound in Paul's Letter to the Romans, yet few have used them as interpretive keys to its mystery.[1] Fewer still take seriously the vantage point of the Gentile converts to a fledgling movement, Paul's intended audience, as a starting point.[2] Yet, that is precisely how Asian American interpreters must approach the letter. Paul is preoccupied in Romans with relations or relationships between ethnic groups, in particular between Judeans and Gentiles, but he seems just as concerned, if not more so, with keeping his Gentile audience in their place. Time and again he reminds them of their humble beginning as pagans. He insists that even after conversion—not to Christianity but to a Jewish messianic movement—Gentiles play second fiddle to the original occupants of the covenant that God established with "our forefather" Abraham (4:1; also 4:12). Using a cultivated olive tree as allegory for the covenant, Paul tells Gentiles, darkly and starkly, "it is not you who support the root but the root you" (11:18). Asian Americans occupy a similar rung of the ladder in

---

1. Exceptions are Esler, *Conflict and Identity*, and Wan, "'To the Jew First and also to the Greek.'"

2. For the Gentile identity of the intended audience, see discussion in Stowers, *Rereading of Romans*, 29–36; Elliott, *Arrogance*, 19 and 177n67; Lampe, *From Paul to Valentinus*, 70n3; and Wan, *Romans*, 15–16. Whether or not the Roman congregation was historically composed of mainly Gentiles is beside the point, even though there is good evidence that was the case. The important point is that Paul *rhetorically constructs* his intended audience as such.

the United States. Ever since the passage of the Chinese Exclusion Act of 1882, the first racially based legislation on immigration, and continuing with the internment of Japanese Americans during World War II, racial discrimination against Asian Americans has been officially sanctioned. If there were doubts that Asian Americans are still racialized as "perpetual foreigners" today, look no further than racist epithets shouted from the highest office of the land during the COVID-19 pandemic.[3]

What Asian Americans and Paul's Gentile converts share in common is their liminality. Liminality has to do with transition. It is an unsettling phase of one's life in which the old has passed away or is no longer relevant but the new has yet to take hold. It can be a creative moment poised to give birth to a new identity or a new structure of existence, but it becomes potentially destructive when the transition is made permanent, forever perpetuating a destabilizing identity construction that robs one of vitality and a valid sense of belonging. Yet, that is precisely where Asian Americans and Paul's Gentile audience find themselves.

The Liminal Gentile

In his self-introduction to a congregation he did not found and holds little sway over, Paul uses his favorite attention-grabbing phrase to announce his intention to visit Rome: "I do not want you to be ignorant, brothers and sisters, that I had often proposed to come to you but have been prevented thus far, in order to reap some fruit among *you* as among the rest of the *Gentiles*" (Rom 1:13, emphasis added).[4] He clarifies immediately what he means by "Gentiles": "To both Greeks and barbarians, to both the wise and the foolish I am a debtor" (Rom 1:14).

The formulation "Greeks and barbarians" is not a neutral formula but part of a rhetorical strategy used to construct a hierarchy of ethnicities. It had its origin in Greeks disparaging non-Greek speakers, but since

---

3. At time of writing, the Stop AAPI Hate website reports a total of 6,603 incidents against AAPIs from March 19, 2020 to March 31, 2021 (https://stopaapihate.org/national-report-through-march-2021). For discussion of the persistent label "perpetual foreigner" (as well as the "model minority") being applied to Asian Americans, see Yee, "Ruth, the Perpetual Foreigner," and Wan, "Asian American Method."

4. Unless noted to the contrary, I am responsible for all translation. Paul's use of the formula "I do not want you to be ignorant" to indicate topics of great import can be found in 1 Thessalonians 4:13; 1 Corinthians 10:1; 12:1; and 2 Corinthians 1:8. He uses it again later in Romans 11:25.

speaking proper Greek was thought to be proof of *logos* or reason, those unable to do so were regarded as stupid, childish, effeminate, uncivilized, and incapable of governing themselves. The phrase is self-evidently ethnocentric in that it assumes a demarcation between smart insiders and outsiders who are weak and dimwitted, thereby giving insiders permission to construct discursive dominance over outsiders, even justification for conquest and enslavement.[5] The Romans found this rhetorical strategy so helpful that they adopted it in service of their imperial ambition. The only exception is that they generalized the concept of barbarians to include all non-Romans, in particular the Germanic tribes against whom Julius Caesar and subsequent emperors waged bloody wars, thus adding an ethnic dimension to linguistic and cultural superiority. The naming of inferior peoples as the Other was central to Rome's military expansion because it justified a self-fulfilling mandate to bring civilization to foreign lands. Virgil succinctly articulates this Roman manifest destiny through the prophetic lips of Anchises:

> Romans, remember by your strength to rule
> earth's peoples, for your ways are these:
> to pacify, to impose the rule of law,
> to spare the conquered, to battle down the proud.
> (*Aeneid* 6.851–53)

Rome could not be the empire without the presence of the "earth's peoples," or the subjugated and the enslaved. Romans, in other words, could not be Romans without the barbarians.

In using the phrase "Greeks and barbarians," therefore, Paul gives a nod to Roman imperialism, but he does so to subvert it. He juxtaposes "Gentiles" to "Greeks and barbarians"—all in the dative—in order to force a comparison, even an identification, between the two. The parallelism between Paul's wish to reap fruit "among you as among the rest of the Gentiles" and his desire to "evangelize those in Rome" (Rom 1:13–15) leaves

5. Isocrates in *Panegyricus* (composed around 380 BCE), for example, attempted to unite the rival *poleis* by calling for a war against the barbaric influences Persia had on the Greeks. The Greeks, he argues, defeated the barbarians in war in order to exert civilizing effects on the conquered subjects. In so doing the Greeks "saved" those who left their homeland to follow them (i.e., the enslaved) and those who by embracing the conquest have received more land than before (Isoc. 4.35–36). This, according to Isocrates, paved the way for eventual Greek colonization and the Ionic migration spearheaded by Athens. See discussion in Dobson, *Greek Orators*, 144–45. A visual commentary on the barbarians can be found in the statue of the Dying Galatian; see discussion by Kahl, *Galatians Re-Imagined*.

no doubt that he regards his audience as Gentiles and that the distinction between Greeks and barbarians must now be folded into Paul's distinction between Jews and Gentiles. Greeks or barbarians, they are all Gentiles! Paul uses the less pejorative "Greeks" to describe non-Jews when he proposes some form of parity between Jews and Gentiles (Rom 1:16; 2:9, 10; 3:9; 10:12; also 1 Cor 1:22, 24; 10:32; 12:13; Gal 3:28), but even then Paul explicitly prioritizes the Jews before the Greeks: salvation or recompense always comes to "the Jew first, then the Greek" (Rom 1:16; 2:9, 10).

To construct his Gentile audience—in all likelihood resident aliens (*peregrini*) coming to Rome from all corners of the empire either through voluntary migration or forced slavery—as "Greeks," Paul appeals to a myth of sameness, according to which all members outside my own ethnic group are all alike. It derives its strength from an essentialism that flattens differences among outsiders by disregarding their places of origins and by imposing on them putative characteristics friendly to insiders. The same can be said of the use of "Gentile" to classify all non-Jews, except it defines outsiders by their status of not being insiders. Such classification legitimates the insiders' occupation at the center of power, yet this is Paul's preferred choice when he addresses his Roman audience explicitly. In 1:13, he calls them "Gentiles" in order to foreground his authority based on a divine commission to preach the good news. Whatever status his recipients might already have in the congregation and whatever might have been their achievements, Paul insists that they are in need of "evangelization" as much as any Gentiles.[6] The question why Paul thinks he should evangelize an established congregation that had a significant history need not deter us;[7] suffice to say it is part and parcel of Paul's self-presentation as an authority figure worthy of respect and, as we learn towards the end of Romans, of financial support for his Spanish mission (15:24, 28). In 11:13, Paul similarly reminds his audience of his superior status as an "Apostle to the Gentiles" who glorifies his ministry just before delivering a blistering lecture on their and all Gentiles' place in the covenant: "Do not boast," he says in his elaborate allegory of the olive

---

6. The verb *euangelizesthai* used in 1:15 has a broader range of meanings than merely conversion. See discussion in Deissmann, *Light from the Ancient East,* 366–67; Georgi, *Theocracy,* 83; Wan, *Romans,* 59–62.

7. The history of the Roman assembly belongs to one of the most contested questions in the interpretation of the epistle, but what follows does not depend on answering this question one way or another. See discussion by Wiefel, "Jewish Community in Ancient Rome," 85–101; and Wan, *Romans,* 9–19.

tree, for "it is not you who support the root but the root you" (11:18). The same effect can be observed in Paul's division into Jews and Gentiles, which appeals to a myth of universalism, a myth structurally similar to the division into Greeks or Romans and barbarians.[8]

The inclusion of Gentiles in the cosmic vision is what enables Paul to transform a Jewish king into a cosmic Son of God, and that turns out to be a critical step in the development of Paul's political-theological thinking. When Paul envisions the eschaton, he is working towards a reign that directly challenges the Empire. In that reign Gentiles play an indispensable role by being incorporated into a new peoplehood. Ethnic issues are not tangential to the purpose of Romans but central to it.

Paul takes the rhetorical strategy of constructing his audience as "Gentiles" most likely because of their liminal status, perceived or real. According to Arnold van Gennep, who first formulated the concept of liminality in relation to rites of passage, transitions in all cultures and societies go through three fundamental phases: pre-liminal rites in which the initiate is separated from an established community, the liminal rites that can be viewed as the transition proper, and post-liminal rites that conclude the transition and incorporate the initiates into a new community with a new identity.[9] Liminality refers to the middle phase where all rules of the old society and its structures have been suspended but the new have yet to take hold. Experiences in this middle phase are both destructive and creative to those undergoing the transition, for they "shape personality, suddenly foreground agency, and (sometimes dramatically) bind thought to experience."[10] The Gentile audience in Paul's letter fit this category as they are going through or have just gone through such a transition to becoming adherents to the Jesus movement and members of the Roman congregation. That is at least how Paul perceives them—recent converts to whom he asserts himself as the superior rabbi.

The ambiguity created by his audience's liminality is at least partly responsible for why Paul constructs his audience at times as full members and at times as supplicants who have yet to earn full membership in the covenant. Addressing the Thessalonians, Gentile converts who "turned

8. See more detailed discussion by Wan, "'To the Jew First,'" 139–41, and Wan, *Romans*, 19–20.

9. Gennep, *Rites of Passage*. It should be noted that Gennep insisted that the tripartite structure of transition is universal; see Thomassen, "Thinking with Liminality," 43.

10. See the summary of Victor Turner's position by Thomassen, "Thinking with Liminality," 46. See also Turner, "Betwixt and Between."

to God from idols to serve a living and true God" (1 Thess 1:9), Paul enjoins them that they ought not submit to their passions "as *Gentiles* who do not know God" (1 Thess 4:5). In evaluating the importance of extravagant feats of spiritual prowess demonstrated by the pneumatics in the Corinthian congregation in anticipation of his critical assessment of glossolalia that comes two chapters later, Paul contrasts his audience's current enlightenment to their former life as "Gentiles [who were] led astray [lit., led and led astray] to mute idols" (1 Cor 12:2). Even in accepting his audience's conversion, however, Paul never ceases to remind them of their original status as Gentiles and their new status as Judeans. In other words, Paul never separates the converts' post-liminal stage of incorporation (into a Jewish messianic sect) from their pre-liminal stage of separation (from paganism). He thereby assumes his position as the quintessential insider, the superior rabbi, the mystagogue, addressing novices and latecomers, all Gentile converts in need of instruction before full integration.

That is clearly Paul's position in his allegory of the olive tree (Rom 11:13–24). He addresses his audience, in an aggressive tone, "To you I speak as Gentiles . . ." (Rom 11:13a). "To you" (*hymin*) is placed in an emphatic position, thus foregrounding his audience's identity *as Gentiles.*[11] But it is not the case that Paul just turns his gaze abruptly to Gentile believers as if he had been preoccupied only with Judeans;[12] his target audience throughout Romans are Gentiles. Rather, Paul destabilizes his audience's false sense of security by calling attention to their liminality, which is the object of the ensuing discussion. The syntax of 11.13b–14, which forms one sentence, is less than clear, but it should be translated as follows:

> 13 To you I speak as Gentiles:
> Although inasmuch as I am indeed an apostle to the Gentiles
> [and] I do glorify my ministry,
> 14 if somehow I might provoke my kinsfolk [lit., flesh]
> and save some of them.

11. The NRSV, "Now I am speaking to you Gentiles," places the emphasis on the wrong place, in my view.

12. So Jewett, *Romans,* 678; Fitzmyer, *Romans,* 612, and the majority of commentators who think the audience of Romans are a mixture of Jews and Gentiles. More recent scholarship has argued, persuasively and decisively in my view, that from the start Paul had in mind only Gentile members of the congregation.

The key lies with the concessive *men oun* ("although") in v. 13b, which "should be understood as a single expression . . . [indicating] what he is about to say is contrary to what [his hearers] will probably be inclined to think."[13] What is contrary to his audience's thinking cannot be his claim that he glorifies his ministry (11.13c), which presumably means his ministry to the Gentiles; he regularly connects ministry to his apostolic appointment (2 Cor 4.1; 11.23).[14] What Paul anticipates as pushback from his audience is expressed in v. 14—that he hopes to provoke his own kinsfolk to jealousy in order to save some of them.[15] In spite of his oft-touted, some say self-arrogated, designation as an apostle responsible for preaching to the Gentiles, here he discloses his innermost wish of "saving" his own flesh and blood. This is not the first time he makes this wish known; earlier he speaks of "great sorrow" and "unceasing anguish" for his "brothers, kinsfolk according to the flesh" that he "could wish or pray (*euchomēn*) that [he] be damned from Christ" for their sake (9:2–3). But the current discussion, going back to 11:11, is the first and only time Paul explicitly connects his ministry to the Gentiles to the salvation of Israel. And the mechanism by which that salvation is achieved—through jealousy—is what is truly surprising.

The reason such a view might be contrary to what his Gentile interlocutors are inclined to think is not so much the surety of Israel's eventual redemption; he states explicitly in 11:1 that God will not abandon the children of the covenant and he assumes, rather matter-of-factly, that Israel will be restored (11:15). Such position will be elaborated later in 11:25–32. Instead, Paul anticipates his audience's objection to his rather instrumental view of his Gentile ministry and, in the allegory of the olive tree, to instating a hierarchy within the covenantal people. The root of the olive tree—the divine covenant with Israel—is holy, says Paul, and that is what makes the branches holy (11:16), not the other way around. He states it explicitly two verses later: "It is not you who support the root but the root you" (11:18). Here his ethnic hierarchy cannot be clearer. Throughout the allegory, Paul likens the Gentile converts to wild olive

---

13. Cranfield, *Romans*, 559.

14. I add "and" to the text in my translation to indicate v. 13c is part of the concessive clause.

15. With most scholars I read both *parazēlōsō* and *sōsō* as aorist subjunctives because of the indefinite *ei pōs* ("if somehow"). The NRSV translation of "*in order to make my own people jealous*" makes Paul's tone more purposeful and definite than is warranted by the presence of *ei pōs*.

branches grafted onto a domestic tree and Judeans to the native branches that have been lopped off, if only temporarily, to accommodate the latecomers. But eventually the domestic tree will revive, and pride of place will be restored to Israel.[16] Paul had earlier disparaged his Roman audience, albeit obliquely, by reminding them of their latecomer status. In a passage that has been wrongly assumed to be addressed to born Judeans, Paul criticizes Gentile converts for taking undue pride in their supercilious adherence to the law: "If you *call yourself* a Judean and take comfort in the law and boast in God . . ." (2:17), and yet commit the very offenses you teach others not to commit (2:21–22). "Do you who boast in the law dishonor God through transgression of the law?" (2:23). Paul's language and the style of his criticism is reminiscent of Epictetus's critique of those playacting philosophers without a corresponding transformation of their inner life:

> Why then do you *call yourself* a Stoic? Why do you mislead the common folk? Why do you playact (*hypokrinesthai*) a Jew even though you are Greek? Don't you see how each is called a Jew, a Syrian, an Egyptian? Whenever we see someone equivocating, we are wont to say, 'He is not a Jew but is only acting.' But when he adopts the inner sentiments of one who has been baptized (*baptizesthai*) and made his choice, then he is both in fact and is called a Jew. Likewise we are also falsely baptized (*parabaptistai*), in name Jews but in reality something else, if we are unsympathetic to our own reason, far from practicing what we say, haughty as if we knew them. (Arrian, *Epictetus Diss.* 2.9.19–21)

Epictetus probably mistook Gentile Christians for converts to Judaism. Jews practiced the rite of ablution, but baptism was what Christianity was known for and what distinguished it from all other philosophies.[17]

---

16. See discussion in Johnson Hodge, *If Sons, Then Heirs,* 143–47. Her statement that Paul uses the allegory "to construct an aggregative and hierarchical relationship between *Ioudaioi* and gentiles as distinct peoples of the God of Israel" (143) is largely correct. Whether Paul is envisioning Judeans and Gentiles as "distinct peoples," however, has not been demonstrated. "In this olive tree passage," states Johnson Hodge, "Paul uses agricultural imagery to arrange Jews and gentiles as related but *distinct* peoples of the God of Israel" (146, emphasis supplied). Against that view is Paul's insistence on the *singularity* of the olive tree, which corresponds to the *singularity* of the covenant.

17. For discussion of this passage and more detailed arguments for Romans 2:1–23 being directed to Gentile converts, see Wan, "'To the Jew First,'" 149–51; and Wan, *Romans,* 16–18. Thorsteinsson, *Paul's Interlocutor in Romans 2,* comes to the same conclusion on the basis of a rhetorical analysis of the epistolary form.

If so, Paul in Romans 2:1–23 derides Gentile converts in the same way Epictetus dismissed those who had the appearance of philosophers but lacked the personal substance or behaviors to be true lovers of wisdom. Without naming them explicitly, Paul indirectly rebuts their overzealousness towards the law by construing an attack on a generic interlocutor whose arrogance is matched by a discrepancy between what they say and what they do. That this is his approach is clear from the diatribe style adopted to mount his critique: "Therefore you have no excuse, O man or woman (*o anthrōpe*), everyone who judges!" (2:1).[18] So when Paul taunts "If you call yourself a Jew" (2:.17), he is addressing Gentiles who regard themselves as full converts to Judaism but whose supercilious adherence to the commandments, in particular circumcision, makes them hyperjudgmental of others who do not share their views. In so doing, Paul assumes the role of a superior rabbi lecturing his Gentile students.

Writing Gentiles into Israel

In support of his criticism of his Gentile converts, Paul cites from the Scriptures of Israel to make a point: "For the name of God is blasphemed among the Gentiles because of you" (Rom 2:24). As seen above from our discussion of 1 Corinthians 12:2 and 1 Thessalonians 4:5, distinguishing converts from Gentiles is part of Paul's standard rhetorical arsenal. It accomplishes two intended results at once: to remind Gentile converts how far removed they are from their former life and, in this particular context, especially to remind them of their liminal status. Paul's purpose in these early chapters of Romans is to establish himself as the superior rabbi, and he does so by inscribing a hierarchy between ethnic groups in the covenant. That strategy is to reach its zenith in the olive tree allegory in chapter 11, but its foundation is being laid early on.

There is a deeper purpose to Paul's appeal to LXX Isaiah 52:5, however.[19] Far from a condemnation of the hearers, the verse is part of Yahweh's promise of restoring Israel. Its original context refers to the exile as cause for the nations to disparage God's name. Just as the people of God have been "taken for nothing"—captured and exiled as the result

18. See Stowers, *Rereading of Romans*, 122–33. For the translation of *o anthrōpe*, the stylized "whoever you are" of the NRSV takes us away from the rawness of the expression.

19. The citation from the Septuagint is not exact, but the modifications appear to be made to fit the new literary context and seem inconsequential.

of violent conquest—God promises that "[they] will know my name on that day, because it is I who am the very one who speaks, 'I am arrived'" (LXX Isa 52:5–6).[20] Since it seems clear that this passage would have apocalyptic signification for Paul, his citation is likely motivated not just by prooftexting the Gentile converts' hypocrisy but also by his desire to co-opt them into the eschatological people of God. Paul is writing the Gentiles into Israel's past and future.

There is ample evidence that throughout his ministry Paul actively incorporates Gentile converts into the history of Israel. He is able even to turn the egalitarianism in the pre-Pauline baptismal formula, "In Christ there is no Jew or Greek, no free or slave, no male and female, for you are all one in Christ Jesus" (Gal 3:28), into a script incorporating Gentiles into the history of Israel, by inscripturating them.[21] In stressing the converts' full status in the covenant and admitting that the liminal rite of baptism symbolizes erasure of advantages associated with ethnicity, social classes, and gender, the formula disclosed an original vision of radical equality. Paul's epexegetical commentary in the very next verse, however, makes clear that for him the formula means incorporating Gentiles into the Abrahamic covenant and the history of Israel: "If you belong to Christ, then you are the seed of Abraham, heirs according to promise" (Gal 3:29). Paul then successfully turns a baptismal formula that is based on a primordial notion a pre- and undifferentiated human figure into a marker of ethnicity based on the genealogy of Abraham.[22] Elsewhere Paul engages in the same type of ethnic construction in 1 Corinthians 10:1–13 and 2 Corinthians 2:14–4:6 by writing Gentiles into the history of Israel. Cavan Concannon calls the result of Paul's construction an "in-between" identity for his Gentile readers, which is equivalent to the notion of liminality I have argued in this essay.[23] In establishing the cov-

---

20. The meaning of *pareimi* is broad: *I am present, I arrive, I am at one's disposal;* BDAG, 773–74. Given the special meaning of its cognate *parousia* in Pauline literature, I have opted for "I am arrived." The MT has "Lo, here I am!" (*hinnēni*).

21. For discussion of Galatians 3.28 as a pre-Pauline baptismal formula, see the classic study by Meeks, "Androgyne," and support by Betz, *Galatians,* 196n122. Bruce, *Galatians,* 189, voices his dissent, however, though without engaging the evidence and arguments marshalled by Meeks.

22. Daniel Boyarin, *Radical Jew,* in fact, takes the primordial human figure to be the starting point of evaluating Paul. But it is clear that Paul was more concerned for the Abrahamic covenant than is generally realized.

23. Concannon, *"When You Were Gentiles,"* 97–116.

enantal credentials for the Gentiles, therefore, Paul reinstates an ethnic hierarchy by placing them under the Abrahamic banner.

In Romans as in Galatians, Paul uses Abraham to incorporate Gentiles into the history of Israel. Why Abraham? Because not only was he the father of all Judeans, he was also revered as the first convert who, according to Philo, heeded the divine call to turn from polytheism to worship the true and living God.[24] As such he is the perfect archetype for all converts, and that is how Paul presents him here as well. Two postulates need to be stated or restated at the outset. First of all, as intimated above, the target audience for this reading of Abraham are Gentile converts who hold an inflated sense of their status and an overscrupulous view of following the law.[25] Paul is decidedly not targeting his fellow Judeans who would regard circumcision as a natural part of growing up and would not be inclined to pit it against trust in God. They would wholeheartedly agree, with no complication, with Paul's statement in 4:12 that circumcision complements trust in God.[26] Circumcision *versus* trust in God was a false choice presented to adult converts to the Jesus movement only as a result of James's insistence on circumcising Gentile converts and Paul's resistance to the move (Gal 2:12).[27] That is why "in-foreskin faith" is emphasized over and over again in Paul's exposition of Abraham, in particular in 4:9–12.[28]

Once we see that this reading of Abraham is intended only for Gentile converts, the second postulate follows: we need to take as our interpretive starting point the position Paul established for his own status among the unseen congregation in the first three chapters of Romans—as the superior rabbi over inexperienced novices. That means all references to the first person plural in this chapter should be understood as Paul speaking in contradistinction from the Gentiles, and all other references should apply to the Gentile converts. When Paul refers to Abraham as

---

24. See especially Philo, *De Abrahamo.*

25. On this see Stowers, *Rereading of Romans,* and Wan, *Romans,* 1–24, esp. 14–19.

26. The paradigm-defining work of E. P. Sanders has made clear that Paul's understanding of Judaism is substantially the same as his contemporaries. It is no different on this matter of circumcision *versus* trust in and acceptance of God's covenantal election. See Sanders, *Paul and Palestinian Judaism.*

27. It can be argued that one without the other would not have created this crisis in the burgeoning movement.

28. *Peritomē* and *akrobystia* literally mean "circumcision" and "foreskin" respectively. They are not always used as circumlocutions for Judeans and Gentiles, even if that is the case in Galatians 2:7, 9.

"our father" (4:12), for example, he speaks as a Judean over against the Gentile converts, a point he makes explicit with the expression "our forefather *according to flesh*" (4:1).

A strict distinction between Paul and the Gentile converts is in fact the most natural way to take the diatribe question that opens the exposition: "What then shall we say, to have found (*heurēkenai*) Abraham our forefather according to the flesh?" Various proposals have been advanced for the subject of the infinitive *heurēkenai*. Some take "we" the Judeans to be the subject. So, for example, Richard Hays suggests translating the question as "Look, do you think that *we Jews* have considered Abraham our forefather only according to the flesh?"[29] This translation has been rightly criticized for being overly subtle, since it requires adding "only" to the text to make it fit the major theme of the chapter, the *Gentiles'* incorporation into the Abrahamic line.[30] Others take Abraham to be the subject of the infinitive but connect it to the phrase "according to the flesh," thus rendering the verse as "What shall we say that our forefather Abraham found according to the flesh?"[31] But that leaves the object of what is found unexpressed. James Dunn tries to solve the problem by understanding the phrase to mean "to find grace or mercy,"[32] but that seems speculative. The NRSV changes the meaning of the verb *heuriskein* altogether, reading it as "to gain": "What then are we to say was gained by Abraham?" That meaning finds no attestation in ancient literature, however.[33]

The most natural way that does justice to the subject matter and the personal dynamics dictated by Paul's diatribe is to take *heurēkenai* as referring to the Gentiles' having found Abraham who, Paul emphasizes, turns out to be "our forefather according to the flesh"—with "our" referring to Paul the Judean distinct from the converts. In that case the perfect infinitive states a present, accomplished fact that the Gentile converts have attained and obtained Abraham as an ancestor, which Paul would not dispute but qualify. The Abrahamic connection, in other words, is a

---

29. So Hays, "Rom. 4.1," 87; emphasis supplied.

30. Jewett, *Romans,* 307. See also criticism by Dunn, *Romans,* 1.199; Fitzmyer, *Romans,* 371. While it is grammatically permissible to take "we" as the subject of *heurēkenai,* it would require taking the question, "What then shall we say . . . ?," no longer as rhetorical but as real. That seems unlikely given the overall diatribe style of Romans and the specific form of the question.

31. So Jewett, *Romans,* 308; Fitzmyer, *Romans,* 371.

32. Dunn, *Romans,* 1.198–99.

33. BDAG, 411–12.

given and forms part of the converts' self-understanding. The supercilious converts claim it and Paul grants it.[34] The only question for Paul is *what sort* of ancestor is Abraham to the Gentile converts. Paul gives a hint what he has in mind when he adds that Abraham is actually *his* biological ancestor, according to the flesh, even as he grants the Gentiles membership in the Abrahamic lineage. To the criticism that "according to the flesh (*kata sarka*)" carries such negative connotation that Paul could not be applying it to Abraham, suffice to say Paul in fact uses the same expression to describe his kinsfolk and even the messiah (9:3, 5), which is his very usage in this context.

Paul's object in Romans 4 is to write the Gentile converts into the history of Israel, but he does so by planting a seed for an ethnic hierarchy that will come to full fruition in the olive tree allegory of chapter 11. For now he is content to demonstrate the converts' credentials by recounting Abraham's own conversion to become the first member of the covenant. Paul suggests that Abraham's lawlessness is blotted out so he could be made righteous not because of any efforts he or anyone else exerted but because he put his trust in God (4:2–5). The underlying principle is transactional. If efforts had been required, the resultant righteousness would have been considered earned wage (4:2, 4). But Abraham exemplifies someone who exerts no self-effort but places trust in the only one who could make him righteous (4:5). Paul anchors that principle with a verse from Genesis 15:6, "But Abraham believed in God and it was reckoned to him unto righteousness" (4:3), the same verse that is cited also in Galatians 3:6.[35]

In Galatians, the citation from Genesis is directed to a Gentile audience preoccupied with circumcision, and it is no different here. As confirmation, God is introduced as one who makes righteous the "impious" or "ungodly" (*asebēs*; 4:5). *Asebēs* and the noun *asebeia* are found among Paul's letters only in Romans, and Paul uses them primarily to refer to Gentiles in need of Christ. Paul states that Christ died for the "weak" (*astheneis*) and the "impious" (*asebeis*) in 5:6 and, again in 5:8,

---

34. Paul himself makes that connection in Galatians 3:29. That raises the question if Paul has assessed the Roman converts' self-perception accurately or whether this is simply Paul projecting his own formulation onto an audience with whom he is decidedly unfamiliar. This question must remain open for the time being, but that does not undermine my reading of Romans 4.

35. The meaning of the Genesis citation and Paul's usage in the present and Galatian context have been the subject of enormous output and debate since the Reformation. But my question on the relation between Judeans and Gentiles is not dependent on the outcome of that discussion.

that "Christ died for us while we were still sinners (*harmartōloi*)," using these three terms synonymously. Use of *asebeia* in 1:18 parallels *adikia* ("unrighteousness, wickedness") and both terms are used to refer to the iniquities of Gentiles. In this connection Paul's usage is typical of Greek-speaking Judaism in which there is no discernible difference between *atheos* ("atheist") or *asebēs* (Philo, *Conf. ling.*, 114; *Det. pot. ins.*, 103). An *atheos* is someone who denies God's existence or believes in polytheism.[36] Even in establishing the Gentiles' bona fides, Paul reminds them of their origins in godlessness and impiety, thus signaling a hierarchy of ethnicity.

Conclusion: The Liminal Asian American

Almost thirty years ago legal scholar Robert Chang assessed the Asian American experience in the context of critical race theory and identified three stages in response to oppression.[37] In stage one Asian Americans denied their racial and ethnic differences with the dominant culture. That proved to be an utter failure, for even after decades of assiduous efforts at assimilation, Asian Americans are today still racialized as perpetual foreigners. That failure made it necessary to move to stage two of their struggle, in which Asian Americans affirmed their racial and ethnic differences with others. In the dominant culture today, inordinate attention is still being paid to such traits as phenotypes, customs, supposed work ethics and successes (real or imputed), language, accents (perceived or otherwise), and the like for determination of belongingness. This is the stage at which Asian Americans seem permanently stuck, making it impossible to move onto the third stage of liberation.

In a state of "permanent liminality,"[38] Asian American readers identify with the intended audience of Romans, the Gentile converts, who are themselves constructed as perpetual converts. Even after having been accepted into a Jewish messianic movement, they still find themselves at the margins. Access to the center of power is promised but forever

---

36. Foerster, "*Asebēs, ktl.*," 7.189. The judgment of Fiedler, "*Asebēs, ktl.*," 1.169, that the use of Abraham to exemplify "the believing *asebēs* is entirely un-Jewish" ignores the Hellenistic-Jewish tradition of taking Abraham as the first convert from polytheism, which was considered a form of *atheotēs* ("godlessness"). *Asebeia* appears in Romans 11:26 as well, though that is part of LXX Isaiah 59.20.

37. Chang, "Asian American Legal Scholarship," 1315–22.

38. "Permanent liminality" is borrowed from Szakolczai, who first coined the term to describe conditions of modernity; see his *Reflexive Historical Sociology*, 220.

deferred. The problem with the Roman converts can be traced to Paul's misjudgment about the state of Judaism and the Gentiles' place in it. His stated desire to suffer anathema for sake of his own kinsfolk (9:3) betrays a view of (or wish for) a linear salvation history whose denouement is being hastened by Christ's resurrection. The mystery that "all Israel will be saved" as heralded in ancient prophecy is being revealed, and the history of Israel is hurling towards a climax (11:25–27). Yet he does not seem to be able to account for the challenges the increasingly Gentile character of the messianic movement presents to Israel. He is of course majorly responsible for the success of the Gentile mission, so much so it is morphing into a separatist movement. The assorted terms he uses to describe his fellow Judeans betray at least an awareness of the brewing crisis. He proudly lists the traditional prerogatives all Judeans share and contribute to the world (9:4–5), he insists on the originality and singularity of the Judean covenant (as symbolized by the olive tree in 11:17–24), and he revels in the election, the patriarchs, and the irrevocability of God's gifts and calling (11:28–29). At the same time, Paul criticizes Israel for being "disobedient" (10:21; 11:30–31), going so far as to call them "enemies regarding the gospel" (11:28). He judges them to have been cut off from the covenant, if momentarily, because of "disbelief" (11:20; cf. 11:23).

Nevertheless, in spite of his awareness that Israel is in flux, Paul's attitude towards the place of Gentiles in Israel differs little from his contemporaries', as the study above shows. Even in the midst of defending Gentiles against the additional requirement of circumcision, he calls them "sinners" in contradistinction from "Judeans by birth" (*physei Ioudaioi*; Gal 2:15). In short, Paul evaluates the Gentile converts in terms of classic rites of liminality and he sees himself as their leader, their mystagogue tasked with guiding them through the rites of passage. The liminal state in anthropological usage is always clearly defined. Two conditions must be met. First, everyone involved is aware of what to expect, when the liminal rites will begin and end, and that incorporation into the new society will be complete. Second, there must be a master of ceremony to guide the initiand through the rituals, which highlights the centrality of leadership.[39] It is clear that Paul sees himself as filling in the leadership role.

The trouble, however, is that the "home society," the Judaism with which Paul is familiar, is itself undergoing its own transition and is

39. Szakolczai, "Liminality and Experience," 148; Thomassen, "Thinking with Liminality," 52.

structurally unstable. The future becomes unknown, and Paul turns out to be a poor master of ceremony because he is personally responsible for contributing to transforming Judaism into a Torah-less movement. That the emergent normative Judaism eventually rejected the Pauline movement, paving the way for independent development of Christianity, does not change the fact that Paul had hoped to take Judaism to a place where "disobedient Judeans" are no longer the "enemies of the gospel" (11:28). As for the Gentile converts, they are shut out from mainstream Judaism and they are regarded as less than full members of the messianic movement.

This is also where Asian Americans find themselves, betwixt and between, stuck in a state of permanent liminality. This liminal moment, becoming "frozen, as if a film stopped at a particular frame,"[40] is fraught with danger but also creativity, because the loss of old structure clears the slate for the creation of the new. So, according to Victor Turner, the liminal can also be the origin of structure.[41] Gentile converts would indeed separate themselves from the Judeans to form their own movement. That is a lesson for Asian Americans who are often constructed as neither Asian nor American though they are both.[42]

---

40. Szakolczai, *Reflexive Historical Sociology,* 220.

41. Turner, *Process, Performance and Pilgrimage,* 95.

42. See Wan, "Wrestling with the 'Body of Christ,'" for a discussion of how Asian American ambiguity could be productive towards transcending tribalism.

Sermon

Romans from an Asian American Perspective

Towards True Unity
Romans 16:17–19

RAYMOND CHANG

The Call to Unity

THE HEARTBEAT OF PAUL'S Epistle to the Romans is the unity of Jewish and Gentile Christians rooted in a gospel so marvelous that such a unity would reveal its splendor. Unity is a significant theme throughout Scripture, from the Old Testament to the New Testament, and there are clear calls to unity that the people of God cannot ignore. Psalm 133:1 declares, "How good and pleasant it is when God's people live together in unity!" In John 17, right before his wrongful arrest and unjust execution, Jesus (in his longest recorded prayer) prays with his disciples. In his prayer, he asks that the Father's will would be accomplished. He then prays that those who believe in him would be one as he and the Father are one, so that "the world may know that [the Father] sent [the Son] and loved them as [the Father] loved [the Son]" (John 17:23). In his final moments, Jesus uses his last words to pray that those who follow him would be unified in ways that reflect his own unity with the Father. Jesus prays for unity because Christian unity, empowered by the Holy Spirit, is a key feature of a Christ-following community and it serves as a testament to

64

the self-giving love and self-sacrificing power of God. Christian unity bears witness of God's glory to the watching world.

Protect Unity

Asian American Christians can hurt or heal the racial divides we see in the American church and society. Though the responsibility doesn't solely rest upon our shoulders to bring about healing that leads to unity, we must understand the role we play in a society that is often segmented into racial categories, which often feature white and Black as the sole categories. These categories often lead to our invisibility and voicelessness, and pressure us to adjust our Asian Americanness to whatever is prescribed as acceptable.

In Romans 16:17–20, as Paul is concluding the letter, he writes, "I urge you, brothers and sisters, to watch out for those who cause divisions and put obstacles in your way that are contrary to the teaching you have learned. Keep away from them" (v. 17). Paul tells fellow believers to be on guard against false teachers who cause divisions, especially when those divisions contradict the gospel message. He calls upon the recipients of the letter to protect the unity generated by the gospel.

The church in Rome was a church divided. Due to the expulsion of Jewish people (including Jewish Christians) from Rome under Emperor Claudius, the gentile Christians who remained in Rome and the Jewish Christians who were expelled developed very different customs and practices. In fact, they developed different ways of interacting, worshipping, and doing life together (Rom 14–15). When the Jewish Christians returned to Rome, divisions emerged between the two communities. This is why Paul called them to unity.

Ordinary Christians are called to display a supernatural fellowship and protect the unity founded in Christ. The body of Christ is called to mirror the unity of the triune Godhead. This unity goes against the patterns of this world and exhibits a vision of God's kingdom. This unity is to be visible and break through social barriers. In our unity, we are to be of "one accord" (Acts 1:14), "likeminded, having the same love, being of one soul and of one mind" (Phil 2:2), making "every effort to keep the unity of the Spirit through the bond of peace" (Eph 4:3), "for we were all baptized by one Spirit so as to form one body—whether Jews or Gentiles, slave or free" (1 Cor 12:13).

To be unified is to be of one mind, one heart, and one will. Unity, however, is not to be confused with uniformity. Unity allows for differences; uniformity does not. You can be different and be unified; you can't be different and be uniform. Unity is to walk in step with one another, bound together in common purpose, rooted in the truth of the gospel.

It is important to note that Paul holds a different posture on disputable matters (Rom 14–15) than regarding false doctrine. For disputable matters, he emphasizes unity, calling the strong to bear with the weak (Rom 15:1). For false teaching, he draws a line in the sand (Rom.16:17).

Unity in the Midst of Racial Divisions

In a racially divided society where the church reflects racial divisions more than it resists them, this call to unity is more important than ever. Well into the twenty-first century, the average church in the United States is still more segregated than the neighborhood it resides in. This echoes the haunting statement by Dr. Martin Luther King Jr. when he said that the worship hour on Sunday is one of the "most segregated hours in America" in the 1960s. The American church was planted and is rooted in racialized soil. Many churches have not adequately contended with this reality. Instead, many have used verses like Galatians 3:28 to promote a colorblind theology and ignore calls to racial justice. Many throughout history have sought to silence those who were actively working against the sin of racism in the form of white supremacy. How do we know this? By the mere existence of the racialized minority churches. The Black church was founded in response to white supremacy within a dominantly white church in the United States. The Black church, in its many faithful expressions, serves as an Ebenezer to God's faithfulness to Black Christians oppressed by the white church's complicity in racism. Sadly, despite some efforts by white Christians to promote racial justice, from slavery to Jim Crow and into the twenty-first century, white churches have, by and large, supported the racialized status quo—a status quo that places those who are racialized as white at the top and everyone else below. This is also why Asian American, Latino/a/e, and Indigenous churches exist as well. If Christians from the racialized majority denounced patterns of dominance and control, and instead took a posture of welcome and embrace, churches would not be so segregated. This is perhaps why so many minority-serving historic churches have a long legacy of activism and advocacy in their DNA. Gospel faithfulness demanded social action and a commitment to social justice in the midst of blatant racial injustice. For example, Christ United Presbyterian Church, founded in 1880, which makes it the oldest Japanese American church in the United States, in addition to advocating for issues pertaining to Japanese American civil rights, sent their pastor to Selma to march with Dr. King. It is in a racialized soil that the American church has been planted, been watered, and has grown.

The Responsibility of Asian American Christians

What is the responsibility of Asian American Christians to promote and protect the unity of Christ? Asian American Christians need to contend with race because Asian Americans are not exempt from racialization. We are both targets of racism and tools used to perpetuate it. The term "Asian American" is a sociopolitical economic term that was coined by college students Yuji Ichioka and Emma Gee in 1968 out of a sense that Asian Americans were underrepresented in the political economy. They realized that various "Asian" American ethnicities shared common experiences of racialization, despite having different languages, customs, cultures, and histories, and that Asian Americans needed to stand together in advocacy. Asian American is not an ethnic category. Asian American is a sociopolitical racial category (like white, Black, Latinx, and Native American). Korean American, Indian American, Filipino American, Chinese American, Taiwanese American, Hmong American, and Vietnamese American are ethnic categories. Thus, to be Asian American means that we are navigating a racial landscape.

To be Asian American is to live with imposed expectations and stereotypes. One of the most common stereotypes is that of the model minority. According to this stereotype, Asian Americans are successful because we are hardworking, intelligent (good at math and science), docile (not rocking the boat), and submissive (willing to accept the status quo). At first glance, this myth seems attractive for Asians because it hails Asian Americans as successful. It gives Asian Americans honorary white status in a racialized hierarchy where white is on top. Not only does this stereotype put significant pressures (to live up to the expectations) and restrictions (limiting the ways we can live out God's calling on our lives) on Asian Americans, but it neglects the challenges of those who aren't "successful" (including, but not limited to some South and many Southeast Asian American communities who came to this country as refugees). Ultimately, the model minority trope does not actually secure our status in this country. In fact, overt anti-Asian racism exposes the reality that the model minority myth only creates an illusion of belonging for Asian Americans as it is used as a vehicle to maintain the racial status quo and underwrite a white power structure.

The model minority myth also weaponizes Asian Americans as a wedge between white and Black/Brown communities. The "success" of some Asian Americans allegedly proves that racism does not exist anymore. Asian Americans are often propped up as the "safe" minority group other minorities should strive to emulate, preserving the racialized status quo. Unfortunately, Asian American Christians are not immune to the temptation to fulfill the model minority role, especially when we personally benefit from maintaining the racial hierarchies (through positions, partnerships, and platforms), even within the church. It is important for the Christian to cultivate an awareness that leads to action, faith that leads to works, and orthodoxy that leads to orthopraxy. This means that Asian American Christians who gain understanding about the ways race functions must decide whether they will perpetuate the harm by maintaining the racialized status quo or promote healing that leads to true unity.

Romans 16:17 warns us to be vigilant of those who cause divisions. The same principle could be applied to those who maintain division as well. The word *division* implies a state where people have been separated into groundless, arbitrary factions. This is what racialization has done. The construction of race has sorted people by arbitrary features. Asian American Christians then have to decide whether they will be used to perpetuate the divisions, falling for the siren song of honorary white status, or resist the racialized status quo. This requires being wise about what is good, and innocent about what is evil (Rom 16:19). We should be wise in what God considers pure. We should be innocent in not perpetuating racialized hierarchies. Knowing and doing good is a common theme throughout Romans (12:2, 9, 21; 15:2; 16:19). It is only when you know what is good that you are able to do it. This is why it's important for Asian American Christians to understand how race, racialization, and racism function inside and outside the church. A unity based on white supremacy (manifested through white dominance, which leads to white normativity) is a false unity. Asian Americans must refuse to be used to support this kind of lie.

One of the ways we do this is by guarding ourselves against those who divide through deceit. In fact, Paul tells his readers to avoid such divisive people (16:17). Then, he identifies three characteristics of those who might shatter such a unity: 1) they teach doctrine that is contrary to the gospel message (16:17), 2) they are self-serving (v. 18), and 3) they deceive through smooth talk and flattery (v. 18). This list is sobering as we consider what it means when it comes to addressing the anti-gospel patterns of the racialized status quo. When it comes to the sin of racism, we are to be on guard for those who create and perpetuate racial divisions, those who say that God does not care about a diverse, multiethnic, multilingual community that reflects God's kingdom, those who care more about their personal image and job security over the radical call to loving God and loving neighbor, and those who say one thing in private and another in public. We ought to check ourselves that we are not such people, and check those around us to make sure they are not falling into such worldly patterns.

We can do this by taking our cues from the text.

1. We can guard against those who cause and maintain division and not allow ourselves to be used to perpetuate racial injustice, both in the church and beyond (v. 17).

2. We can grow in knowledge and wisdom. We need to develop a sober-minded, gospel-saturated race consciousness. We cannot be wise and blameless if we perpetuate the racial problems that exist. We must grow in consciousness about how race divides people.

3. We can protect and preserve unity. Standing up for what is just will seem divisive to those who have grown accustomed to and benefit from a racialized status quo. However, instead of being used as wedges that maintain racial hierarchies, we can be ramps that propel the cause of racial justice and unity. This will require us to speak up against inequities and injustices, build bridges with other communities of color, and demonstrate a kingdom unity for the sake of God's glory.

May we, like the believers in Rome, be known for our obedience to Christ (Rom 16:19). May others hear about Asian American Christians who stand against the racialized status quo, not being satisfied with what Martin Luther King Jr. called a "negative peace" or a superficial unity, but a positive peace where justice is present. May others hear about Asian American Christians who are not silent before racial injustice, but active in racial righteousness. Asian American Christians can be a tool to divide or a force to unite. Whether we buy into the racial hierarchy will determine whether we draw people towards unity or maintain our present divisions.

Sermon

Romans 15:1–13

GERALD C. LIU

[1] We who are strong ought to put up with the failings of the weak, and not to please ourselves. [2] Each of us must please our neighbor for the good purpose of building up the neighbor. [3] For Christ did not please himself; but, as it is written, "The insults of those who insult you have fallen on me." [4] For whatever was written in former days was written for our instruction, so that by steadfastness and by the encouragement of the scriptures we might have hope. [5] May the God of steadfastness and encouragement grant you to live in harmony with one another, in accordance with Christ Jesus, [6] so that together you may with one voice glorify the God and Father of our Lord Jesus Christ.

The Gospel for Jews and Gentiles Alike

[7] Welcome one another, therefore, just as Christ has welcomed you, for the glory of God. [8] For I tell you that Christ has become a servant of the circumcised on behalf of the truth of God in order that he might confirm the promises given to the patriarchs, [9] and in order that the Gentiles might glorify God for his mercy. As it is written,

"Therefore I will confess you among the Gentiles,
and sing praises to your name";
10 and again he says,
"Rejoice, O Gentiles, with his people";
11 and again,
"Praise the Lord, all you Gentiles,
and let all the peoples praise him";
12 and again Isaiah says,
"The root of Jesse shall come,
the one who rises to rule the Gentiles;
in him the Gentiles shall hope."

13 May the God of hope fill you with all joy and peace in believing, so that you may abound in hope by the power of the
Holy Spirit.

For Paul, in Christ, the powerful are obligated to serve the powerless.
Yet who has power over whom shifts and isn't always clear. Power is contested. Power is conflicted.

Paul wrote to the congregations in Rome nearly two thousand years
ago. Let's say around the spring of 57. He did not found the churches
there. But he knew them. He understood what they were going through.
So, he addressed them candidly.

What the churches were going through was something like this. In
the year 49, the Emperor Claudius expelled Jews from Rome, including
Jewish and Jewish Christian leaders. New Testament scholar Robert Jewett suggests that the ban against the Jews provided an opening for Gentile
converts to replace them and to establish new assemblies of worship. In
54, after the death of Emperor Claudius, Jews were allowed to return to
Rome. But their leadership was no longer welcomed nor respected as it
once had been. Hence, Paul pleads for the strong to welcome the weak
from Romans chapter 14 onward.

Yet a twist for careful readers of Romans is that Paul never clearly states who is strong and who is weak. He is oblique. This is maybe
because it is not as simple as associating the Gentile majority with the
strong and the returning Jewish minority with the weak.[1] It is a jumbled
affair. It is contested and conflicted. Many of the Greco-Roman churches
led by Gentiles had Jewish origins. Paul was a Jewish apostle of Jesus to
the Gentiles. Plus, Roman churches were small. Paul could not therefore

---

1. See the post-supersession essay in this volume by Brian Robinson, which also
discusses this topic.

afford to stoke further division. So, he keeps his audience wondering to ease them toward unity.

It's as if he is using sleight of hand with the identifiers "strong" and "weak" in order to catch the attention of his hearers by appealing to what they cannot resist defending with displays of honor—their egos. In actuality, who is strong and who is weak is immaterial for Paul. What he wants from the Roman churches is for them to fulfill the more important call to embrace one another with overflowing hope for the world in Christ.

Asian Americans have been seen as weak ever since we stepped onto the shores of what would become the United States. The white majority dominated by males has seen itself as strong against us.

The first immigration ban was the Chinese Exclusion Act of 1882. Initially strictly against the Chinese, its precedence also led to limited immigration quotas for the entirety of Asia and much of Europe. The effects of that ban were not repealed in full until the Immigration and Nationality Act of 1965, over eighty years later. That is also why even though there are multigenerational Asian American families in the United States, the majority of Asian Americans begin their American heritage in the middle of the twentieth century. Much of what it means to be Asian American has formed from 1965 onward. The entire time most of America has seen us as weak, especially Asian American males.

The first time the US experimented with being a global superpower began on Asian shores. The United States took control of the Philippines after the Spanish-American War. Not knowing what to do with the islands, President McKinley told the *The Christian Advocate* in 1903 that he got down on his knees and prayed to God after receiving "little help" from Democrats as well as Republicans.[2] And it came to him from God that "there was nothing left for us to do but to take them all, and to educate the Filipinos, and uplift and civilize and Christianize them and by God's grace do the very best we could by them, as our fellow men for whom Christ also died." As a result, the United States government saw to it that European priests in the Philippines replaced the Filipino ones. The Muslim sultan in the southern islands was allowed to keep his power as long as he ended the practice of slavery. The US transformed the culture of a nation by infiltrating its deepest held beliefs through the exportation of the American ideal of religious freedom and a president's hallucinogenic prayer. The US tasted for the first time how it could shift critical

2. General James Rusling, "Interview with President William McKinley," *The Christian Advocate*, January 22, 1903, 17.

pieces upon the geopolitical stage and assert its political influence to the farthest reaches of the globe, and in this case, alongside an so that it reads an imperial white and male vision putatively driven by the gospel.

The first and only use of nuclear weapons during warfare happened against Asians. Colonel Paul Tibbets flew the *Enola Gay* bomber that decimated Hiroshima, Japan on August 6, 1945. The *Enola Gay* was named after his mother. Major Charles W. Sweeney piloted *Bockscar* to annihilate the town of Nagasaki three days later. The original target was the town of Kokura. Yet lore has it that steelworkers in Kokura burned coal tar to produce a thick smoke to cloud any possibility of an air campaign upon their town.[3]

President Harry Truman, a Baptist, was reported to be aboard a submarine praying and singing hymns only hours before annihilating the Japanese with atomic fire. Domestically, Japanese American citizens were imprisoned on remote tracts of land across the country until a year after the bombings took place. The US has never apologized for massacring nearly a quarter of a million people, most of them civilians. President Reagan did issue a formal apology for the Japanese Internment with the signing of the Civil Liberties Act. That legislation also compensated more than 100,000 people of Japanese descent with $20,000 for each surviving victim, a paltry sum. With just a casual glance of American wartime action during the twentieth century, one can see that the vilest and what I would call the weakest actions of the country we call home have also been laced with distorted understandings of heritage, faith, and national strength.

Asian American identity is exponentially broad, multicentered, often multiracial, and eludes precise consensus. I have named only three national transgressions against particular Asian identities. There are also stories of unprecedented achievement, such as the election of Kamala Harris to the vice presidency. Yet remembering national sins is crucial for all Asian Americans, especially when we consider what it means to be faithful to God as Asian Americans. What the three examples show is how the "strong" and "weak" rhetoric of Paul for the Roman churches still maps onto the predicament of forging Asian American identity, especially given the historical treatment of Asians alongside the formation

3. Katherine Hignett reports how former steelworker Satoru Miyashiro told the *Mainichi Shimbun* about the efforts to divert an attack upon Kokura in "The Devastation of Nagasaki and the Luck of Kokura: A Tale of Two Cities," *Newsweek*, August 9, 2018.

of the United States as a nation and its establishment as a global super-power. Put another way, forging Asian American identity requires understanding the strengths and weaknesses of American history, history undertaken in God's name. With a sobering look at the past, we can revise a future where Asian American identity is affirmed, even embraced, perhaps even empowered, and where living together as God would desire in the US becomes the norm.

For Asian American Christian identity in particular, we must disentangle our faithfulness from the kind of white and male Christianity that created the need for domestic missions to a marooned bachelor class as a result of the 1882 Chinese Exclusion Act. We must spurn the kind of prayer that led President McKinley to his knees for the Philippines, and eradicate the kind of worship that made it okay for President Truman to sing hymns while entire populations of Japanese were burned alive. Even today Asian American Christians will have to overcome and correct cultural scorn against them as transmitters of a "China Virus" that has weakened every aspect of life as we know it.

While Paul never identified clearly who was strong or who was weak, Asian American Christians today must call out the weaknesses of white and mostly male American Christianity in all of its array. Being strong as an Asian American Christian means amplifying Paul's candor to the Roman churches and making it more precise so that we fearlessly name the specific, continuous, and venomous truth of American xenophobia and racism against Asian Americans performed in the name of God. Being strong as an Asian American Christian will require a surgical approach to Christian unity that may mean witnessing to the judgment and wrath of God as much as the promise of divine grace. Amen.

North American Indigenous Perspective

RAYMOND ALDRED

Introduction

WHEN APPROACHED TO SUBMIT this essay, one of the claims or observations put forward by the editors was that Romans is the most influential New Testament book for Christian theology in the history of the church.

I remember thinking, "Maybe where you're from, but not around here!" I do agree that Paul's occasional letter to the Romans has had a significant influence in shaping how the Protestant evangelical Euro-American and Euro-Canadian Church presents the gospel. Think about the classic North American evangelical "Roman Road to Salvation" evangelistic plotline, starting as it does with texts that reinforce the human condition of sin—Romans 3:32 ("all have sinned"), 6:23 ("wages of sin are death"), and 5:8 ("while we were yet sinners"). And this tradition of reliance on the text of Romans to narrate a pathway out of an individual sense of lostness, despair, and/or depravity (personally owned or as promulgated from the pulpit) has a venerable history reaching back to a founding father of European Protestantism, Martin Luther. It also has a prominent place in the conversion stories of Augustine and John Wesley (who was "strangely warmed" in hearing Luther's commentary on Romans).[1] But it is not just in personal conversion narratives that Romans looms large, but in the task of Western theology generally. Perhaps this emphasis on Romans comes out in similarities between the Western

---

1. Augustine, *Confessions*, 8.29; Wesley, *Works*, vol. 1, 113.

church and Paul's Roman audience. And Paul is a bit combative (as he so often is)—throwing down the challenge of his interpretation of the gospel and how law does or does not fit into it. The Romans loved law—it was their great cultural achievement—and they loved to go to war over law. This seems to me how much of the church has spent a significant amount of their time the last few hundred years, going to war with others over the meaning of the gospel. For this reason, perhaps the Letter to the Romans is a good choice for the Western church to focus upon. I will not spend much time trying to change anybody's mind about this reality. I will, however, offer a couple of observations from my thirty years of ministry as an Indigenous person in the church in North America.

My plan for the essay is to offer a lens through which to view Romans, as understood in the Indigenous church. This lens is the lens given to me by my Indigenous relatives, both living and those who are part of the venerated ancestors. When I listen to the voices of the elders, I see a different emphasis upon how we understand the gospel and therefore how we understand Romans. For the Western church, Romans is read either in the context of personal conversion narrative or it is read as "theological treatise." Within an Indigenous context, the gospel is one great story that is taken in by Indigenous people and that takes in Indigenous people.[2] When approached from the angle of Jesus and gospel as the central narrative, Romans is then testimony to how Jesus can be seen in the Hebrew Scriptures and how he is meaningful to the Romans in their Roman context. The story of Romans is then another witness of Jesus being present in an Indigenous context.

Not only is Romans narrative, it is also poetic in its rhetoric. In Romans, Paul (or whatever authorship we want to attribute to the letter) is trying to capture mystery. Like smoke in a bottle, Paul tries to communicate something that clearly goes beyond one or two or ten propositions. Through it all, the gospel is in the center and as important as reading Romans is, my Indigenous sensibilities means that I must hear it in a group setting. The apostolic faith is contained in a story and to be a story there must be a teller and there must be a listener. In the midst of these two or three, then comes the presence of Christ. It seems to me that for many Indigenous people, Christ is what is most important for the gospel. Perhaps it is like Irenaeus and the early church, who did not present Christian faith as a "system of beliefs" but about encountering Christ in

2. See Lindbeck, *Nature of Doctrine*, 33.

Scripture.[3] The gospel is always in the center, so that Jesus will come into our midst.

Finally, I want to remind people that when doing theology or preaching from Romans, it is important at this point in time to help people see and hear the good news of the gospel. In the Indigenous world we are still recovering from colonial Christian mission's emphasis upon the total depravity of man. This focus upon the thorough sinfulness of humanity was used to rationalize attempts to destroy Indigenous culture and identity. There is need for a corrective or a shift in emphasis. Perhaps this can occur by paying attention to creation throughout Romans and in particular how salvation and creation are intertwined. As we noted above, the evangelical world loves Romans 3:23—"the wages of sin is death, but the free gift of God is eternal life." Or, perhaps, Romans 5:1, "having been justified by faith, we have peace with God." These are important texts but for much of the Indigenous church when Paul points out in Romans 8:38–39 that nothing can separate us from the love of God, Indigenous hearts are moved. Indigenous people like Romans 8:22 when it talks about our mother the earth in childbirth waiting for us to be revealed as true humans, children of the creator. In classic Western use of Romans, creation is not core—perhaps apart from Romans 1 where the failure of humans to recognize God's revelation in creation is met with particular emphasis. Otherwise, God's act of creation is hardly more than an answer to a primary Sunday school class pupil asking where we come from. It is not absent; it is just secondary and not the stuff of classic "Romans-based theology." Creation, however, is the context within which Indigenous eyes hear the gospel proclaimed and discover Jesus living within Indigenous lands. His real presence appearing again and again in the proclamation of the gospel.

Reading through Indigenous Eyes: This Is a Story

A great conversion in my biblical and theological education occurred at the midpoint of my studies for my master of divinity degree (and did not involve Romans, unfortunately). I remember the moment that I was reading the Genesis 23 story of Abraham buying a cave in which to bury his wife Sarah. At that point I remember that I was having trouble finding the joy of reading the Bible and that my faith had become primarily an exercise in reason and rational thought, which meant it was dry and

---

3. Saint Irenaeus, *On the Apostolic Preaching*, 7.

from my perspective a bit lifeless. I remember deciding that morning that I would read the Bible like an "Indian." That is, otherwise than I had been trained to read the Bible within a Western academic context—that is, looking to take the text apart, then try to understand what was behind the text and what all the individual words would mean and after that come to a conclusion on "the main point of the text." Instead, I decided to read or try to hear the text according to the narrative tradition of my own Indigenous people. I would enter the story and read with "Indigenous" eyes. I remember reading and feeling something. I felt humor where I had not seen this in the story before. I understood the intricacies of how people negotiated, where I had missed that before. In this story I understood, because it is just this way in Indigenous culture, that the person selling the field, even though he said that Abraham could have the field, had every intention of not giving the field to Abraham but of selling it to him. They were just going through the appropriate cultural negotiations.

The point here is not whether this is the appropriate reading of the rhetorical setting of Genesis 23. My point is that the narrative tradition of my own Indigenous background, the intuitive Indigenous understanding of how story works, provided additional resources, a different lens with which to see and feel and enter the story. And that is what I want to propose for my reading of Romans. Romans is a story, set within a larger story, and for Indigenous people, there needs to be reciprocal entering into of both the gospel story and Indigenous story. This sort of intertextuality may be along the lines of Paul Ricoeur's two horizons.[4] The text will change because of its interaction with the Indigenous community and perhaps for the better. At the same time, the text could change people, maybe for the better as well.

Of course, to bring up the Indigenous concept of "story," you end up having to deal with the fact that Indigenous stories are first and foremost "oral." I remember the occasion when the narrative quality of all the New Testament and in particular the oral quality of Romans was driven home. I was listening to my daughter Catherine giving a paper on the similarities between Cree orality and the oral nature of New Testament Greek, trying to prove her point that the qualities of narrative or story can be found throughout the New Testament.[5] Her conclusion was that the marks of Cree orality—repetition, the presence of a change in register

4. Ricoeur, *Time and Narrative*, 77.
5. Aldred, "Let Me Tell You a Story."

of the voice, and the placement of particles—are there within the New Testament. There is an oral quality that the writing is trying to capture. This presence of these oral qualities means Romans is closer to poetry when Paul is "waxing" eloquent, than to a theological treatise. Or, perhaps better to say, it is a theological treatise that is written to be presented orally, like a poetic recital.

The implication I want to draw from Catherine's point is twofold. First, as with my previous example, Indigenous story tradition helped me to hear the text in a different way, so Indigenous language and in her case, translating the Bible into an Indigenous language, helped her to see the presence of narrative devices in the writings of all the New Testament writers, including Paul. My second point is that since Paul's letters can be read as story, or at least fitting into story, this has implications for how dogmatic we become about our own conclusions from the text. As "story" (instead of, say, "treatise"), it is more apparent that there is a surplus of meaning within the text, to borrow a phrase from Ricoeur, and Indigenous understanding and culture draw out that surplus.[6] The surplus of story creates a different hermeneutic than an interpretation that focuses upon finding the core of the teaching and transferring that core into a different context. Rather, the interest in Indigenous hermeneutics is upon telling and hearing the story in a manner that allows for a plurality of possible meanings.[7]

Drawing on translation theory and oral composition theory, Catherine identified several storytelling techniques that are present within Cree translation of the Bible and also within the original Greek New Testament writings. This includes the repetition of ideas and phonetic repetition, with both giving the listener an opportunity to better remember what is being said. Others have noted Paul's use of repetition, particularly with regards to law—like F. F. Bruce for instance.[8] However, what Catherine points out that F. F. Bruce does not is the way that it sounds when spoken. Again, this is about attention to its oral qualities because "stories" are "oral" if you are Indigenous. We understand that most of the early church were not literate people but it was about hearing and doing the word of God. Thus, for the project of this book, the Indigenous

---

6. Ricoeur, "Rhetoric—Poetics—Hermeneutics," 71.

7. McLeod, *Cree Narrative Memory*, 92–95.

8. Bruce, *Epistle of Paul to the Romans*, 52.

contribution to "how to read Romans" would be to remind the reader
that it is about listening.

A turn back to orality is occurring and Indigenous mother tongue
speakers and Indigenous language have a contribution by reminding us
that it is the words that are spoken and heard or received. Cree is meant
to be spoken and heard. Cree has a sound system of syllabics, with each
symbol representing the sound so that you can make Cree sounds.[9] While
syllabic codes are a step toward the type of written texts created with the
Roman alphabet of European languages, the written representation of
Cree is still firmly grounded in Cree orality, based on what is said aloud.
For English speakers, their English texts represent "written practice" and
as such is "read" with little thought of it being spoken aloud.

So then, turning to Romans. If we read Romans paying attention to
the story, we can make a couple of observations. First, when reading Romans, one is reminded of its relation to the stories within Hebrew Scriptures. In Romans 1:18–32, Paul could have in mind the stories of Genesis
3–11. Sin has entered into creation and society is powerless to stop its
spread and degradation upon society. Romans 1:21—"For although they
knew God, they did not honor him as God or give thanks to him, but they
became futile in their thinking"—could be understood as referring to the
story of the man and woman exchanging the glory of God for the snake
and listening to the snake and treating creation with disrespect by violat-
ing the proper treatments of the trees within the garden. It could also be
understood within the context of the stories in the Gospels. Those who
should have known, both the Jewish religious leaders and the Gentile Roman leaders, after witnessing the invisible attributes of God in creation
but also in the second act of creation, the incarnation of Jesus Christ,
they should have known but they rejected Christ and God and crucified
the Lord.

This reading or hearing is consistent with an Indigenous understanding of land or creation. My Indigenous reading of Genesis 3 points
out that the first sin humanity makes is not only against God but against
creation itself. This theme is picked up in Romans 8 with Paul's pointing
out that salvation will impact in a positive way our mother, the earth,
who is groaning as in childbirth. A hermeneutic flowing out of the Reformation would focus on finding the "one right meaning" of Romans 8
(Ricoeur). With that approach, the mother earth metaphors are not the

9. Okim*asis, Ratt, and University of Regina, Cree, Language of the Plains, vol. 1,
xiv.

primary focus of the core of the message. However, with Indigenous per-spective and its interests, the metaphor of mother earth gets thicker and rich and begins to draw out the implications of how creation is impacted by human salvation. Wolfhart Pannenberg, a Lutheran theologian, how-ever, points to the reality that creation itself must be saved by a human, and this is done through the human, Jesus Christ. Paul's writing, then, as Ricoeur points out,[10] is cut off from the original context, and when encountered by Indigenous Cree people, it is not improbable for them to ascribe greater significance to the role or involvement of mother earth with regard to salvation. Indigenous attention to creation would add to a richer, fuller meaning of the text as our mother the earth longs for the revealing of God's salvation brought about by Jesus.

I need of course to make a statement about Paul's observation that many humans worship creation. Indigenous people respect mother earth but they do not worship the earth, whatever the suspicions of Western ears that hear the term "mother earth" spoken by Indigenous speakers. It may seem counterintuitive, but perhaps there is a great tendency among those who are cut off from the land to worship creation. Walter Bruegge-mann makes this observation about Israel in his book *Land*.[11] As Israel moved away from living in tents upon the land to cities, the incidence of idolatry seemed to increase. Perhaps Paul's words to those who are cut off from land rightly indicate a caution to not fall into worshipping creation but to those who live with land as a relative, worship of creation is less of a temptation.

Reading with Indian Eyes: Indigenous Law and Romans

For the Indigenous people of the Northern Plains the circle is of great significance. Our teepees are circular, we dance in a circle. The circle reminds us that we are related or connected to all things. Harmony is assumed as the starting point for how we see the cosmos. Indigenous Archbishop Mark MacDonald teaches that the most important things for people are placed in the center of the circle. Lakota people place the pipe in the center. On the other hand, the Anishinabek and Cree people place

---

10. Indigenous author Neal McLeod points out the similarity in thinking about surplus of meaning between Ricoeur and Indigenous storytellers. McLeod, *Cree Narrative Memory*, 16.

11. Brueggemann, *Land*, 53–59.

the drum in the center. For the Indigenous Anglican church elders, they also place the gospel. When you do ceremony, you begin by acknowledging that all things are related and that it is a good creation or good world. In acknowledging all things, we are now creating sacred space. The proper relatedness of all things is recognized by Indigenous people because our Indigenous law flows out of creation—at its heart a network of relations(hips).[12] Appropriate ways of relating to things, if followed, assured an ongoing harmonious relationship in the land. Two examples of this reality can be understood from the Lakota "making relatives" ceremony and from historic negotiations of Treaty 6 in Canada between the British Crown and the Saskatchewan First Nations. Both of these examples illustrate how bringing harmony to relationships was seen as key to healing the land.[13] These examples help illustrate how Indigenous law, rooted in the interrelatedness of creation, allows us to hear Paul's emphasis upon Law or Torah as flowing out of Christ not as a puzzle ("How do gospel and law fit together? Are they not opposites?") but rather as good news or gospel.

In the first example, Black Elk, a holy man of the Oglala Sioux, describes to Joseph Epes Brown the Lakota making relatives ceremony as a way to work out historic enmity that had existed between two Indigenous tribal groups. By becoming relatives, the good of both groups was assured. According to Brown, as told to him by Black Elk, the two groups come together for the ceremony. There are objects or mnemonic actions to remind both parties of the basis for the hard feelings between the groups. There is a ceremonial smudging with burning sweetgrass to all the directions and then a prayer is offered affirming that in this ceremony these two groups are now becoming relatives to live out in peace. They were making peace and they were committing themselves before the Creator to live out this peace in the land as relatives.

> O Grandfather, Wakan-Tanka, behold us! Here we shall make relatives and peace; it is your will that this be done. With this sweet grass which is Yours, I am now making smoke, which will rise to You. In everything that we do, You are first, and this our sacred Mother Earth is second, and next to Her are the four quarters. By making this rite we shall carry out Thy will upon this earth, and we shall make a peace that will last to the end of

12. MacDonald, "Reclaiming Our Culture."

13. Ottmann, "First Nations Leadership and Spirituality." Morris, *Treaties of Canada*, 194.

time. The smoke from this sweet grass will be upon everything in the universe. It is good![14]

A second example that also points to the reality of Indigenous law being primarily about maintaining or repairing relationships is provided by historic Indigenous treaties. Making harmony in the land through treaty would increase the possibilities not only for the Indigenous generations who negotiated the treaty but those who would come after. Indigenous treaty was an agreement between three entities—First Nations, Newcomers, and the Creator.[15] As such a treaty took on a covenant status. Through the treaty negotiations the First Nations and Newcomers became like relatives and they promised to live in the land harmoniously.[16]

Now Indigenous law flowed out of creation—a point well made by MacDonald. The Europeans, however, had long relied upon practices of doctrines of *terra nullius* or the doctrine of discovery. The Newcomers claimed that Indigenous people had no law, no nations, and thus were uncivilized people. This denial of Indigenous law is, of course, a racist doctrine that was ultimately used to deny the humanity of Indigenous people.

This recognition of Indigenous law is very important for a reading of Romans. Paul points out that, although he is not denying the importance of the Jewish people, there is a law working within the Gentiles (Rom 2:20ff.). Again, European Gentile nations would continue to deny that Indigenous people had a law, but Romans draws out the reality of God working within the Gentiles, including the Indigenous people. This is a point that Irenaeus draws out in his writing, that the "barbarians" (the nations who do not speak Greek), do believe and have salvation written on their hearts. They show that they have true faith, the marks of that true faith being belief in Christ and in one creator God.[17] Irenaeus's emphasis on God as creator and linking that to the incarnation draws a line from the gospel and salvation back to God's identity as Creator. Thus for Irenaeus, the answer to the question of which God is the true God—that answer is, as it is throughout the Hebrew Scriptures and the Christian Scriptures, the creator. Indigenous people's understanding that the law of relationships is displayed or understood by learning from creation—this echoes and resonates in those opening words in Romans.

---

14. Black Elk, Brown, and Steltenkamp, *Sacred Pipe*, 103.

15. Ottmann, "First Nations," 83ff.

16. Miller, "Compact, Contract, Covenant," 33.

17. Irenaeus, *Against the Heresies* 3.4.2.

So, as we have discussed, Indigenous law, flowing out of creation, means living in harmonious relationship with all of creation. Indigenous spirituality then begins with the goodness of all of creation and an understanding that thankfulness is a proper response. I have seen this in the conversations I have had with other Indigenous people from my own territory. A friend of mine once related to me that the heart of our spirituality and ceremony was to pray in the fall for good hunting and, in the spring, to give thanks for good hunting. Thankfulness is a key component for maintaining respect and harmony spiritually as well as materially. These two, of course, are not divided in the Indigenous context. Spirituality flows out of a proper understanding of creation, the material. This idea is echoed in Romans 1:20–21, where Paul makes it clear that the proper response to seeing the eternal power within creation ought to produce thankfulness toward the Creator. Paul's further explanation of the judgment that will come upon those who do not honor the Creator is in keeping with Indigenous understanding of what proper spirituality involves. According to the Cree, for example, those who are truly spiritual, engage in actions that make clear that they indeed have the spiritual power they claim to have.[18] This point Irenaeus also understands—namely those who reject the Creator and law flowing from or displayed in creation will tend to find their entire life wracked by sin, a point Paul makes as he develops his argument in Romans.

This understanding that the goal of life is about understanding and living out proper relatedness has been understood for centuries among Western scholars such as Émile Durkheim, Richard Preston, Alasdair MacIntyre, James McClendon, and many others. Preston notes that the Cree people had an innate understanding of how every one of their personal actions impacts every other relationship. Therefore, they understand that the goal of law is being properly related and this is what Christ has come to impress. This Indigenous understanding then allows me to see Paul's emphasis upon law in those terms. That law can only be properly understood if one sees the law as located in Christ, who brings about proper relatedness through his life, death, and resurrection, and this then becomes the pattern for our own lives. This can be traced through Romans. The eternal life ("life of the age") will bring about proper relatedness between human beings and creation (Rom 8) as our mother the earth groans as we are slowly changed to be who we were created to be.

18. Waugh and Roan, "On Concepts and 'the Best Place.'"

Proper relatedness between people and Creator comes as we have peace with God through Jesus Christ (Rom 5). Proper relatedness between peoples, Jew and Gentile, comes as we occupy the same creation and are brought together through the gospel of Jesus Christ. Proper relatedness to ourselves is raised in Romans 12. Rather than worshipping our body's false identity, we are able to see that our lives are poured out for one another (Rom 12) as we live out this proper relatedness in Christ, God, the Creator, is glorified. In Christ then all relationships and all of creation is healed. Bringing Indigenous identity and understanding allows me to hear and see this in Romans.

Reading with Indigenous Eyes: Seeing All My Relatives

Through thirty years of ministry in Indigenous contexts I have found that when preaching and teaching the most helpful texts have usually been from the Hebrew Scriptures and from the Gospels. Discipleship in the Gospels and discipleship within the Indigenous church are both based on shared experience and story rooted in the present and the past. Perhaps this section of the essay seems out of place but it is in keeping with an Indigenous way of understanding Scripture. In Western contexts, the "gospel of Romans," once distilled by theologians, feels very much like a stand-alone entity that does not need the rich narrative of the Gospels. The "Romans Road" evangelistic path is a single-track trek through Romans! From an Indigenous perspective, it might be better to say Romans helps the gospel but you cannot forget the gospel. Preaching and reading needs to be from the "whole counsel of God." A. W. Tozer reminded people of the holiness movement that "truth always has two wings" and so you should remember what all Scripture teaches.[19] I am pressing for the idea of reading Romans beside the Gospels because I think you end up with something that is "better news" for Indigenous listeners than the narrow "Romans Road" gospel.

First, in the Indigenous church, we are trying to impart or model how life is lived or taken into the gospel. Hans Frei in *The Eclipse of the Biblical Narrative* points out that this pattern of having life taken into the biblical story was the pattern at least up until the Reformation but faded to the background of the mainstream North American church.[20] Indig-

19. Tozer, *That Incredible Christian*, 18.
20. Frei, *Eclipse of Biblical Narrative*.

enous oral story culture helps to bring this to the forefront again. Paul's life is modeled in Acts (as are that of all the other apostles) as following the pattern of Christ's life. We, however, might not know the way the story goes for Paul apart from Luke-Acts. We understand the trajectory of Paul's life and his ministry from the stories related in Luke-Acts and we understand that Paul is very much a Jew who is following the Hebrew Scriptures come in the flesh, Jesus Christ. The words of Paul in Romans, then, are coming from the one who is situated in the story told in Luke-Acts and whose life follows the pattern of Christ as told in the Gospels. "Paul the theological writer" of modern Western scholarship who some consider to be the "true Paul" (versus the Paul who speaks in Luke-Acts) is set apart and of another mode than the narrative writers/tellers of the Gospels. Western exegetes frequently assume Paul has little interest in the Gospel narratives (and even conservative exegetes who would not outright make that claim follow suit in terms of reading Paul narrowly within the Pauline corpus only).

Second (and related to the first), I think by placing Romans as supporting the Gospels, rather than as the book that provides the definitive summation of the gospel, we end up with a different story and we might have ended up with a different story of first encounters. Both the early evangelical mission workers and mainline mission workers were keen to point out the lostness of Indigenous identity and culture. Throughout this task, Romans was used to draw out the way that sin was completely dominating everything in the culture. To be fair, many saw their own life as completely sinful and so it made sense that they would see their preaching as necessitating an emphasis upon the lostness of humanity. Reading the journal of David Brainerd, for example, his spirituality is often expressed with acknowledgement of his sinfulness.[21] For many in the early evangelical church, the Bible began, in a manner of speaking, with the serpent enticing human beings to rebel against God and quickly all things are cast down and relationships broken so that the starting point for all humanity is the alienated individual.

The Capetown Commitment from the Third Lausanne Congress shows how the evangelicals saw the world in such negative terms. In citing the reasons for God's mission, it points out that "Human beings are lost and stand under the just judgement of God in our sin and rebellion" (5). The importance of the goodness of creation is discussed later in the

---

21. Brainerd, Edwards, and Howard, *Life and Diary of David Brainerd.*

document, but the emphasis is clearly on the brokenness of the world. This stands in contrast to an Indigenous understanding that it is a good world and that we function from harmony to harmony. In a contemporary context, reiterating the sinfulness and fallenness of humanity and the brokenness of the world to a people who have lived with generations of missionaries all telling us that our identity and culture is sinful and wrong—this makes it difficult to hear the gospel as good news.

This emphasis upon the brokenness of the world is found across the spectrum of the church. The Reconciliation Network wrote in a paper in 2005, "The mission of God in our fallen, broken world is reconciliation".[22] This sentence shows how heavily the emphasis falls on the world as fallen and broken. I am certainly a fan of reconciliation and the world certainly needs more of it—but what I see in statements like the one from these forty-seven scholars is that the starting point is always a fallen and broken world. Maybe it is a Western fixation with "problem-solving" and creating principles to solve problems and so the first principle is always the problem to be solved. I understand they are attempting to point out the seriousness of the problem of sin and of the need for reconciliation, but I wonder if it ends up condemning everyone and everything because of its one-sided emphasis.

Indigenous people, on the other hand, begin and end with the goodness of creation. Salvation and reconciliation, then, are to affirm the harmony that exists within a good creation. Things do go wrong, but relationships are warped and damaged—not completely severed. As MacDonald points out, there is a part of us that the elders taught is deeper than sin. It is the part that God still calls to and we hear the voice of the Creator calling us to reconciliation and healing. Indigenous people are not naïve about the state of humanity or of our world, but we believe that a good Creator made a good world, and that we are called to live out the goodness of creation and Creator in the world around us.

The idea that something is deeper than sin can be found throughout the Scripture, but in Romans the whole idea of the gospel is that the love of God is deeper and stronger than anything that may attempt to separate us from the Creator (Rom 8:37–39). This, however, will make some nervous (or elated) and think that it harkens back to classic liberal ideas of the divine spark within each person. Does this take us down a pathway where we completely discount personal sin and responsibility? I would

---

22. "Reconciliation as the Mission of God," 5.

counter with an argument from the language of the field of addiction and recovery. Gabor Maté relates that to the alcoholic, someone whose brain is damaged and cannot stop drinking, the idea that they could take responsibility free from "toxic self-judgment" is an opportunity for living a new life.[23] In another paper I likened this taking up of responsibility to that of repentance.[24] The grace to respond to the urging of the Spirit comes from the Creator, as all of life does, and so cannot be reduced to works or heroic human effort. This is where the Indigenous perspective on the interrelatedness of all things matters. While Western theological suppositions built on Romans relentlessly point to the chasm between God and humanity generated by human sinfulness, starting with a more hopeful view of the Creator and the bonds of love and relationship within creation shifts the contours of the story. Where there is only a chasm between Creator and human, everything humans do and try must be consigned to sin and fallenness. And so it is that missionary efforts premised on this dark starting point consign Indigenous culture and identity and any understanding of the spiritual world within Indigenous cultures to sinfulness. Christendom muddied the waters as to whether the missionaries' own culture and identity were equally lost—a story for another day—but certainly the individual self-loathing as the starting point of the gospel was projected as a whole on the cultures they encountered. You can read Romans this way, but do you have to? What if you take it as a given that the writer of Romans is also the preacher at Athens in Acts 17, where he endorses the Athenian creation theology and that God's expectation of the nations is that they would seek him and find him (Acts 17:22–28), that all genuine insight of humanity into the nature of the Creator and the relationships of creation has not been lost? What if we assume that the genuine relationship between God and Israel in the Hebrew Scriptures are also there and available between the Creator and those who recognize the Creator and the laws of creation? What if we read Romans with that starting point? What if we take it as genuine testimony that the Indigenous "law of creation" comes out of a right response to the Creator who reaches out and calls for humanity to reach back?[25]

Returning to the idea of story, my own practice of reading Romans and any of the occasional letters of Paul, I follow the pattern of trying to

---

23. Maté, *Realm of Hungry Ghosts*, 332.

24. Aldred, "Indigenous Reinterpretation of Repentance."

25. I gained this idea from a discussion with Dr. Andy Reimer circa August 2021.

locate the rhetorical setting of the letter within the story of the gospel. Romans is difficult because we do not know from Scripture whether Paul made it to Rome or how this letter was received—we just have Paul's statement about his desire to eventually be present with the believers located there. We do know, however, that the issue of the relationship between Jews and Gentiles was something Paul needed to talk about. By the end of the book of Acts, the church is primarily focused upon the mission to the Gentiles. This explains Paul's extensive use of the word "law." He wants to emphasize that there is an inner law working in Gentiles that fulfilled the same purpose or goal as the Torah or Law for the Jews—and this law is a good thing—but that there is still a need for a savior. Thus, his goal could be read, through Indigenous eyes, not only to point out the sinfulness of all humanity, but to point out that all peoples approach the Creator of the universe through the same savior, Jesus Christ. A proper reading of creation or law leads to the same conclusion. This should produce humility in people, as they realize that without understanding granted by the Creator, there is no real understanding at all. There is an understanding from the law, genuine and good, but the Creator must join us for an in-person revelation of his limitless love—and this is something the good law prepares us for. This "second act of creation" comes from the same Creator and is recognized by those who already were seeking good relationship with Creator and the rest of creation.

Let me continue for a bit more. Paul seems intent, according to my good friend Andy Reimer, on reminding the Romans that the promises to the Jews are extended to the gentiles. Although they are Romans, part of the most powerful earthly kingdom and gentiles, ascending in control of the church, they do not replace the Jewish people. In keeping with the teaching of Christ in the Gospels, Paul is not advocating for the creation of some earthly kingdom (that would inevitably eclipse and not create the kingdom of God). Paul writes to remind the Romans that the kingdom is always in the now but not yet. We are to give ourselves away in love for each other. The ethic of the gospel as expressed by Paul brings us to the Indigenous value of using our freedom of choice for the good of the group, not to merely advance our own desires. This makes better sense of Paul's focusing in on those who fail to understand the significance of the creation and the second act of creation, that it is sacred in that it reveals the eternal reality of the Creator. Those who focus primarily on human beings' existence and bodies end up turning to all kinds of licentiousness in an attempt to find meaning.

To ensure that we do not end up focusing only upon our favorite passages of Scripture, the Indigenous Anglican Church follows the lectionary in its gospel-based discipleship approach. At regular meetings, as stated above, we read the Gospel, as laid out in the lectionary, and reflect how the Creator in Christ is directing our lives to hear and do or live the word that is enfleshed again as we gather together in groups of two or three. This, as Romans puts it, is what living out our lives in worship to God and service to one another is about. It is the natural outflow of the life lived in thankfulness to the Creator.

Conclusion

Romans has been a favorite text of the Euro-American and Euro-Canadian church in spreading the gospel among Indigenous people. Through it all Indigenous people heard the story of Jesus and saw how it lined up with their understanding of creation and the law that the Creator had given to them via creation. Indigenous people received the gospel and continue to find Jesus throughout their spirituality and hear this same Jesus proclaimed throughout the gospel story. The assumption by the Newcomers has been that what Indigenous people really needed was to understand their sinfulness. The emphasis on "individual alienation from God" that they felt and found in Romans became projected onto the Indigenous people as a whole. But of course the alternative to Indigenous cultures (assumed to be intrinsically fallen) was Western culture. And so the move from gospel to assimilation became seamless. But with a different starting point there can be a different outcome. I have shown that the Indigenous understanding that has influenced how I see the gospel has allowed me to see again that Christ is the center of what Paul proclaims in Romans. Law flows from the Creator and is related to living in right relationships with one another. The gospel is about healing the wounds of human beings and all of creation. An Indigenous reading will also push the North American church to remember that this is a good world and this understanding pushes us to give thanks.

Sermon

Restoring Harmony with Creation

Reading Romans 8:18–23 with Indigenous Stories[1]

T. Christopher Hoklotubbe

A MALAISE ARISES WHEN I think about the trajectory of our current environmental predicament. While I'm generally an optimist, I've grown quite cynical about our prospects for stopping the apocalyptic climate change that awaits us, and especially the world that awaits my children and those presently living in ecosystems most threatened by this coming change.

By the year 2050, the average global temperature is expected to rise three to seven degrees Fahrenheit.[2] In Iowa, where I now reside, on land that formerly made up the trading and hunting grounds of the Baxoje ("Ioway") and Meskwaki nations,[3] the trend has been to get an increasing amount of rain in the spring and less in the summer. This weather pattern has been a boon for corn and soy, but as it gets more extreme, heavy rains and flooding are feared to cause more soil erosion, shorten the window for planting, and leech more nutrients and nitrates from the soil and

1. This sermon is a combination of two sermons I preached for Sanctuary Community Church in Coralville, Iowa and represents original expansions and modifications of my essays "Native American Interpretation of the Bible" and "A Native American Interpretation of Romans 8:18–23."

2. Irfan, Barclay, and Sukumar, "Weather 2050."

3. For a helpful map on the world that details the traditional lands and territories of Indigenous peoples, see https://native-land.ca.

pollute our drinking water, and further down the rivers, contribute to the polluted dead zones of the Gulf of Mexico.[4] Let us hope and pray that the flooding that devastated Cedar Rapids in 2008 and the hurricane-like winds that destroyed crops, trees, and powerlines in the 2020 derecho storm don't become the new normal.

Now while most of us will be able to adapt and it really isn't so end-of-world gloomy for us (at least I hope), we should be more concerned about the quarter of the world's population that lives on or near the coastlines, which will be impacted by rising sea levels and more intensifying cyclones, hurricanes, and typhoons. We should be especially concerned for those who can't so easily adapt and migrate to more sustainable environments.[5]

And climate change isn't the half of it. There really seems to be no end to our throwaway culture of plastic.

No end to the industrial waste and toxic chemicals that are byproducts of our consumer goods.

No end to our dependence upon deep-water drilling, fracking, and pipelines to extract and transport fossil fuels.

No end to the inadvertent and yet expected oil spills that pollute our oceans, rivers, and land.

In our rapidly changing society that seeks quick and easy profit and whose economy and status is wrapped around consumption rather than sustainability, there seems little hope.

Yes, we recycle, but is that enough? What good does driving a Prius do in light of the fact that over two-thirds of greenhouse gases are generated by a mere one hundred transnational corporations?[6] Are we deluding ourselves in our naïve presumptions that we can stop this machine, propelled by corporate profit and our own habits of consumption, and dismissed by pseudoscience and government officials?

What Might an Indigenous Reading of Romans *Teach Us* in This Moment, Here?

Indigenous peoples have long held that our lives are interconnected and woven together with all that is around us—this includes the animals,

4. United States EPA, "What Climate Changes Means for Iowa"; Boulter, "An Uncertain Future."

5. Sengupta, "This Is Inequity at the Boiling Point."

6. Griffin, "CDP Carbon Majors Report 2017."

plants, trees, and even rocks. In the Lakota language spoken by the Oceti Sakowin who also occupied parts of Iowa, there is a beautiful expression that captures this vision that we are who we are in relation to all of creation: *Mitakuye Oyasin*. This sacred phrase can be translated as "all my relations" or "we are all related," and often closes prayers and ceremonies. Animals are not considered to be lower subspecies compared to humans, but like humans are, in Lakota, *oyáte* or "nations"; creatures are nonhuman persons.

According to the Haudenosaunee (or "Iroquois") creation story, it is the animals that come to the rescue of a young pregnant woman who has fallen from the skies and literally pave the way for her to survive. Birds catch the woman and other animals, most notably the toad, retrieve mud from the bottom of the ocean, and craft the first patch of land on the back of a turtle—eventually creating North America, which is referred to by the Haudenosaunee as Turtle Island. Such narratives contrast with common readings of Genesis 1:28, wherein the Creator is understood to have instructed the first humans to dominate and subdue creation. Such interpretations have been complicit with and used to rationalize our deforestation and scarring of the earth in order to extract its resources at unsustainable rates. At the heart of Indigenous creation stories is a calling to live in harmony with creation, which entails practices of sustainability and reciprocity. However, Genesis 1 isn't the only or even last word on creation in our Christian Scripture.

Paul of Tarsus has an underappreciated understanding of creation that many Indigenous theologians have noticed in Romans 8:18–23. Now a quick note about Romans: this is Paul's self-introduction and fundraising letter to the Roman churches. He writes this from Corinth in the spring of 52. He is just about to depart for Jerusalem to deliver a collection of money to be donated to the church there, after which he plans to share his gospel in Spain, with Rome being his launching point. This letter is his attempt to respond to *a lot* of bad press that has preceded him and Paul wants to lay out his gospel to put the haters to rest—who are mostly fellow Christians who think he's being too syncretistic with a foreign culture—a common charge brought against Indigenous Christians! His opponents hold that Paul is going against Scripture in preaching that Gentiles don't have to be circumcised or keep kosher—convictions that seem to be based on Paul's *vision* of Jesus—a story and experience that certainly resonates with many Indigenous readers! Romans 8 falls along the climax of Paul's damning indictment of the incapability of all humanity, both Jews and pagan Gentiles, to follow God's law, and his assertion how the Spirit of God and participation in the Messiah's perfect faithfulness are humanity's only hope of being declared to be in right covenantal standing with the God of Israel. Chapter 8 is the fireworks, the grand release of the tension he has been building up in his first seven chapters of telling his Roman audience how they are lost and utterly depraved in their sin. Chapter 8 is about hope—the hope that the Creator is going to make things right in the world through the resurrection despite the present suffering that results from our sin.

Romans 8:18–23 is a dense and rich text, such that I offer my own loose translation to help us better hear Paul's message:

Our present suffering is *nothing* compared to the glorious state of affairs the Creator has in store for us. Even creation *cannot wait* for the restoration of all things. (BTW: it's our fault that Creation has been reduced to its futile state.) All nature hopes to be free from the cycle of death and to take part in the glorious resurrection. It's as if creation is like a mother in labor; in fact, it's as if we were all mothers in labor, groaning in pain, knowing that something amazing is right around the corner, the restoration of Eden in the resurrection.

Paul describes creation as a nonhuman person, who stands in solidarity with our suffering, suffering alongside of us—knowing that God has something in store. When Paul talks about the redemption of our bodies, he is referring to the ancient Jewish hope that at the resurrection of the dead, the earth itself would also be resurrected and restored to its original Edenic state.

Here in Romans, Paul seems to affirm the Indigenous conviction that our present livelihood and destinies are tied together with creation— that we inter-exist and are interrelated and so should treat the world around us with an attitude of appreciation and strive for balance with our nonhuman kin in the greater kin-dom of God.

There is another Indigenous story that resonates with Romans' themes of sacrifice and solidarity with creation, namely that of Corn Mother.[7] Of special note is a particular retelling found among the Penobscot tribe in Maine, wherein the first generation of humanity overhunts the land, nearly killing every living creature, and finds itself on the brink of starvation. The First Mother, their respective "Eve" figure, is distressed at the cry of her children and tells her husband to kill her so that her

---

7. On reading the story of Corn Mother and Christ together, see also Tinker, "Christology."

children might live. He does so, but only after consulting with the Creator and agreeing to follow his wife's strict instructions to drag her body across the fields such that her flesh, blood, and bones might comingle with the soil. As a result of the Corn Mother's sacrifice, corn begins to grow and the people are saved from starvation. In words reminiscent of our Christian Eucharist, the First Man tells his people: "Remember and take good care of First Mother's flesh, because it is goodness become substance. Take good care of her breath, because it is her love turned into smoke. Remember her and think of her whenever you eat, whenever you smoke this sacred plant, because she has given her life so that you might live."[8]

Reading Romans alongside of Indigenous creation stories inspires a deep sense of gratitude for everything that the Creator and creation has given and sacrificed in our behalf. We can recognize that we are indebted both to the life-giving gift of Christ and to the life-giving nourishment of Christ's creation. And so, out of hearts that overflow with honor for all our relations, let us stand in solidarity with creation as we both wait and long for the final restoration of all things. And in our waiting and longing, let us strive to walk along the Harmony Way[9] as we seek out a more sustainable and right relationship with creation. We owe this to Christ. We owe this to creation. We owe this to our ancestors. We owe this to our children.

8. Erdoes and Ortiz, *American Indian Myths and Legends*, 13.

9. On the Harmony Way as an "interchangeable construct" with the Israelite notion of "shalom," see Woodley, *Shalom and the Community of Creation*, xiii–xv.

Sermon

Who Are You Weeping With?

H. Daniel Zacharias

Rejoice with those who rejoice, weep with
those who weep. —Romans 12:15

No one really wants to weep. In fact, much of our North American culture seems bent on making sure that we avoid deep places of pain and lament. It is only in the past few decades, for instance, that many funerals have now stressed celebratory elements, in attempts to both honor the dead and also minimize communal lament. While these "celebrations of life" amidst the death of a love one may be a good way to honor those who have departed, they can also curtail the grieving process. We have also become a highly entertained society in which amusing ourselves has become a predominant passion for many, helping us to limit our exposure to the real world—and suffering is part of the real world.

This aversion to lament has also taken root in the communal gatherings of the church. It seems that the modern worship enterprise has declared an indefinite moratorium on lament. This is deeply ironic given that fifty-nine of the 150 Psalms in the Old Testament are categorized as lament. If our communities wanted to be "really biblical," we may need to consider making 50 percent of our corporate worship expressions of lament from now on. The psalmists certainly recognized that suffering was a part of life, and that communal times of worship needed to embrace lament in order to work through these embodied realities.

I suspect part of the fuel driving this aversion to lament goes beyond our natural desire of not wanting to suffer, and exposes one of the diseased roots of the Western worldview: dualism. Indigenous peoples have long recognized this fundamental difference in worldviews between colonial-rooted nations and Indigenous nations. Euro-Western dualism, which places the mind and the body into separate realities, inevitably downplays those feelings, like lament, that arise deep within our physical selves. Yet we increasingly are learning through books like *The Body Keeps the Score,* by Bessel Van der Kolk, that our physical bodies hold on to trauma. Our pursuit of happiness attempts to downplay, or outright ignore, these material feelings. Lament is too carnal and too primal to be afforded our time, effort, and attention. This perspective breeds disintegration within an individual and within communities. Lament is a call to integrate fully, to feel our feelings and to feel the feelings of others. It is a call to recognize our interconnected reality that entwines all of creation together.

The apostle Paul too recognized grief, and recognized not just the reality of grief but the importance of joining together corporately to grieve. Rather than transcend our feelings in avoidance of pain, Paul instead states that fully entering into our own lament and the lament of others is a mark of a Jesus-shaped community. In an extended section of exhortations in the book of Romans, Paul states in Romans 12:15, "Rejoice with those who rejoice, weep with those who weep." If this is not already hard enough for modern people, it is compounded further by the grammatical structure of this statement, as the commands to rejoice and to weep in verse 15 seem to be elaborations upon the command in verse 14 to "bless those who persecute you." Perhaps you and I should not be so shocked at an exhortation like this. After all, Jesus himself radically advocated for love of enemy in Matthew 5:44. Paul, that radical Jesus follower, now helps the Christians in Rome to envision what obeying Jesus's command might look like. Loving your enemy is not simply about non-retaliation or refraining from harsh words, but actually joining oneself to the grief of one's enemy. In the words of some disciples in John 6:60, "This teaching is difficult; who can accept it?"

Given Paul's exhortation in Romans 12:15, we need to attune our ears to the surrounding sorrows, observing how these sorrows may manifest themselves in certain actions or reactions, and seeing how we might join in. I want to help attune our ears by looking to the context of the apostle Paul, and then to the Letter to the Romans itself.

Paul wrote Romans for several different reasons. Behind this theological masterpiece sits well-established ministry relationships, such as with his ministry partners Priscilla and Aquila, mentioned in Romans 16:3. There were also inner-community relational dynamics that Paul hoped to encourage. This is clear in Paul's discussion about the strong and the weak in Romans 14 and 15. There is also the desire to cultivate further relationship with the Roman church, as he hopes to come to Rome and move forward with his gospel work into Spain, something he discusses in Romans 15:22–29. I want to suggest that it is quite plausible that Paul saw the Jewish Christians in Rome as a group that may have been in a season of sorrow and struggle. We know from the Roman historian Suetonius and from Acts 18:2 that Jews and Christians were expelled from Rome in 49 CE, likely from internal conflicts around the preaching of Christ by some. This is how Paul came to meet Priscilla and Aquila. This edict by Claudius ended in 54 CE, which allowed Priscilla and Aquila to return to Rome. These historical realities suggest a level of group trauma that the Jewish community may have endured, and it is more than likely that those returning Jewish Christians may have encountered yet another struggle in attempting to integrate with the Gentile church in Rome that had grown and established itself during the period of their expulsion. As mentioned before, Paul also addresses the church regarding those who are "strong" and those who are "weak," in Romans 14 and 15. While scholars have debated the makeup of these groups, most agree that the "weak" were Jewish Christians who continued to uphold their ancestral Jewish traditions stemming from the Mosaic law.[1] Perhaps Paul saw his fellow countrymen in Rome as ones who were in a season of lament as he exhorted the community to weep with those who weep.

Joining in lament can take both individual and corporate expressions. Just as Paul probably had in mind this marginalized community from his own ethnic kin, I think today about ways in which the Indigenous peoples of the lands now called Canada continue to be marginalized, and especially how sorrow has situated itself deep into our communal psyche as the Indigenous peoples of these lands. Colonization dispossessed us of our ancestral lands, banned our cultural traditions, demonized our worldviews and spiritualities, and came for our children.

---

1. For a different perspective, see the post-supersessionist essay by Brian Robinson in this volume.

While Canada has gone through a Truth and Reconciliation Commission to reckon with the realities of the Indian Residential Schools, Canada continues to half-heartedly engage in the resulting calls to action. And in the midst of this, lands are still unjustly occupied, treaties are still dishonored, and unmarked graves of children near residential schools are still being found. In the midst of these graves being uncovered, National Indigenous Anglican leadership put out a call for several days of prayers at each finding, and gathered people throughout Canada to pray. It was a lot of lament. And as the media began covering the issue less and less, and the shock of the findings wore off, Indigenous followers of Jesus kept joining themselves to the lament. We continue to do so. The First Peoples of these lands are strong and resilient—and that is why they continue to mourn deeply as they work through this intergenerational trauma. I did not experience residential school, nor did my maternal ancestors. But I am compelled to join myself to the sorrows of those who did, to commemorate things like the National Day for Truth and Reconciliation, and to drum and sing the songs that are used by the communities who mourn the loss of their children.

The second context I want to consider is the Letter to the Romans itself. The specific Greek verb for *weep* used in Romans 12:15 occurs nowhere else in Romans, but several conceptually similar words do occur that also convey the idea of lament. One of these is in Romans 14:15, "If your brother or sister is being *injured* by what you eat, you are no longer walking in love. Do not let what you eat cause the ruin of one for whom Christ died." This supports the first context that I mentioned above, as this verse takes place within the discussion of the "strong" and the "weak." The other place where we have a cluster of words that also signify lament is in Romans 8. Romans 8:15 says, "For you did not receive a spirit of slavery to fall back into fear, but you have received a spirit of adoption. When we *cry*, 'Abba! Father!'" We then encounter Romans 8:22–23: "We know that the whole creation has been *groaning* in labor pains until now; and not only the creation, but we ourselves, who have the first fruits of the Spirit, *groan* inwardly while we wait for adoption, the redemption of our bodies."

Understandably, Romans 8:18–27 is an important section of the New Testament for eco-theology and green readings of Scripture. You will find major discussion and interaction with this text in almost every book on creation care and environmental stewardship produced by theologians and biblical scholars. It is also an important passage for Indigenous followers of Jesus, not only for the issue of earth care, but because the creation is spoken of, rightly, as one with agency, awareness, and feelings. The language from verse 22 clearly conveys maternal descriptions of creation. This is something Indigenous folks know well, as we have always recognized mother earth as alive and caring for us. How could we not take care of the land when the land takes care of us? So many efforts for climate justice today, as good as they are, continue to fail at this one thing: they do not first change the way they relate to the land. They do not move from viewing creation as a resource for our use to seeing creation as something with which we are in a deep and symbiotic relationship. In Romans 8:22–23, Paul actually provides an example of weeping with those who weep—joining our groans to the groans of creation. This example from Paul ought to encourage us to expand our scope to the wider community of creation as we seek to join in lament. Does not the earth cry out when we blow up mountains to get the ore? When we poison and pollute the waterways? When we permanently destroy whole ecosystems for resource extraction or pipelines? Should we not lament when entire species go extinct because of our greed?

And should not lament, whether it be joined to human or nonhuman creation, change our hearts, our minds, and our actions as we move towards right relationship and right relatedness?

Feminist Perspective

Melanie A. Howard

Introduction

Embarking on an endeavor to codify *the* feminist perspective on Romans is doomed before it even begins. Thus, in this essay, I hope to offer only *a* feminist perspective on Romans that might allow preachers of Paul's text to be faithful not only to the words of the apostle, but also to the lives, voices, and experiences of women from the first to the twenty-first centuries.

The multiplicity of feminist hermeneutical approaches means that there is a corresponding multiplicity of ways in which to read the text. Thus, after briefly introducing feminist hermeneutical trends and exploring the hermeneutics of suspicion and hermeneutics of retrieval among those trends, I turn to an exploration of Romans 8:1–30 from a feminist perspective, since this text, rich in feminine imagery, deserves greater attention from a feminist perspective. Applying both a hermeneutics of suspicion and a hermeneutics of retrieval to this text, I argue that a feminist perspective on Romans must contend with the complexity of the biblical text and the lives of female interpreters in order to remain faithful to both in the task of preaching the good news.

Feminist Hermeneutics and Romans

Feminist hermeneutics take a variety of forms that are alternatively identified by a host of titles from liberal/socialist/radical[1] to conformist/ resistant/rejectionist/transformational.[2] Similarly, Phyllis Trible identifies three trends in feminist biblical scholarship: observing oppressive texts, recovering neglected women, and telling women's stories *in memoriam*.[3] This multiplicity of labels confirms Philomena Njeri Mwaura's observation that "although there are major identifiable categories of a feminist biblical interpretation, there is no single method of a feminist biblical hermeneutics of liberation."[4] Thus, following Mwaura's caution and recognizing that it is beyond the scope of this essay to compare these various categories of feminist approaches to biblical texts,[5] I wish instead to identify two larger hermeneutical stances that tend to be prevalent within feminist readings: a hermeneutics of suspicion and a hermeneutics of retrieval.

A feminist hermeneutics of suspicion does not shy away from asking difficult questions about how a given text might be oppressive to women or might erase the voices of women. Such a hermeneutical stance might call into question oppressive structures of power and patriarchy that both obscure the role of women in societies behind the text and limit the opportunities of women in front of the text. Furthermore, a hermeneutics of suspicion might seek both to identify and to overcome the androcentrism that pervades the biblical text and its interpretation.

Unlike a hermeneutics of suspicion, a feminist hermeneutics of retrieval focuses on the ways in which the voices and experiences of women might be reclaimed. Within the biblical text, voices of women are often silenced. Furthermore, in the epistolary genre, the reader necessarily encounters only the voice of the epistle's author, and if the words of others are included, they are always filtered through this authorial voice. A hermeneutics of retrieval, then, seeks ways in which these erased female voices might be recovered.

---

1. Ruether, *Sexism and God Talk*.

2. Polaski, *Feminist Introduction to Paul*, 2–4.

3. Trible, "Feminist Hermeneutics and Biblical Studies."

4. Mwaura, "Feminist Biblical Interpretation," 77.

5. For a thorough collection of essays covering a wide swath of issues related to the feminist interpretation of the Bible, see Brenner and Fontaine, eds., *Feminist Companion to Reading the Bible*.

Beyond recovering the voices of women *behind* the text, a hermeneutics of retrieval might also attend to the ways in which the experiences of women *in front of* the text can also be recovered. This can happen through tracing the reception history of a text through its female interpreters or through inquiring about the ways in which contemporary women's experiences might offer a new lens through which the text might be interpreted. While such a process might be dismissed as a focus on something other than the text itself, as Dale Martin observes, "[M]ost scholars believe that new directions in scholarship will emerge more from new questions and perspectives on the part of scholars than from new 'raw' data."[6] In other words, by bringing women's views and experiences into conversation with the text, one opens up the potential to discover new insights in the ancient words.

Having briefly outlined feminist hermeneutical concerns, I turn now to the application of such a perspective to Romans. In what follows, I will be gesturing toward the ways in which a hermeneutics of suspicion and a hermeneutics of retrieval might be applied specifically to Romans 8:1–30. However, before embarking on that enterprise, it is important to note that when these twin hermeneutical approaches are applied together, they highlight a trend identified by Sheila McGinn for feminist interpreters "to show a certain amount of ambivalence to the Pauline corpus."[7] On the one hand, parts of those epistles can be degrading, demoralizing, or downright dehumanizing of women. On the other hand, Paul's letters as a whole, and Romans in particular, are esteemed by both women and men in the Christian tradition.

I want to suggest that the application of both a hermeneutics of suspicion *and* a hermeneutics of retrieval can produce a more well-rounded picture of feminist perspectives on Romans. One image for how feminist interpreters might engage the biblical text appears in Silvia Schroer's appeal to a Matthean parable:

> If we can liberate ourselves from the necessity to view the biblical texts themselves as normative then they can become a treasury, a *thesauros* (Mt 13.52) of our religion and our beliefs. We are then the women scribes that bring out something new and something old and confront the new with the old. We will find worthless, worm-eaten and even harmful things, but also delicacies and

---

6. Martin, "Social-Scientific Criticism," 137.

7. McGinn, "Feminist Approaches to Paul's Letter to the Romans," 166.

> treasures. . . . In order to neutralize something poisonous or
> harmful it is often sufficient merely to leave it in daylight.[8]

To borrow from Schroer's imagery, I intend to recognize both the problematic and the life-giving elements of Romans 8:1–30, trusting that in doing so, even the difficult parts might be made less challenging by naming them as such. Furthermore, I hope that this dialectical engagement with Romans 8 offers preachers a model to consider as they prepare to proclaim the good news from Romans.

Applying a Feminist Perspective to Romans

Having identified a hermeneutics of suspicion and hermeneutics of retrieval, I offer here one way in which these twin feminist approaches might be applied specifically to Romans 8:1–30 before gesturing more broadly toward other directions from which a preacher might take a feminist perspective on Romans. However, let me first comment on the choice of this passage, since many feminist interpreters of Romans have focused more attention on places in Romans where women are explicitly mentioned (e.g., Romans 1:26–27; 7:1–6; 16:1–16). While such texts have much to offer, Romans 8:1–30 abounds in feminine and feminist-friendly imagery that makes it a rich preaching text.[9] Furthermore, preachers following the Revised Common Lectionary will encounter texts from Romans 8 (eight times total throughout the three-year lectionary cycle) more than from any other single chapter in Romans. Thus, preachers are likely to encounter selections of Romans 8 throughout their preaching careers.

A Feminist Perspective on Romans 8:1–30

Romans 8:1–30 abounds in images and ideas that lend themselves easily to a feminist approach. In what follows, I focus on just two of these: Paul's familial imagery and Paul's use of subordination language. In both cases, I offer interpretations of these characteristics with both a hermeneutics of suspicion and a hermeneutics of retrieval, as a way of suggesting the complexity of taking a feminist approach to this passage.

8. Schroer, "'We Will Know Each Other by Our Fruits,'" 14.

9. Likewise, Schottroff suggests that the whole of Romans 8 "especially . . . clarifies the interdependence of liberation and the Holy Spirit" in a way that is consistent with feminist liberation readings (*Let the Oppressed Go Free*, 31).

Familial Imagery

Familial language and imagery permeates Romans 8:1–30. For example, Paul identifies "sons of God" (vv. 14, 19), celebrates adoption (vv. 15, 23), points to the use of the familiar father-language of "Abba" for God (v. 15), claims the title "children of God" for fellow believers (vv. 16–17, 21), uses labor/birth imagery to describe creation (v. 22), and identifies Jesus as a firstborn son (v. 29). In short, familial imagery dominates much of the landscape of Romans 8. From a feminist perspective, then, it is important to ask how both a hermeneutics of suspicion and a hermeneutics of retrieval might address the prevalence of this familial imagery since, as Polaski observes, such familial metaphors "may be turned in a direction that reinforces hierarchy, stressing inherent inequality and relationships of control and dependency. They may also be turned in a direction that stresses the intimacy and tender nature of these familial relationships."[10]

Although the choice of familial imagery may point in positive directions, a feminist hermeneutics of suspicion might identify problematic elements of this imagery related to the prevalence of masculine-gendered "son" language. That is, while Paul occasionally uses the neuter "children" (τέκνα), which could presumably include women (vv. 16–17, 21), the language of "sons" predominates (vv. 3, 14, 19, 29). Beyond that, the particular term for adoption that Paul uses (υἱοθεσίαν, v. 23) might more literally be translated as "son-placing."[11] As Kathleen Corley has suggested, Paul's choice of this term rather than the more gender-inclusive τεκνοθεσία (evidenced in other ancient literature) points to an image that is a "gender-specific one, as it probably presupposes the priority of the privileges of sons over those of daughters."[12] These privileges would include not only a place within the familial structure but also the economic benefits of inheritance rights. Given Paul's own use of "heir" language (v. 17), the masculinizing tendency of this language could have the effect of being exclusive of women. In short, then, a hermeneutics of suspicion

---

10. Polaski, *Feminist Introduction to Paul*, 80.

11. For further discussion of Paul's use of an adoption metaphor, see Burke, *Adopted into God's Family*.

12. Corley, "Women's Inheritance Rights in Antiquity," 121. Paul's earliest audiences may have also seen in this term a connection to the inheritance rights of sons rather than daughters. With Emperor Augustus's adoption of his male grandchildren as "sons," Augustus essentially annulled any claim to inheritance that his daughter Julia might have hoped to make. I am grateful to Mary Schmitt for suggesting such a connection to me.

would raise questions about the degree to which Paul envisions a reality in which women can participate as full equals with men in relating to God and sharing in God's inheritance.

While these problematic elements of Paul's familial imagery should not be undermined, a hermeneutics of retrieval might be able to identify ways in which women's experiences might still be evident in this text. Indeed, the choice of familial imagery is itself a gendered one. Paul turns not to the structural organization of the masculinized political setting but of the feminized home setting in order to explain what he understands as the significance of Christ's work. This move is essentially a nod to female realms of influence. As Cynthia Long Westfall observes, "The fact that women were secluded or restricted to the home . . . did not mean that they held no authority; rather it was recognized that the domain of women's authority was in the domestic sphere, while the man's authority was in the public sphere."[13]

Beyond the potential for locating this familial imagery within the domain of women, a hermeneutics of retrieval is also possible in celebrating the places where Paul does use more inclusive language. As noted above, "son" language as applied to believers is certainly prevalent in this passage. However, "children" (τέκνα) language nonetheless appears in verses 16, 17,[14] and 21, including the claim "*we* are children of God." The use of this first-person plural has the effect of underscoring mutuality in relationships among believers.[15] Further, if "all creation" in verse 22 encompasses all of humanity as well, as Gaventa argues,[16] this includes both male *and* female humans who would be anticipating adoption (υἱοθεσίαν, v. 23). Such "children" language, then, serves to counteract some of the hierarchical and male-privileging familial language that appears elsewhere in this passage.

In sum, the familial language that Paul uses in Romans 8 can be read both with a hermeneutics of suspicion and a hermeneutics of retrieval.

13. Westfall, *Paul and Gender*, 23.

14. Polaski suggests that this language in verses 16–17 may hint at a more inclusive view (*Feminist Introduction to Paul*, 89).

15. Mutuality among believers is a theme that appears again in Romans 14–15 as Paul discusses differing cultic and culinary practices among believers. As Kathy Ehrensperger observes of this mutuality, "Mutuality can only be ensured when minorities are respected and protected" ("New Perspectives on Paul," 240).

16. Gaventa, *Our Mother Saint Paul*, 54–55.

Both lenses are necessary in order to encapsulate a range of feminist perspectives on this aspect of the text.

Subordination Language

In addition to familial imagery, the language of subordination or subjection is also prevalent in Romans 8:1–30. Paul notes that the disposition of the flesh is not subordinate to the law of God (v. 7), but creation is made subject to futility (v. 20a) by one who performs this act of subjugating (v. 20b).

From a feminist perspective, the dangers of this language are immediately apparent when viewed with a hermeneutics of suspicion. Language of subjection might easily be fused with Paul's language of co-suffering and co-glorification with Christ. Such an amalgamation has the potential to produce untold harm in the lives of women who experience intimate partner violence and may be encouraged to remain in dangerous situations because their suffering mimics Christ's. Beyond this concern, a hermeneutics of suspicion might join with Elisabeth Schüssler Fiorenza in noting that Paul's language of subordination insidiously "stands in the ideological service of domination" and could encourage interpreters not only to identify with Paul but to promote such dominating structures in their own contexts.[17] In short, a hermeneutics of suspicion could easily find fault with the language here.

Paul's subordination language undoubtedly presents problems for feminist interpreters. Nonetheless, it is ultimately not subjugation, but freedom, that Paul seems to understand as an end goal (vv. 2, 21). Thus, a hermeneutics of retrieval might suggest that subjugation is only a stopping point on the way to future liberation. Seen in this light, subjugation might be understood as a form of care that intends to lead to freedom, much as a mother might "subjugate" her children under her care until they are old enough to fend for themselves. This possibility might be evident both in the particular verb that Paul uses here (ὑποτάσσω) as well as in the birthing and relational imagery that appears in the text.

In verses 7 and 20, Paul uses variants of the verb ὑποτάσσω to describe the lack of the fleshly disposition's subjection to the law of God and creation's subjection to futility. This term is a common one in the New Testament household codes for describing how wives are to relate to

17. Fiorenza, "Paul and the Politics of Interpretation," 53.

their husbands (Eph 5:24; Col 3:18; 1 Pet 3:1). In those contexts, it is right
to consider what the term might indicate in terms of hierarchical power
relationships that are at work between spouses.

However, beyond its use in these settings, ὑποτάσσω also appears
as a description of the relationship that a recipient of care has with a
caregiver. For example, the psalmist celebrates the subjection of creation
under the care of humanity (Ps 8:5–6; LXX 8:6–7), a sentiment that the
author of Hebrews echoes in quoting this text (Heb 2:7–8). Even more
explicitly illustrating such a relationship between a caregiver and their
charge is Luke 2:51. In this text, the young Jesus who stayed behind in
the Jerusalem temple after his family's departure, returns home with his
parents and is subordinated to them. Given the story that Luke is telling, this subordination is not a case of one party exercising power over
another. (Indeed, it seems clear that even as a young boy Jesus commands
a significant level of authority [cf. Luke 2:47].) Rather, Jesus's subordination to his parents seems to indicate his acceptance of their parental care.

While the verb ὑποτάσσω itself can point to nurturing relationships,
beyond that, Paul makes use of the language of giving birth to reinforce
this image. Such imagery further suggests that the use of subordination
language is not about illustrating dominating power relationships but is
more indicative of relationships of care.

Birthing imagery is most explicit in verse 22, as Paul describes creation groaning and laboring. What is particularly fascinating here is that
Paul describes creation not only as "groaning and laboring," but rather as
"co-groaning (συστενάζω) and co-laboring (συνωδίνω)."[18] These particular
verbal forms are quite rare, not appearing anywhere else in biblical literature. However, their limited appearance in other ancient Greek literature
points to a connection between these verbs and nurturing relationships.
The verb συστενάζω appears only once in pre-Pauline literature where
Euripides uses the term to describe friends weeping together after dis-
cussing the death of a child who was born (Ion 932–35). Furthermore, the
verb συνωδίνω appears only twice in pre-Pauline literature where it is used

18. Rehman highlights both the relational and the apocalyptic elements of Paul's
language here: "This is how the experience of innumerable women can be expressed in
the terminology of apocalyptic, namely that the good ending does *not* happen *without
collaboration* and active exertion. The new earth does not simply fall from the sky;
justice does not come about without our cooperation" ("To Turn the Groaning into
Labor," 81). For a thorough treatment of maternal imagery throughout Paul's letters
and the connection of this imagery to apocalyptic elements, see Gaventa, *Our Mother
Saint Paul*, 85–160.

by Euripides to describe the proper behavior of a servant co-rejoicing and co-sorrowing with a master (*Hel.* 727) and by Aristotle, who (seemingly contradicting Euripides's point) suggests that the sorrow that slaves might share with their masters is not a true sorrow in the way that mothers grieve for their children or birds co-despair (*Eth. Eud.* 1240a).[19] Thus, while Paul's use of these specific compound verbs is unusual, their limited attestation elsewhere suggests that Paul, whether consciously or not, is picking up on an idea of care and compassion in relation to these terms.

Beyond the birthing imagery in these verbs, these particular compounds with a συν- ("co-") prefix point to the collective and relational nature of the actions that Paul envisions here, such that a hierarchical understanding of subjugation might also be minimized. This verbal prefix points back to the many verbs in verses 16–17 that made use of the same prefix ("co-witnessing" [συμμαρτυρεῖ], "co-inheriting" [συγκληρονόμοι], "co-suffering" [συμπάσχομεν], "co-glorifying" [συνδοξασθῶμεν]). Likewise, it looks ahead to verses 26–29 ("co-helping" [συναντιλαμβάνεται], "co-working" [συνεργεῖ], "co-formed" [συμμόρφους]). In short, the proliferation of the prefix throughout this passage points to the mutual relational connections that Paul perceives among humanity, creation, the Spirit, Christ, and God.

This is a relationality not best defined by hierarchical and subordinating relationships. Rather, it is a relationality that capitalizes upon cooperation for the sake of the good (v. 28). As Thomas Vollmer puts it, "There is an interconnectedness between the hope for creation and Christians along with the subsequent work of intercession and prayer offered by the Spirit. This interconnectedness does not equate to a subordination of one to another; rather, it signifies a relationship between each, with a subordination to someone or something else."[20] In short, the abundance of "co-" language here undermines the concern of an enforced subjugation. Furthermore, taken as an invitation to act with the Spirit in this generative and liberating activity, female interpreters in front of the text who are practicing a hermeneutics of retrieval might hear this language as an imperative to resist subjugation and work toward the ultimate goal of liberation toward which Paul points (vv. 2, 21).

19. This latter text that juxtaposes mothers and birds is especially fascinating when held together with other biblical texts that imagine divine care using maternal avian imagery (e.g., Deut 32:11–12; Ps 17:8; 57:1; 91:4; Matt 23:37; Luke 13:34).

20. Vollmer, "Theocentric Reading of Romans 8, 18–30," 793.

When understood as a relational image, then, creation co-groaning and co-laboring (v. 22) is a complex maternal image that points to a wholistic and life-giving reality. However, beyond applying merely to creation, there is a sense in which the Spirit itself is deeply involved in a sort of "birthing" or midwifery practice in relation to human prayers. In verse 26, Paul notes that given the limitation of human knowledge of how to pray, the Spirit intercedes with wordless groaning (στεναγμοῖς ἀλαλήτοις).

The term for groaning that Paul uses here (στεναγμοῖς), while rare in the New Testament,[21] is moderately attested in the Septuagint. Surveying these appearances, John Bertone concludes that the term is "always used to express intense emotion."[22] Of especial interest is the use of the term in relation to childbirth. Throughout Romans 8:18–30 there are echoes of the curses in Genesis 3:14–19. In particular, the use of στεναγμοῖς in 8:26 is reminiscent of the same term in the Septuagint of Genesis 3:16, which describes the pain of the woman in childbirth. This, in turn, suggests a relationship between the word's use in Jeremiah 4:31, which describes the pain of a woman giving birth to her firstborn (πρωτοτοκούσης), and the description of Jesus as the firstborn (πρωτότοκον) in Romans 8:29. Beyond this explicit connection to the Spirit's work in birthing, throughout Romans 8, Paul frequently juxtaposes the language of "life" and "Spirit" (vv. 2, 6, 10–12), highlighting the Spirit's presence in life-giving arenas. In short, then, Paul's use of this term in relation to the Spirit's activity connects the Spirit to birthing practices.

To summarize, the subordination language that Paul uses throughout Romans 8 cannot be overlooked. Read with a hermeneutics of suspicion, this language points to dangerous trends both in the early church and in contemporary settings of making women inferior to their male counterparts and potentially encouraging them to remain in dangerous situations. However, such language might contain the possibility for a more affirming interpretation of this passage that is in line with a feminist hermeneutics of retrieval that seeks to find the ways in which traditional interpretations of the text might be obscuring the experiences of women. The prevalence of relational and birthing imagery provides a firm connection to just such experiences.

---

21. It is only otherwise found in Acts 7:34.

22. Bertone, "Experience of Glossolalia and the Spirit's Empathy," 58.

Other Directions for Preaching Romans from a Feminist Perspective

This application of a feminist perspective represents only one possible avenue for a preacher. Several others exist. Even within Romans 8:1–30, one might capitalize upon the potential for an eco-feminist reading of the text that would highlight a concern for creation and sustainability. In an essay that explores the groanings of the Spirit, creation, and humans, Vollmer offers a reading in this vein that connects Romans 8 with the world's contemporary ecological circumstances.[23] Given the ways in which women's experiences and the natural world (as an often feminized object ["Mother Earth"]) are connected, such an eco-feminist reading could be developed more substantially.

Beyond Romans 8, a preacher might also consider exploring Paul's use of Sarah in 4:13–25 and 9:1–18. In both cases, Sarah appears more as an accessory to Paul's argument rather than a central component of it. Applying a hermeneutics of retrieval to her contribution to the larger thrust of Paul's argument and connecting the mention of her name to the larger account of her story in Genesis 12–23 could allow the preacher to breathe life into Paul's otherwise rather flat portrayal of Sarah as a barren woman who eventually gives birth.

Beyond that, the preacher might similarly engage in a hermeneutics of retrieval by seeking to expand the picture of the "married woman" whom Paul uses as a part of his analogy in 7:1–6.[24] Although this figure serves the rhetorical purpose of helping Paul to make a point about the relevance of the law, the preacher could explore Paul's choice of a married woman to make this point and might consider reflecting on how this trope might gesture toward the experiences of real women in Paul's time.

Finally, as many feminist readers have already done,[25] the preacher could explore any number of the women named in Paul's final greetings in chapter 16 (Phoebe [16:1–2], Prisca [16:3], Mary [16:6], Junia [16:7], Tryphaena/Tryphosa [16:12], Persis [16:12], Rufus's mother [16:13], Julia

23. Vollmer, "Theocentric Reading of Romans 8, 18–30," 789–97.

24. For a feminist treatment of this pericope, see Thimmes, "'She Will Be Called an Adulteress . . .'"

25. For discussions of the named women in Romans 16, see Gench, *Encountering God in Tyrannical Texts*, 135–61. For a discussion of women in 1:26, 7:2, and much of chapter 16, see Koperski, "Women in Romans." See also Mathew, *Women in the Greetings of Romans 16.1–16*.

[16:15], Nereus's sister [16:15]).[26] Of especial interest for many feminist readers have been Phoebe (named as a deacon) and Junia (named as a prominent apostle). Unlike Sarah or the "married woman," these women in chapter 16 provide fertile ground for exploring the ways in which real women advanced the work of the early church. Recovering their contributions may provide occasion for the preacher to reflect on the similarly unnamed or unappreciated women in contemporary Christian settings.

Conclusion

Depending upon how one views the task of the preacher, the application of a hermeneutics of suspicion could rest uneasily alongside of the imperative to preach good news. After all, how can the omission of and oppression of women ever be called good news? Nonetheless, I want to suggest that when used with caution from the pulpit, a hermeneutics of suspicion can offer the preacher an opportunity to engage in the necessary task of truth-telling. That is, it may be that "good news" for some is finally hearing their reality named publicly. For some congregations, the preacher's identification of the dearth of female experiences in Paul's Letter to the Romans and centuries of marginalization of women will come as a welcome acknowledgment of the ways in which the biblical text and the church have been held "captive to the law of sin" (Rom 7:23). In this way, preachers engage in the same task as Paul himself in identifying the corrupting power of sin (cf. Rom 5:12–21; 6:1–23; 7:7–25).

However, just as feminist interpreters have not relied only on a hermeneutics of suspicion, preachers too can make use of a hermeneutics of retrieval in preaching Romans from a feminist perspective. The use of this approach would allow the preacher the opportunity to explore the ways in which women's experiences might be lurking within the text, even when traditional interpretations of the text have obscured those experiences. This, in turn, allows contemporary female audiences to hear the good news that their experiences, viewpoints, and values might be affirmed by Paul's words.

How, then, might Paul's Letter to the Romans be preached from a feminist perspective today? The astute reader will note that while I have offered my own exegesis of this text from Romans 8, I have not provided

26. For a discussion of the importance of these women in Romans 16 to African American interpretation, see pages 31–34 of this volume.

clear guidance on how this text might be preached. This avoidance is intentional. By offering a reading of the text that takes into account both a hermeneutics of suspicion and a hermeneutics of retrieval, I have attempted to demonstrate the complexity of a feminist perspective on Romans.

This multiplicity of feminist viewpoints means that there is no one "right" way to preach Romans from a feminist perspective. Rather, the hallmarks of such a perspective might be eschewing easy answers and trite theology. Indeed, feminist views on the Bible have developed and become increasingly attuned to the intersectional aspects of identity that include issues of race, class, and sexuality, in addition to gender. This increased nuance has meant that the development of womanist, *mujerista*, and Asian feminist perspectives has been able to shed light on the complexity of both contemporary women's experiences and the biblical text itself.

For the intrepid preacher of Romans, taking a feminist perspective on the task of preaching this complex theological text might simply mean not trivializing the complexities. The lives and experiences of women today cannot be easily boiled down to a single paradigm, and nor can Paul's words to the Romans. Thus, we might honor the voices of both women and Paul by embracing the tensions of both even as we trust in the faith(fulness) of Christ to sustain our work in the task of preaching the good news.

Sermon

Does Anybody Really Know What Time It Is?

Romans 8

Cheryl Johns

Years ago, the group Chicago produced a hit song asking the existential questions: "Does anybody really know what time it is? Does anybody really care?" The song began with these words:

> Does anybody really know what time it is (I don't)
> Does anybody really care (care about time)
> If so, I can't imagine why (no, no)
> We've all got time enough to cry.

These days I catch myself singing the lyrics to this song and reflecting on its haunting questions. These are strange times. COVID, political unrest, the devastating effects of global climate change, are but a few events that mark our era. The #MeToo and #ChurchToo movements have revealed that we continue to live in slavery to the ancient order of patriarchy. My Twitter feed is full of stories of abuse of women and the exclusion of women from the ministries of the church. It seems these days we've all got time enough to cry.

As Christians, we live between two eras, or two dimensions of time—the present reality of a world under the curse of sin, and the new order of creation inaugurated by the coming of Jesus. Sometimes we get absorbed into the pain and angst of what the apostle Paul, in his letter to the church at Rome, described as "the sufferings of this present time" (8:18).

When we get bogged down in this present era it is all too easy to let go of the wonder and joy found in living in Christ's new creation. We become people who live out of the flesh and exhibit the fruits of the fallen order: fear, anger, and a need for control. To deal with these issues, instead of getting at their root causes, we choose to put Band-Aids of legalism over our deep, festering wound. In doing so, we perpetuate the very sins that Jesus came to deliver us from!

As we read through Paul's Epistle to the Romans, it becomes clear that contemporary Christians are not the first to have difficulty grasping the implications of living in the realm of the coming kingdom while existing in a world dominated by the old order. We can take heart knowing that we are not the first ones to find it easier to acquiesce to the old order of things.

In the first century it was easy for Christians to revert back to the old order of things. After all, this old order, with its laws and ordering of human relations, was a comfortable place for them. It was "the way things have always been." They had not only reverted to the old ways of relying on the law, some were even boasting about how they were superior in keeping its regulations, all the while living sinful lives.

The church at Rome had leaders who were so confident in their righteousness that they saw themselves as "a guide to the blind, a light to those who are in darkness, a corrector of the foolish, a teacher of children, having in the law the embodiment of knowledge and truth" (2:20). Yet, these teachers were living in a manner that went against the very things they preached. They were stealing. They were committing adultery. They were abusing and slandering others. Sound familiar?

Paul reminded these ancient Christians that the way of Christ was the way of faith in the power of Christ's death and resurrection. The Christian way was life-giving and transformative. He reminded them of the significance of their baptism, noting that in the waters of baptism their old lives were put to death; they were raised with Christ so that they might "walk in the newness of life" (6:4). This new life was not the Band-Aid approach of the old order of the law. Rather, Christian baptism ushered believers into a whole new, grace-filled era and a new way of being in the world. In fact, in baptism, Christians were ushered into a new dimension of time—the eschatological time of the Spirit. Only by the power of the Spirit could they live the transformed life found in the kingdom. They were living in the world dominated by the powers of sin, yet they could live lives characterized by the "new life of the Spirit" (7:6).

In chapter 8 of Romans, Paul gives a beautiful and poignant description of this new life. The key to this new life is the power of the Holy Spirit to set believers free from the bondage of sin and death. "For you did not receive a spirit of slavery to fall back into fear, but you have received a spirit of adoption" (8:15).

In 8:18, Paul moves into a description of the time yet to come. It will be a time of glory and a time when all creation will be set free from its bondage to decay, obtaining the freedom of the glory of the children of God (8:21). Paul reminds his readers that the creation is even now groaning for that day, a groaning not of despair, but of labor pains. Paul notes that we "who have the first fruits of the Spirit, groan inwardly while we wait for adoption" (8:22–23).

Here's the key to living in this new dimension of time: we who are baptized in Christ have the first fruits, the first tasting of what is coming. We live in the great feast of Pentecost. It is the harbinger of the new creation—the filling of everything with God's glory and presence. As Pentecost people, we are signs of that which shall one day cover the whole created order. Moreover, we groan for that day, and as a mother in labor, we live into that day, working with the labor pains, knowing that our prayerful work is productive.

Paul wrote, "In hope we were saved. Now hope that is seen is not hope. But who hopes for what is seen? But if we hope for what we do not see, we wait for it with patience" (8:24). Groaning does not exclude hope. In fact, as in childbirth, we groan with hope for that which is being born. The Spirit of the future lives in us, and it is the taste of that future that gives us hope.

Does anybody know what time it is? It's time to get in tune with things. It's time to groan with the creation, longing for the coming of Christ. It's time to live in hope for that which we cannot see. It's time to live out of the future and not in the past. It's time for people living in the old order of bondage to be set free!

Women, in particular, acutely feel the effects of the old order that is dying. Our bodies bear the scars of the trauma of childbirth. Many women's bodies bear the scars of domestic violence. Most of us bear the scars of the oppression of the old order that wants to put us under the law and "in our place." We are lamenting. We are groaning. The Spirit within us is sighing and longing for a better day.

Like many in the early Roman church, there are those today who choose to live in the old order of things. They are the so-called "benevolent patriarchs" who boast in their ability to lead and protect women, all the while viewing women as lesser than themselves. Instead of living in the new creation found in Christ, and co-stewarding this creation, benevolent patriarchs glory in the old order and their privileged place in that order. *Revelations of abuse and misuse of power reveal that the old order of men ruling over women only has the power to reveal sin. It cannot transform and heal brokenness and oppression.* You can't dress up the old ways and make them beautiful enough, benevolent enough, to set people free and change their lives. Only the power of the Spirit—the Spirit that raised Jesus from the dead—can break such bondage!

In her insightful book *African American Readings of Paul*,[1] Lisa Bowens points out how many enslaved African Americans did not capitulate to their white masters' interpretations of Paul's writings. They refused to read Paul as one who promoted slavery. They rightfully understood how Paul struggled to live between the times of the old order and the coming new world. They saw Paul as pushing the church toward living out of the new world that he had so boldly proclaimed: "There is no longer Jew or Greek, there is no longer slave or free, there is no longer male and female: all of you are one in Christ Jesus" (Gal 2:28). Those precious saints who were enslaved chose to live in the hope of that new world, all the while groaning in their present sufferings. It is a choice Christian women need to make: reading Paul through the lens of the coming kingdom, all the while groaning and doing the hopeful work toward that which is coming.

Yes, these days we all have time enough to cry. Ours is a time for lamenting with the broken and the hurting. Let us also remember to groan, joining with the creation and the Spirit in the work of productive labor pains. Paul told the Roman Christians: "Likewise the Spirit helps us in our weakness; for we do not know how to pray as we ought, but that very Spirit intercedes with sighs too deep for words" (8:26).

In the end, while we groan, let us have time enough for hope. May the words of the apostle Paul to the church in Rome be our benediction: "Do not be conformed to this world, but be transformed by the renewing of you minds, so that you may discern what is the will of God—what is good and acceptable and perfect" (12:2).

---

1. Bowens, *African American Readings of Paul.*

Sermon

Romans 5:1–5

A Feminist Text of Hope

AMY PEELER[1]

IN MANY LITURGICAL TRADITIONS, the long season after Pentecost, thrillingly termed "ordinary time," includes readings from the Epistle to the Romans. What better book than this to instruct believers how to live regular life, day in and day out, in light of the good news of the gospel? The first half of Romans 5 offers that kind of instruction, with particularly good news for those who identify with feminism.[2]

Romans is one of the few letters of Paul written to a congregation he did not found. That is one reason why Romans is so comprehensive, why it is often used to teach people the basics of the Christian faith. Paul lays out here his understanding of God in the hopes that the Romans might

---

1. I learned a great deal about Paul, Romans, and women in several classes with Beverly Gaventa. My debt to her teaching is evident in several insights here.

2. *Feminism* is a complicated term, open to many different definitions and instantiations. Historically, scholars categorize its movements organized into three waves, the first focused upon equal legal rights, chiefly the right to vote, the second focused upon equal vocational rights, and the third, more diffuse, focused upon full flourishing for all. It is rightly differentiated from ethnic expressions because historically white women did not take into account the different experiences and desires of women of color. Feminism is not limited to biological females. Any who support the humanity and dignity of women may take up its banner. As a white woman, I identify as a Christian feminist, committed to the idea (and the advocacy that stems from it) that the triune God inestimably values women.

learn from his message, approve of his message, and then support him in future missionary endeavors.

After a pretty typical epistolary opening in which he outlines the thesis of his gospel—that it is God's righteousness revealed to the Jew first and also to the Gentile that creates a life of faith (1:16–17)—he moves to an explanation of that gospel. And he begins with dark intensity.

1:18: "For the wrath of God is revealed . . ."

In chapter 1 he catalogues the stereotypical sin of the Gentile world, namely idolatry, only to turn the tables on the Jewish audience in chapter 2, those who might have thought themselves to have escaped divine wrath because they are not sinners from among the Gentiles. He shows, however, their equally damning culpability when they fail to keep the law God has given them. By chapter 3, he presents a catena of Israel's Scriptures, text after text that leaves all the world silent, unable to offer any defense of their imagined righteousness before a holy God.

By 3:19 every mouth is shut and all the world comes under judgement, guilty before God.

Creation was insufficient to drive humanity to worship God alone, and the law brought the knowledge of sin. The good news won't be that good unless Paul is honest about the dire nature of the human condition.

Therefore, in that silence, when all the world has nothing it can say for itself, Paul writes this: "But now, apart from law, the righteousness of God has been disclosed, and is attested by the law and the prophets, the righteousness of God through faith in Jesus Christ for all who believe. For there is no distinction" (Rom 3:21–22).

This is the genesis, I think, of the "Sunday school" answer, that moment when you ask precious children anything in Sunday school and they answer enthusiastically with "Jesus!"

Just because this answer is simple doesn't mean it is simplistic. Jesus the Messiah, the Son of God, through his incarnation, death, resurrection, and ascension, is the answer to the deep and pervasive human problem, for Jews, for Greeks, for people in the past, for people in the present, for everyone, the answer is faith in God who revealed Jesus.

In chapter 4, Paul explicates that answer with the story of Abraham. Abraham had faith and that was accounted to him as righteousness. Being in a right relationship with God comes by trusting in God because God is worthy of such trust.

That brings us to Romans 5, which starts with this idea: "Therefore, since we are justified (*dikaioō*) by faith, we have peace with God through our Lord Jesus Christ."

Notice the contrast. In chapter 3, he brings forth the sacred Scriptures of Israel to assert, "There is no one who is righteous (*dikaios*), not even one" (3:10), but here he says that they have attained that which was impossible.

And there's more! Having been made right before God from faith, he proclaims that they have peace with God. If righteousness carries connotations of a forensic declaration, it is not a legal fantasy, but has real implications for the emotive reality of lived experience: a deep peace.

If all this comes through faith, what does it exactly mean to have faith?

Faith certainly includes intellectual assent—"I believe that Jesus who was God lived, died, and rose again," à la the ecumenical creeds—but it is also something more. These Romans relate to God in a different way because they have believed and that means that they have taken on a new Lord that is Jesus Christ. This is faith, which is not only mental assent, but also trust that results in a changed life. There is a pledge here to *follow* him. And at the same time this pledge is a response to God who has already acted.

In my church I grew up singing "I have decided to follow Jesus," but that tune raises a seeming paradox. If Paul and many others in the NT say that you cannot *work* your way to God, how is it that faith, choosing to follow Jesus, is not also a work? This perceptive question pushes toward a better picture. What if true faith—fruitful trust—is not something you do, but something you *stop* doing? Instead of going your own way in life, struggling in your inadequacy to meet your need for a right standing with God, to create a peaceful life, you stop and exercise faith by acquiescing, relaxing into what God has already done for you? What if faith is pledging to God's sovereignty, not out of strength but out of weakness?

Feminism offers a particular purchase on this conceptualization of faith. In eras past women were considered, or at least told, that they were weaker. Possibly the picture of faith I'm suggesting resists a "macho" concept of being active, strong, and grabbing faith for oneself out of strength.

But to slot pictures of faith as more "masculine" or "feminine" may only solidify stereotypes that many feminists resist. More recent conversations make ideas of feminine weakness and the eras in which they flourished now seem very much a thing of the past. In current settings, no one would publicly say that women are weaker (without condemnation), and so women are invited to do all things.

But the ancient assumption lingers, and so many women feel the pressure to prove themselves. Not just to do well, but to do better than well so that no one can say the old idea was actually right. Romans' concept of faith, trust through surrender, frees everyone, but in a particular way, it frees women from the need to earn favor. And this pressure is nowhere stronger than in the realm of faith where very often women are assumed to be disadvantaged, due to poor but powerfully enduring interpretations of certain Pauline passages. For women *ek pisteōs* means collapsing into the sufficiency of God in weakness-as-strength resistance to any internalized or external voice that demands women to prove themselves.

This is real belief, and this is where we have peace with God.

Moreover, as we lean on God, our Lord Jesus Christ leads us (*prosagōgēn*) into an arena of grace in which we are given standing. Some secular feminists have expressed concern that Christianity keeps its followers—especially women—weak and dependent, unable to express agency or maturity. Admittedly, Christianity urges submission to God, but this grants not weakness but true power.[3] Certainly, oppression has happened in Christian history, but that is an aberration of the text. This text shows that Christ does not enervate us or keep us weak, but gives us divine strength to stand confident in our righteousness and boldness. Those who are trusting in Christ can not only stand, but also boast, and not just about our present standing before and experience with God but also about our future reality, the hope of God's glory, a glory before which previously all humanity continually fell short.

Even that's not all! We also can boast in our . . . tribulations.

Wait a minute, we might say, this was all sounding really good: righteousness, peace, grace, hope, glory. Those are all really positive, wonderful things. Tribulation is the one thing that is not like the others. It just doesn't belong. Didn't Paul do all the bad news already? Maybe he is confused as to which section of the letter he is now writing.

But the presence of tribulation here is one major reason I love the Christian gospel. It is real. It is honest about the human condition. It doesn't water down the awesome goodness of God, nor does it sugarcoat the challenges of the Christian way. Though you have peace, standing, righteousness, boldness, hope, and glory, there will also be tribulation.

---

3. I am indebted to the insights of Christian feminist theologian Sarah Coakley, especially her work *Power and Submissions*.

The Christian gospel allows both celebration and lament. This recognition in Christian faith frees women from the cultural bind of constantly "playing nice."

The people to whom Paul was writing had real life experience with tribulation. When one became a Christian there was an immediate and tangible social cost. Some Jewish groups persecuted Jews for believing in a criminal Messiah. Some Greco-Roman groups persecuted them for no longer showing their allegiance to Caesar or the local gods. For those who had endured such things and not given up on the confession of Jesus as Lord, they knew that these situations worked in them the quality of endurance. They had found that God and his people had not left them, and as they relied on God, they did not fail.

Since they had endured, they stood as proven, tested, often translated as having "character." They were not an unknown quantity but were trustworthy. They knew they would be able to go through more hard times when those came. And because they were trustworthy in their trust in God, they had hope. They could hope that God would continue to be faithful to them in the midst of tribulation, and they had hope that, since they had already done so, they would continue to pass the tests that came and endure.

Whereas the cultural burden on women demands strength that can eventually burn out in exhausted weakness, the Christian gospel allows honest acknowledgment of weakness followed by divine power that results in enduring strength. Freed from the *need* to prove oneself to earn favor, we are given the power to prove ourselves as we depend upon God.

In this list from tribulation to endurance to character to hope, Paul has worked his way back to the good with which he began this chapter. You do have hope, not as some pie-in-the-sky impossible dream, but sure hope because God acted first, providing the righteousness of Christ and the gift of the Holy Spirit. This is why Romans 5 is a post-Pentecost text. God has given us the Holy Spirit as well. We are already experiencing the presence and glory of God which is the content of our hope. This hope, Paul says, does not disappoint, literally, it does not include shame (*kataischunō*).

As a woman navigating the world, I am often aware of shame that waits to pounce upon my soul. I feel this with most acuity in my vocation, when I stand as professor or pastor to proclaim the word of God. "Women can't do that! You better not mess up! You better do better than any of your peers or you will only confirm what everyone thinks, that women can't do that!"

For many years now, I have lived in a hope that does not disappoint. I have withstood the imp of shame. I have nothing to prove to anyone, no favor I need to curry. If someone doesn't like what I do or who I am, they are welcome to take it up with the God in whose image I am made, the God who deigned to come to humanity as a human *born of a woman*. And in that place of dependence upon the triune God I have found great strength, endurance, character, and therefore hope.

My prayer is that all who read this text will find such strength, for everyone in some way struggles with shame.

But if God's enemy has particular enmity against women (Gen 3:15), and human history up until the day in which I write seems evidence of this fact, we women may be in special need of this message of God's peace.

Post-Supersessionist Reading of Romans

Brian J. Robinson

Section 1: What Is a Post-Supersessionist Reading and Why Does It Matter?

FOR MUCH OF THE Christian tradition, especially in its various Protestant forms, supersessionism exists as a nonnegotiable assumption upon which many key theological constructs, especially those pertaining to the gospel, are built. To propose changing such an assumption, then, is both audacious and overwhelming because of the far-reaching impact it will necessarily have in reshaping the tradition. Such work should not be undertaken lightly, but a growing sense from both the academy and many Christian traditions is that such a reevaluation is long overdue in light of historical, textual, and ethical evidence.[1] Paul's letter to the believing Gentiles in Rome gives us ample room to explore the impact of a post-supersessionist reading, both in terms of how a post-supersessionist

---

1. As will be obvious from the current chapter, Mark Nanos has and continues to inspire my work with his careful and critical interpretations of the New Testament. The very best ideas are probably his; any lapses in thought are strictly of my own making. I would like to thank Mark for recommending me for this project and the editors for accepting his recommendation.

Mark D. Nanos provides examples from both Roman Catholic and Protestant traditions of such an awareness and the difficulty of integrating such a change into these traditions. See his "Romans 11 and Christian-Jewish Relations."

approach impacts our reading of the text as well as for thinking about what it means to claim the label *Christian* in our contemporary settings.[2]

The current chapter begins with a brief introduction to the issues and how a post-supersessionist approach reshapes thinking about Paul's own religious identity. I will then show how a post-supersessionist approach impacts readings of several key passages in Romans, particularly those intersected by issues of Torah and identity. Ultimately, a post-supersessionist reading of Romans expresses Paul's vision for an ethnically diverse community that embodies a Torah-shaped obedience overcoming racial animosity as the people of God embody the kingdom of heaven on earth, now. Although I cannot tease out all of the details or their implications, I hope that the current chapter provides interest and energy for readers to continue this work in their own communities.[3]

But what is a post-supersessionist approach? R. Kendall Soulen defines post-supersessionism as:

> [N]ot a single viewpoint but a loose and partly conflicting family of theological perspectives that seeks to interpret the central affirmations of Christian faith in ways that do not state or imply the abrogation or obsolescence of God's covenant with the Jewish people, that is, in ways that are not supersessionist. Positively expressed, a theology is post-supersessionist if it affirms the present validity of God's covenant with Israel as a coherent and indispensable part of the larger body of Christian teaching.[4]

Conversely, an approach could be labeled supersessionist if it undermines the ongoing vitality and legitimacy of Judaism and/or seeks to replace Judaism with Christianity in the plan of God. In supersessionist readings of the New Testament, Judaism, and the Torah specifically, are negative foils that show the insufficiency and inability of human works in

---

2. I will use the terminology of *believing Gentiles* and *believing Jews* rather than *Christian* because of the way such language traditionally functions to form an essential separation between Christianity and Judaism.

3. For an introduction to key ideas and voices, readers interested in continuing the conversation should see Nanos and Zetterholm, eds., *Paul within Judaism*. For a focused introduction to understanding Paul without appealing to later Christian developments, see Eisenbaum, *Paul Was Not a Christian*. For a broader overview of the impact of a post-supersessionist approach to Romans, see Tucker, *Reading Romans after Supersessionism*. Soulen offered an important, early articulation of the way that supersessionism functioned within Christian theology. See his *God of Israel and Christian Theology*.

4. Soulen, "Supersessionism."

earning or securing one's status in the people of God (i.e., justification or righteousness). This failure, then, becomes an opening act that prepares people to enthusiastically receive *the* gospel, that is the newly available offer of grace and forgiveness through Jesus Christ. In such an approach, Judaism and the Torah are purposefully "left behind" as Christianity and the gospel take their place and address the problem of sin that the Torah could not.

I assume that many, if not all, readers are currently wondering whether most readings of the New Testament are, therefore, supersessionist. That suspicion is correct. That such readings are dominant should not, however, be taken as evidence that they are accurate historically or exegetically or be used to excuse their negative ethical implications.

A post-supersessionist approach must, therefore, move past supersessionism by understanding that the believing community is in continuity with, even falling under the broad umbrella of, the Jewish tradition;[5] whatever it means for Gentiles to receive the Spirit and become members of the people of God must make sense within the framework of Judaism. In fact, the basis for a post-supersessionist reading comes from a group of scholars working under the "Paul within Judaism" banner. What Paul writes, and the Gentiles upon whom he expects his argument to affect, should be understood as a part of the hope that the Jewish God will act to fulfill the promises made to the Jewish ancestors and recorded in Jewish texts and voiced by Jewish prophets and brought to fulfillment by a Jewish messiah.[6] Furthermore, it is necessary to appreciate that in our present settings, especially following the Shoah but also the resurgence of anti-Semitism in the US, one cannot articulate a non-supersessionist approach. The effects of supersessionism, both on the Christian and Jewish traditions as well as our world more broadly, are too pervasive to ignore. Although beyond the scope of the present study, a post-supersessionist

---

5. Tucker distinguishes supersessionism into two types: the first type necessarily excludes any ongoing significance of Jewish identity as a whole and a second, softer, type that allows for Jewish ethnic identity but removes the privilege such identity previously carried. In both hard and soft constructions, the privileges and commitments previously belonging to Judaism have been transferred to Christianity, which now takes Judaism's place as the primary loci of God's grace and action.

6. That such a construction is novel reveals the lengths to which Christian readings go to separate the early believers from the Jewish identity by assuming an essential difference in religious identity. See Eisenbaum, "Paul, Polemics, and the Problem of Essentialism."

approach, then, should also look toward addressing the ongoing damage inflicted by supersessionist approaches.

Section 2: But Didn't Paul Convert from Judaism to Christianity?

Supersessionist approaches often employ Paul as a star witness in this story, understanding his personal journey as one from the Jewish Saul to the Christian Paul and his encounter with Jesus as prompting him to recognize the temporary nature or insufficiency of his Jewish religion as he claims the new offer of God's grace in Christ. In this approach, Paul was Jewish and suffered under the burden of Torah and, when confronted with God's grace manifested in and offered uniquely through the Christian gospel of Jesus, left Judaism and joined Christianity. Although such readings vary, they share an assumption about the insufficiency of Judaism to address the problem of sin, which leads God to replace Judaism with Christianity. Such a reading of Paul's life and the caricatures of Judaism that accompany it, however, are patently incoherent when looking at the textual and historical data.[7]

Although defining Judaism is a notoriously slippery task,[8] a general rubric for assessing Jewish identity, especially during the Second Temple period,[9] emphasizes the centrality of Torah, temple, and God. Not all Jews understood or interacted with these three aspects in the same ways, but to call oneself a Jew required some personal stake in each. Even a cursory glance at the Pauline Epistles, and especially if you include the Acts of the Apostles, shows Paul engaged with the Jewish Scriptures as authoritative sources, continuing to use images and practices of the Jewish cult and temple, and, most obviously, focused on the power and plan of the Jewish God. Most striking is the portrayal of Paul, post-Damascus, not only taking a Jewish vow and worshipping in the temple, but also

---

7. Eisenbaum, *Paul Was Not a Christian*, 5–98.

8. Cohen, "'Those Who Say They Are Jews and Are Not.'" More recently, Boyarin has provocatively challenged even the usage of the moniker "Judaism" for people from before the end of the Second Temple period, in *Judaism*. Eisenbaum also demonstrates the difficulty of defining an essential nature for religious identities, especially for the purposes of distinguishing Jews from Christians. See her "Essentialism," 233–38.

9. For helpful introductions to the history of Second Temple Judaism, see Grabbe, *Introduction to Second Temple Judaism*, and Cohen, *From the Maccabees to the Mishnah*.

helping other Jews complete their vows expressly to verify his commitment to Torah (Acts 21:17–27). A Paul who saw Judaism and Torah as
superseded by a Christian gospel could not undertake such actions. Even
more problematic for supersessionist approaches is Paul *circumcising*
Timothy so that Timothy will be able to accompany Paul on his missionary journeys (Acts 16:1–5). Such actions appear to fundamentally
conflict with Paul's proclamation in Galatians that undergoing circumcision voids the effects of the gospel. If you, however, pay close attention to
the relationship between Torah and identity, you see that such actions are
consistent with Paul's writings in affirming the ongoing vitality of God's
commitments to the Jewish people as he commands his audience to obey
Torah, albeit in ways appropriate to each person's native identity.

This *apparent* tension between Torah observance and commitment
to the gospel of Jesus is a product of later definitions and essentialist approaches to religious identity. Even E. P. Sanders, whose work was instrumental in the genesis of the New Perspective on Paul by showing how
thoroughly Paul fit within Rabbinic Judaism,[10] assumed an inherent break
between Judaism and Christianity, and was left to assume an ideological
break rather than having evidence for one. Pamela Eisenbaum, among
others, demonstrates that such assumptions rely on later misreadings of
the New Testament and misunderstandings of how religious identities
are constructed and maintained.[11]

The most important concept in the discussion of Jewish identity
and the New Testament is a rather bulky term coined to express how
Judaism balances the concepts of justification and obedience: covenantal
nomism. Simply put, covenantal nomism is a covenantal approach to the
Jewish Torah (*nomos* in Greek). This covenantal approach acknowledges
that God establishes the covenants with the Jewish ancestors not because
of their merits or any special characteristics,[12] but because of God's uni-
lateral prerogative. Although a modern term, the concept of covenantal
nomism pervades the Jewish tradition, especially in texts that are near

10. Although Sanders worked with rabbinic texts, his goal was to establish a sufficient connection with Pharisaic Judaism to show that Paul's thinking makes sense
within the movement with which he himself identifies. See *Paul and Palestinian
Judaism*.

11. Eisenbaum, *Paul*, 33–55.

12. Abraham is the main exception, with some parts of the Jewish tradition saying
that Abraham's refusal to worship his family's idols was an act that singled him out. See
the discussion in Levenson, *Inheriting Abraham*, 18–35.

contemporaries of the New Testament. In the Hodayot, a collection of prayers in the Dead Sea Scrolls, the author writes:

> As for me, my justification is with God. In His hand are the perfection of my way and the uprightness of my heart. He will wipeout my transgression through his righteousness . . . My iniquities, rebellions, and sins, together with the perversity of my heart, belong to the company of worms and to those who walk in darkness. For mankind has no way, and man is unable to establish his steps since justification is with God and perfection of way is out of his hand. (1QII.2–22)

Notice the author's rather bleak self-assessment regarding their ability to merit justification. The idea of legalism, that is earning one's place, is nowhere to be found. This is balanced by the idea that it is in response to this gracious act that justifies that people respond in obedience to the Torah. Obedience, then, becomes the proper demonstration or outworking of the identity that God has freely and graciously bestowed upon an individual and is necessary for maintaining that identity. Said more provocatively, justification is an act of God's grace while salvation is an act of human obedience. The resonance such an approach has with the New Testament, especially Paul's letters, balances acknowledging God's grace in freely welcoming people into the people of God with the necessity of those people to demonstrate an obedience that is oriented to the Jewish God (e.g., Rom 6).

Rather than a Paul who leaves Jewish identity and abandons Jewish privilege, the New Testament shows a Paul that is fully coherent within Judaism and working to make space for others, that is Gentiles, within the Jewish tradition by teaching them how to orient their lives toward the God of the Jews. In fact, we will see how Romans can be understood as arguing towards precisely this goal as Paul writes of God's offer of justification and the requirement for his Gentile audience to respond with Torah-shaped obedience that fulfills the Torah in ways appropriate to them as non-Jews.

To be clear, this is not the same as advocating Gentiles become Jews,[13] as was the case for proselytes who were individuals who *became* Jews by converting from their native identity. Paul's Letter to the Galatians clearly opposes such a change. No, what Paul communicates is that because the God of the Jews has triumphed over the present age and the forces that

---

13. Nanos, "Paul's Non-Jews Do Not Become 'Jews.'"

rule over Gentiles, these Gentiles are now free to orient their lives in the service of the God of the Jews rather than the lower principalities and powers to which they were formerly enslaved.

Section 3: The Chronometrical Claims of Paul's Apocalyptic Gospel

Some of the most important developments in Judaism during the Second Temple period were those that resulted from Judaism's encounter and interaction with apocalypticism. Prior to the Babylonian exile, Jewish thought was basically sapiential, meaning that the world was thought to make sense as presented with life working out following a rational system of cause and effect. The books of Proverbs and Deuteronomy are prime examples of such logic, where life is said to be ordered by clear rules and consequences are appropriate to one's actions.

The exile and resulting suffering of God's people strained this logic to the point of breaking. To maintain their beliefs in God's goodness and election of the Jewish people, their current and ongoing suffering needed to be explained rationally. Such a shift can be seen in the book of Job, which finds a way of breaking the connection between suffering and angering God. Job's friends take the sapiential point of view that understands Job's suffering as a direct result of his acting against God. Job denies such a charge and is forced to defend his righteousness even in the midst of his suffering, by positing that God's ways are mysterious.

Such a line of thought pervades the Jewish Apocrypha and Pseudepigrapha. Wisdom of Solomon is a particularly helpful example because of the parallels with key parts of Paul's argument in Romans. Most important for our discussion is the way that the present suffering of God's people is framed as a temporary part of God's purification of God's people while God allows the sins of outsiders to accumulate (e.g., Wis 3:1–13). The result is that on the day of judgment, those who had been purified would be welcomed into the next age while those who had not would be destroyed.

The expectation of a transition from the current age to a future age or turning of the ages as Paul describes it (cf. 1 Cor 10:11), is another key development in Second Temple Judaism and is essential for understanding Jesus's message in the Gospels and Paul's writings. The idea was that the current age is dominated by forces that are not God, which is why evil currently triumphs over good. God will not, however, allow such an arrangement to continue indefinitely and will one day defeat the powers that currently rule the world. The future age that will follow is one where God is king, evil is defeated, and the righteous thrive.

The New Testament, and Romans in particular, clearly manifests these expectations. Their main innovation, and one that is at the heart of Paul's thinking, is that rather than a clean break that separates the two ages, there is an overlap where the old age lingers on while the new age takes effect. The most important consequence of this overlap is that Gentiles are no longer under the control of their lesser gods but can become worshippers of the Jewish God without having to become Jews. That what should only be true in the future can be a present reality is what Mark Nanos refers to as the chronometrical claim of Paul's gospel.[14] Nanos's use of the chronometrical claim provides a helpful and nuanced update to the more familiar "already but not yet" terminology that is likely more familiar to students of the New Testament.

The most important consequence of Gentiles shifting their orientation away from their native gods to the Jewish God is that their life and worship should now appropriately reflect the concerns and obligations required of the Jewish God. The most direct evidence of this, especially in Romans, are Paul's references to Gentiles who have the Law written on their hearts and his expectations that his Gentile audience will fulfill (i.e., do) the Law by loving their neighbors as themselves. Paul's reference to Gentiles who have the Law written on their hearts is a helpful detail because the expectation of God writing the Law on a person's heart is part of apocalyptic Judaism's expectations of what would happen in the future age (e.g., Jer 31:33; Jub 23:24–30). Paul stating that such a person presently exists is just one sign that he understands the future age as a present reality.

Section 4: Romans 1–6, from Torah-Free to Torah-Shaped

The most immediate impact of a post-supersessionist approach to Romans is an awareness of how positive Paul is about Torah and Jewish identity more broadly.[15] As mentioned above, supersessionist approaches require Judaism have a deficiency or at least a transient function tied to an understanding that the Torah's main function is to make people aware

14. Nanos, *Reading Paul within Judaism*, 22–23.

15. Fredriksen, "Why Should a 'Law-Free' Mission Mean a 'Law-Free' Apostle?"

that they are sinful and need God's grace. But this is not at all how Paul talks about or uses Torah in Romans. In fact, throughout Romans Paul emphasizes the need for his Gentile *audience* to fulfill the Law.

Paul's opening rhetorical salvo involves indicting human failure to act according to what one knows to be appropriate. Paul begins with condemning an unidentified person, whom current scholarship considers to be a fictitious interlocutor in the form of a philosopher, who knows what is right, judges the behavior of others based on that knowledge, but ultimately fails to act according to that knowledge (Rom 2:1–5). Paul's point is that simply knowing what is right is not enough; a person's life must demonstrate that knowledge through appropriate action.

> For [God] will repay according to each one's works. To those who by patiently doing good seek for glory and honor and immortality, [God] will give eternal life, while for those who are self-seeking and who obey not the truth but wickedness, there will be wrath and fury. There will be anguish and distress for everyone who does evil, the Jew first and, also, the Greek, but glory and honor and peace for everyone who does good. *Because God shows no partiality.* (Rom 2:6–11; emphasis added)

Again, Paul's point is *not* that God sets a moral trap in order to be able to condemn everyone (contra Martin Luther), but to emphasize God's impartiality in *judging and rewarding* without regard to ethnicity. Paul then reiterates this by pointing to Gentiles who have the Torah written on their hearts and, consequently, are able to instinctively *fulfill* the Torah and are, therefore, rewarded for their fidelity (Rom 2:14–15). I will return in the final section to address what type of Gentiles could have the Torah written on the heart.

Paul then shifts to address a person who can claim Jewish identity (2:17).[16] Although this person knows Torah, their failure to embody its precepts and bring glory to God results in their condemnation (Rom 2:18–24). Paul then reiterates this point by using a key marker of Jewish identity: circumcision.[17]

> Circumcision indeed is of value if you obey the law; but if you break the law, your circumcision has become uncircumcision . . . Then those who are physically uncircumcised but keep the law

---

16. There is debate about whether this would be a natural-born Jew or a proselyte; see Rodriguez, *If You Call Yourself a Jew*, 47–72.

17. Cohen, "'Those Who Say They Are Jews,'" 39–49.

will condemn you that have the written code and circumcision
but break the law. (Rom 2:25, 27)

Paul's point is that simply having a marker of a privileged identity is
insufficient because a person must embody that identity through fidelity
to the Torah. In fact, obedience is so important that Gentiles who lack
the mark of identity (i.e., circumcision) but who fulfil the Torah, will be
counted among those of the privileged identity.

A supersessionist perspective is incapable of accounting for the fact
that not only is the reality of fulfilling Torah used in the text, but that
doing so allows Gentiles to be counted among the Jewish people. Rather
than Paul arguing that these Gentiles have replaced Jews or that there
is a new religious identity that accomplishes what Judaism could not,
Paul argues for Gentiles being able to enact the very thing that Moses,
the prophets, and the vast majority of the Jewish tradition consistently
expect: fidelity to Torah.

Section 5: Romans 7–8, the "I" and the Law

Identifying the speaker in Romans 7 and understanding their relationship
to the Torah is notably complex, with a long and winding interpretive
history. Indeed, some of the statements can be read as directly supporting
a supersessionist approach that understands Torah as either inadequate
or intentionally designed to provoke human guilt. The two main questions that scholars have raised in reassessing the traditional reading are
what assumptions are used in approaching the text and who the speaker
is. These will be addressed in order, below.

Few names are more important in reassessing assumptions about
Romans 7 than Krister Stendahl. Writing in 1963, before the New Perspective on Paul, Stendahl effectively challenged many of the long-held
assumptions necessary to read Romans 7 as Paul's autobiographical
renunciation of his Jewish identity. Stendahl effectively demonstrates
how later theological and psychological concerns, concerns that could
not have been present in a first-century Mediterranean text, had come to
dominate interpretations of Paul.

> The Pauline awareness of sin has been interpreted in the light of
> [Martin] Luther's struggle with his conscience. But it is exactly
> at that point that we can discern the most drastic difference
> between Luther and Paul, between the 16th and the 1st century,

and, perhaps, between Eastern and Western Christianity . . .
Where Paul was concerned about the possibility for Gentiles to
be included in the messianic community, his statements are now
read as answers to the quest for assurance about man's salvation
out of a common human predicament.[18]

In contrast to a Paul whose acute awareness of his moral failure
drives him to convert to Christianity, Romans 7 presents an individual
who is aware of and wants to do good, but whose body is still enslaved to
sin and, therefore, cannot embody faithfulness to the Torah. The problem
is the body, not Torah or Judaism, which is why Paul's answer to the problem in Romans 8 is not the creation of a new religion but addressing the
problem of sin in the flesh (Rom 8:1–4). Furthermore, Stendahl points
out that this declaration of sin is not the rhetorical point of Paul's argument.[19] Rather, Romans 7 focuses attention back on a point that comes
up repeatedly in Romans: the relationship between Jews and Gentiles in
the people of God. Furthermore, Stendahl's comments about the messianic community fit into our discussion above about the results of Paul's
chronometrical gospel, where Gentiles become equal participants in the
Jewish community.

Scholars have built on Stendahl's insights by questioning the identity
of the "I" in Romans 7. Consider Stanley Stowers, whose use of ancient
Mediterranean rhetorical models has significantly impacted interpretations of Romans. Rather than the I being Paul, Stowers argues that Paul
employs the I to answer a long running ethical conundrum of Greek philosophy: why do people do things that are ultimately bad for them and
how do you stop them from taking such harmful actions?[20]

In contrast to the Stoic response of education, Paul's approach identifies the problem as the body that is trapped in the old age and is unable
to follow the Law. As Paul states, the problem is not the Law itself or
human desire to follow it but the inability of those who are still under
the control of the powers of the former age, namely sin and death. The
resolution is not to abandon the Law or condemn the individual but to
have the body set free from the old age by the obedience of Jesus. This
shift then brings the Law into contact with a body under the power of the

---

18. Stendahl, "Apostle Paul and the Introspective Conscience of the West," 200,
206.

19. Stendahl, "Apostle Paul and the Introspective Conscience of the West," 200–202.

20. Stowers, *Rereading of Romans*, 271–76.

Spirit, which serves as a sign of the new age, rather than the Law under the power of sin.

A post-supersessionist approach makes sense with this reading of Romans 7–8 by not framing the transition that frees the "I" from the inadequacies of Judaism but the powers of the current age. The resolution is not a required shift to Christian identity but a shift to a body that has been transferred to the next age *and is able to fulfill its desire to uphold the Law*, a shift possible because of Christ's defeat of the powers of the current age.

Section 6: Romans 9–11 and Israel, the Law, Gentiles, and the Tree of God

No section in Romans offers as many key divergences between supersessionist and post-supersessionist readings as Romans 9–11. Because of space, we will only have time to highlight the three most relevant to our current study: the identity of those who are truly Israel (9:6), Christ as the *telos* of the Law (10:4), and a discussion of how Gentiles received a place in the people of God (11:11–36). It is crucial to note that Paul's rhetorical burden in this section is to explain why it is that some Gentiles are responding positively to the message of Jesus while some Jews are not. In other words, why would some Jews reject the message of how the Jewish God fulfills the promises made to the Jewish ancestors?

Paul's opening comments regarding Israelites, his kinspeople according to the flesh, includes a series of statements about what belongs to them as a matter of birthright (9:4–5). These rights are clarified later when Paul says that these are obligations made by God to the Jewish people and are, therefore, unbreakable obligations that will be kept (11:29). Taken together, these statements can be read as Paul affirming God's commitment to the Jewish people and the covenants and Law while explaining why not all of the Jewish people have acknowledged the inbreaking of God's new age in the person and work of Jesus.

The main point that must be addressed in distinguishing a post-supersessionist reading is Paul's statement that, "For not all Israelites truly belong to Israel, and not all of Abraham's children are his true descendants" (9:6b–7a). The main question is whether the category that Paul drives toward, those who truly belong to Israel, includes all those labeled Israelites and believing Gentiles or whether some Israelites do not truly belong to Israel. Without connecting this statement to the obligations just outlined by Paul, this statement could be read as part of a redefinition of Israel so that those Jews who are not currently participating in the new age are excluded while Gentiles who are participating are included. Most notable in this vein would be N. T. Wright, who argues that Paul's redefinition of Israel is solely around those currently exhibiting faith.[21] Such a reading clearly fits the definition for supersessionism because it removes Judaism by itself as a valid category for relationship with God and requires that it be combined with Christianity.[22] While Paul certainly centers faith, Wright's argument requires overlooking Paul's emphasis on the obligations made to Jews regardless of their current response to the message of Jesus. More importantly, including Gentiles into the people of God as Israelites overlooks Paul's broader burden of maintaining ethnic particularity in the new age.

If Paul's statement is read that it is not *just* all Israelites who truly belong to Israel, then Paul could maintain the independent validity of Jewish identity and *expand* the boundary of those belonging to Israel to include Gentiles without needing to call these newcomers Israelites or Jews. Although Paul clearly argues for the full inclusion of Gentiles, such a move comes later and includes Paul expressly warning the Gentiles from thinking that they are replacing Jewish priority or ethnic particularity.

Paul's statement, "For Christ is the *telos* of the law so that there could be righteousness for everyone who has faith," is equally problematic (10:4). The Greek word *telos* (τέλος) can be translated as end with the meaning of point of cessation or goal with the meaning of fulfillment. The former of these meanings is clearly in line with a supersessionist reading since ending the Law would require ending the validity of Jewish identities defined by observance of the Law. Such a reading would also fit the supersessionist story that Jesus signals a shift from the Law and Judaism to grace and Christianity as Jesus ends the Law's function as demarcating those who are declared righteous (i.e., given membership in the people of God). No longer are the people of God defined by the Law but by faith.

But a supersessionist reading cannot account for Paul's ongoing use of the Law as a metric for behavior throughout Romans and his other letters, or for his continued personal observance of the Law. If Christ had,

---

21. Wright, *Paul and the Faithfulness of God*, 539–41.

22. For a different view of N.T. Wright's work, see John Anthony Dunne and Eric Lewellen, eds. *One God, One People, One Future: Essays in Honor of N.T. Wright*. Minneapolis: Fortress Press, 2018.

in fact, ended the Law, then why continue to appeal to it as a goal to which Gentiles should aspire? A post-supersessionist reading would take Paul's meaning as Christ, and what Christ accomplishes, as the goal to which the Law pointed, which Paul has explicitly stated twice already in Romans (1:2, 3:21). This would also fit nicely with Paul's statements in Romans 7 and 8, discussed above, where the problems of Gentiles and the Law in the old age is solved by Jesus making possible the chronometrical reality of God's new age. Furthermore, Paul's comment "so that there could be righteousness for everyone who has faith" would be read as expanding the boundary of the people of God to now include both those whose identities are defined by the Law (i.e., Jews) and those whose are not (i.e., Gentiles).

In the conclusion of this section, Paul directly confronts the consequences for those Jews who have currently rejected the gospel, the details of which directly contradict supersessionist readings.

> So I ask, have [Jews who have currently rejected the gospel] stumbled so as to fall? By no means! But through their stumbling salvation has come to the Gentiles, so as to make Israel jealous . . . For if their rejection is the reconciliation of the world, what will their acceptance be but life from the dead! . . . But if some of the branches were broken off, and you [Gentiles], a wild olive shoot, were grafted in their place to share the rich root of the olive tree, do not boast over the branches. If you do boast, remember that it is not you that support the root, but the root that supports you. (Rom 11:11–18)

Paul's statements are explicitly designed to rebut Gentile assumptions that Jews who have not accepted the gospel have abrogated their place in the people of God. On the contrary, Paul says that the rejection of the gospel by some Jews is necessary to create the opportunity for Gentiles to be joined into the family. Within this discussion, Paul uses the metaphor of branches; God's causing some Jews to reject the gospel is understood as God creating a bend in the branch that allows foreign branches (i.e., Gentiles) to be grafted into the host plant.[23] Horticultural references aside, Paul's meaning is clearly to emphasize Jewish priority: the host plant is Jewish and Gentiles are included as foreign guests. As Paul states, the point is to prevent Gentiles from feeling superior to Jews, since it is a Jewish community that these Gentiles have joined.[24] What-

---

23. Nanos is especially helpful on the rhetoric and translation of these passages. See "Romans 11," 14–20.

24. Nanos argues that the early believing communities did, in fact, meet under

ever else Paul thinks of the believing community, he clearly envisions the continuation of a Jewish community, albeit one that now includes Gentiles as Gentiles. Recalling the earlier discussion of the problems created by essentialist approaches to religious identity, we see how supersessionist approaches that construct a firm boundary between Jew and Christian fail to account for Paul's argument and imagery.

Section 7: Romans 14–15 and the "Strong" and "Weak"

Paul's comments about the strong and the weak in Romans 14–15 are traditionally read as framing strength as a mindset and life that are free from the constraints and practices of the Law and weakness as continuing to feel bound to them. In this construction, freedom from the Law is the more desirable or enlightened position to which all people, Paul included, should aspire. As such, this has been a classic text to contrast Paulinism with more Jewish forms of Christianity and, therefore, is a key text for supersessionist readings.

There are multiple problems with such a reading that are overcome by a post-supersessionist approach and closer attention to Paul's rhetoric and usage of strength and weakness. As Beverly Gaventa demonstrates, Paul's use of strength and weakness do not fit the neat parallel necessary for the traditional reading to hold.[25] Yes, Paul describes those who are weak in faith using patterns and practices that correspond to observance of the Jewish Law,[26] but strength is not characterized as those who are free from such patterns and practices. Rather, strength is defined as being able to set aside one's preferences for the preservation of the Other.[27]

Such observations help explain how Paul can identify the practices of each group, those observing and those not, as equally valid before God. If Paul identifies observance of the Law with weakness it is hard to imagine him then labeling such practice as acceptable before God. In such a construction, it is not the practices themselves that are at issue but

---

the umbrella of local synagogues and were under the authority of Jewish leaders. He applies this construction to Paul's comments in Romans 13 to argue Paul argues submission to synagogue authorities, not to Nero and the Roman state. See *Mystery of Romans*, 321–28.

25. Gaventa, "Reading for the Subject."

26. Nanos, *Mystery*, 119–43.

27. Such a construction relies on a careful reading of the Greek text. See Gaventa, "Reading for the Subject," 9–10.

judging and making distinctions of value based on those practices that are the target of Paul's rhetoric.

The power of a supersessionist approach is apparent in the fact that Gaventa, despite outlining many of the above points, retains a supersessionist assumption that Paul must label those who follow Torah as weak, which broadly follows a strength-as-Christian-and-weakness-as-Jewish paradigm.[28] Such a conclusion is not required, or even casually supported by the text, but by a history that assumes a firm definitive break where Christianity becomes the natural and rightful replacement of the Jewish tradition.

In contrast, a post-supersessionist reading does not require Paul to identify Law observance with weakness and so does not require positing Christian strength and Jewish weakness. Paul's comments, then, are about freedom from making value judgments based on ethnic particularity, since each person is judged individually by God based on the practices and standards relevant to their particular identity (e.g., 14:4). The goal of such an argument comes in the quotations where Jews and Gentiles stand together and praise God with one voice (15:8–13). The main difference is that these Jews are still fully Torah observant Jews and these Gentiles are still ethnically distinct Gentiles who have nonetheless oriented their lives to obedience of the Jewish God. They are equal and united, but they are not the same. Such a vision for the people of God has a tantalizing overlap with the apocalyptic narrative within which Paul thinks. These Gentiles no longer must serve their native gods because these gods have been defeated and are contained within the old age. This means that Gentiles who have received the Spirit as a marker of their participation in the new age can now become full members of the people of God without needing to change their identities.

Although I can only point in the direction of the implications of Paul's thinking, Paula Fredriksen details the social, economic, and political perils that awaited Gentiles who engaged in such subversive behavior.[29] Abandoning one's native gods without coming under the protection of new gods, which required a conversion of identity, left Paul's Gentiles in a dangerous position. This could be one reason why Paul earlier framed

28. Gaventa, "Reading for the Subject," 5–6. For a different assessment of Beverly Gaventa's work, see David Downs and Matthew Skinner, eds. *The Unrelenting God: God's Action in Scripture: Essays in Honor of Beverly Roberts Gaventa.* Grand Rapids: Eerdmans, 2013.

29. Fredriksen, "Why Should a 'Law-Free' Mission."

the gospel as something of which he, and hence also his audience, is not ashamed, and framed this obedience in terms of worship (Rom 1:16, 12:1–4, respectively). These Gentiles were being asked to imagine a world in which their native identities did not determine the course of their worship, where all people were invited into a community oriented toward a God best described as love and an awareness that differences in race and worship did not determine one's value. It was a truly radical idea then, as it is now, and one not designed to make us comfortable but to set us free.

Section 8: Conclusion

Although the current chapter could only highlight the most salient points of a post-supersessionist approach to Romans, I hope that the readings described and contrasts offered with traditional approaches to Romans offer some insight and have piqued the reader's interest. There are a wealth of resources for further exploration, many found in the footnotes of this essay. If readers take anything away from the possibilities offered by a post-supersessionist reading, I hope that it is a sense for the radically inclusive possibilities that such a reading makes possible as Paul's gospel no longer frames Judaism as weak and defunct but offers a way to see all people, in their particularity and unique expressions of worship, as equally valued and celebrated before the God who rules over all creation.

Sermon

To the Jew First

David Rudolph

When my daughter, Miryam, was little, I would tuck her in bed at 8:30 PM, turn off the lights, and say, "Good night, I love you." But as she got older, she began to think to herself, "Wait a minute, why do I have to go to bed at 8:30 while my sisters get to stay up until 10:30, and my parents don't seem to have a bedtime? That's not fair!" One day she shared with me her reasoning. So I said, "You're right. We have a different standard for you, for your sisters, and for us as your parents. It all depends on age." Miryam replied, "Well, why do you get to decide this? Why can't I decide?" And I said, "Because I'm your daddy." Then Miryam said, "Why do I have to listen to my daddy?" And I said, "Because the Lord said so." Then she said, "How do you know that?" And I said, "In Exodus 20 the Lord says, 'Honor your father and your mother.'" I remember curiously waiting to see whether she was going to ask why she had to listen to the Lord. Fortunately, she was satisfied with my answer, and that was that.

All of us at some point in our lives voice the words, "That's not fair!" But not all of us pause to consider that fair doesn't always mean equal, and by equal I mean having the same privileges and opportunities. This is something that we need to keep in mind when we are blindsided by Paul's declaration in Romans 1:16 that the gospel is "to the Jew first." How should we understand this seemingly unfair principle that our father in heaven has put in place?[1]

Let's look at the context first. Paul identifies himself as an "apostle to the Gentiles" (Rom 11:13) and in Romans 1:13 he explains that he intended to come to Rome as part of his mission to the Gentiles:

> I do not want you to be unaware, brothers, that I have often intended to come to you (but thus far have been prevented), in order that I may reap some harvest *among you as well as among the rest of the Gentiles.*[2]

What does Paul mean by "Gentiles"? The term "Gentiles" derives from the Hebrew word *goyim*, which means "nations." It often refers in the Scriptures to all the nations except one, the nation of Israel. Paul's reference to "Gentiles" reminds us that Paul was a Jew. From Paul's perspective, the world was divided into two groups: Jews and non-Jews (Gentiles). Gentiles who became followers of Jesus remained Gentiles and did not become Jews. They did not become a "third race" that was neither Jew nor Gentile, as some theologians suggest. Rather, in Paul's view, Gentiles who become followers of the Messiah of Israel become Gentile members of the people of God (Rom 11:13, 17–24; 15:10).

In Romans 1, Paul communicates three times that the gospel is for the Gentiles and that he is called to serve the Gentiles. We hear this loud and clear in verses 5, 13, and 14. And lest his readers have still not gotten the point, he says a fourth time—in verse 16—that the good news of Jesus the son of David is for the salvation of "*everyone* who believes," and that "everyone" includes the Gentiles. Paul has stressed this again and again because he wants the Gentiles to be secure in the knowledge that God loves them, that Paul loves them, and that nothing will change that.

It is at this point, after establishing God's commitment to care for the Gentiles, that Paul introduces the subject of divine priorities. He shifts gears to focus on the Jewish people, his own people, when he says in Romans 1:16 that the gospel is "*to the Jew first* and also to the Greek." Why does Paul say this?

---

1. For a broader discussion of the issues involved in Romans 1:16, see Rudolph, "To the Jew First."

2. All Scripture quotations are taken from the ESV (2011) unless otherwise indicated.

Notably, Paul uses the expression "the Jew first and also the Greek" three times in his letter to the Romans. The first is in Romans 1:16 and the other two are in Romans 2:9–11:

> There will be tribulation and distress for every human being who does evil, *the Jew first and also the Greek*, but glory and honor and peace for everyone who does good, *the Jew first and also the Greek*. For God shows no partiality.

In Romans 2, "the Jew first" is not about mission chronology or strategy. Rather, "the Jew first" is another way of referring to Israel's election. God's standard of judging the world will be: to whom much is given, much is expected. And because Israel has been given much in the way of prerogative due to her election and covenant relationship with God (Rom 3:1–2; 9:4–5; 11:28–29), the Jewish people will be judged by a different standard than the nations. Here Paul describes God's approach to Jews and Gentiles as fair but not the same. In light of Romans 2, and Paul's identity as a Second Temple Jew, a compelling case can be made that, in Paul's thought, the gospel is first for the Jewish people because there is a covenantal priority (cf. Acts 3:25–26; 13:44–46; 14:1; 17:10; 18:4–6; 19:8ff.).

But is this a continuing priority? The normative Christian view over the past two millennia has been that the election of the Jewish people expired sometime in the first century CE and that the church has replaced the Jewish people as the people of God. Romans 1:16, however, calls us to reject this way of thinking. The words "to the Jew first" are Paul's rallying cry for the continued prioritization of Israel in the Gentile wing of the church, despite supersessionist arguments to the contrary.

The primary reason Paul included "to the Jew first" in Romans 1:16—even at the risk of alienating some of his non-Jewish readers—appears to be that the Gentile believers in Rome needed to hear that God's covenant relationship with Israel was "irrevocable" (Rom 11:29). Some Gentiles were saying that God had given up on the Jewish people and that Israel's election had expired (Rom 11:1). In Romans 1:16, Paul fires the first shot in his attempt to push back against this wrong teaching, a teaching that continues to circulate in the church today. "To the Jew first" should be understood in the wider context of Paul's defense of Israel's ongoing covenantal relationship with God—a defense that begins in Romans 1:16, continues in chapters 2–3, climaxes in chapters 9–11, and concludes in chapter 15.

How do we apply this text in the twenty-first century? How do we prioritize Israel in the life of the church? This is something that each of us needs to pray about. We need to be led by the Lord in this. Let us also remember that the gospel involves bearing witness to the Messiah in word and deed; it is an incarnational reality, hence the weight that Paul gives to the collection for the poor in Jerusalem (Rom 15:25–27; cf. Gal 2:9–10; 1 Cor 16:1–4; Acts 24:17). Here are some questions that Gentile Christians can ask themselves in light of our discussion on Romans 1:16: Do I have a sincere love for the Jewish people? Has replacement theology shaped my understanding of the gospel? When was the last time that I shared with a Jewish friend about Jesus the son of David? Is Jewish ministry a priority of my local church? Do I encourage Jesus-believing Jews to retain their Jewish identity as a matter of calling and covenant fidelity, or to assimilate for the sake of "oneness" in Christ? Do I have relationships with Jewish followers of Jesus? If so, are these relationships characterized by interdependence, mutual blessing, and mutual humbling? Do I give to Jewish charities and advocacy organizations? Do I fight antisemitism in the church and the public square, or look the other way? Do I regularly pray for Israel and the well-being of the Jewish people worldwide? All of these are spheres of life that will be impacted when we experience Spirit-led vision to bring the gospel to the Jew first.

Sermon

Two Acts of Service, One Servant

Joel Willitts

LAST SUMMER I WAS in St. Paul visiting friends. Some months before tremendously destructive race riots broke out after George Floyd's death. My friend showed me around St. Paul and the destruction that happened there. The Target was looted and a couple of businesses were burned or looted. I was amazed at what had been done. I would soon realize things can be much worse. We then drove to Minneapolis and walked by all the destruction done in the ethnic fallout. Many buildings were burned to the ground. The police station was burned. A liquor store was burned. A post office was burned down. I had never seen anything like that. It was truly overwhelming to see the violence ethnic tension can wreak. I've looked back over those images captured on my phone. The pictures cannot do justice to the reality.[1]

I came again to Romans 15:7–13 with those pictures in my imagination; I was thinking about the destructive nature of ethnic tension and especially ethnic tension in the church. The apostle Paul would not tolerate

---

1. See the essay in this volume, "Looking Back to Move Forward," for a historical context for the unrest in Minneapolis and around the nation in response to George Floyd's murder. The ongoing destruction of black bodies and black life and the historical pattern of ignoring cries for justice, refusing to recognize blacks' right to live and breathe, as well as the repeated refusal to hold those in power accountable played a huge role in the unrest. Despite calls for peaceful protests from Floyd's family and others, some took advantage of the situation and engaged in violence.

it. I think he might say that the ethnic tension that gave rise to the fires of Minneapolis and St. Paul, are no more destructive than ethnic tension in the church. If left unattended, ethnic tension can destroy the church's foundation.

In Romans 15:7–13, the apostle Paul taught the necessity of reconciliation between different ethnicities in the churches in Rome. Paul argues that Christ-believers can overcome ethnic tension in the church. His message was that Christ-believers must embrace each other across ethnic lines. His teaching can be divided into three units: (1) the imperative to embrace one another, (2) the explanation of Christ's service for different ethnicities, and (3) a concluding statement of Gentile hope.

I need to provide a bit of the context for Romans 15:7–13. Over chapters 14 and 15, Paul dealt with ethnic division between Messiah believers in Rome. The issues related to the question of what makes a Jew a Jew and what defines a Gentile. Apparently, one or both groups were discriminating against the other because of the distinct markers of their race/ethnicity. Paul walked through the issues that were most important. The bottom line was a lack of empathic respect for and understanding of the ethnicity of another believer. At the beginning of chapter 15, Paul drew the trump card when he appealed to Christ's refusal to please himself when he gave himself over to humiliation for the world. In verses immediately before those of our passage, Paul wrote,

> May the God of steadfastness and encouragement grant you to live in harmony with one another, in accordance with Christ Jesus, so that together you may with one voice glorify the God and Father of our Lord Jesus Christ. (15:5–6)

Romans 15:7–13 flows perfectly from these opening verses of the chapter. We will see similar themes in our passage: (1) live in harmony with one another, (2) live in accordance with Christ Jesus, and (3) with one voice glorify the God and father of the Lord Jesus Christ.

I think that this passage has much to contribute to the ethnic challenges we see playing out daily from our smart phones.

I. Paul's Command: Embrace One Another (15:7)

Paul's command in verse 15:7 summed up what he had said since the beginning of chapter 14. "Welcome one another, therefore, just as Christ has welcomed you, for the glory of God." The command here adds little to what he has already stated. In verse 5, he said, "live in harmony with one another." What's important is not the observation that the two commands are parallel. What's important is why they are parallel. The idea in the command is important enough that Paul states it twice. So, this is not of little importance. Embrace each other. "Embrace one another!" The verb "embrace" is beautiful. An embrace. Intimacy. Welcome. Love. Affirmation. Gift. Peace. Laughter. Knowledge. Touch. Grief. Acceptance. Understanding. Forgiveness. Patience. Hope. The Five Senses. This is embrace. We are to embrace each another.

Keep in mind the context. Paul is writing to churches in Rome struggling with ethnic tension between Jewish and Gentile Christ-believers. The issues were related to patterns of life that defined their ethnicity. Paul stated emphatically, "Embrace each other." Notice what Paul then said, "just as Christ has embraced you." Christ's pattern of life provided the example to follow and a command to obey.

The embrace of two uncomfortably joined ethnicities considering Christ's own example of the acceptance of us brings God glory. Ultimately, it is for the glory of God that two ethnicities embrace. The embrace of one another across ethnic lines brings glory to God.

What do we do with this imperative in 2023? In the US, we are experiencing an unprecedented time in race relations. The cultural trends in our cities and neighborhoods and country are reflected in our churches, with some in our church supporting law enforcement while others are in support of Black Lives Matter. As with most of our society today, the church is experiencing crippling polarization around ethnic issues. But this is not purely an issue of black and white. As we have experienced in recent years, Mexicans and Latinos experience ethnic struggle in the US. And all this is to say nothing of the plight of Asian Americans.

Paul's command to embrace each other across ethnic lines is as relevant today as it was two thousand years ago in these Roman congregations. It's a message as well that speaks beyond the church to the wider society.

What might embrace look like in our time? It of course begins with our relationship to Jesus. Humiliation and servanthood structured his life. Elsewhere, in Philippians 2, Paul speaks of the Messiah having equality with God, but still humbling himself to become human to the extent that he would die. Paul no doubt has that early Christian hymn playing on his Spotify playlist. It's Jesus. Begin by reading the Gospels. Make it a habit of reading a bit of a Gospel every day. Ask how Jesus was a servant in this story or in this teaching. Make the Gospels familiar. Let Jesus' life lead you, his words, his deeds, his priorities. Let him point out areas where you need to grow. Let him give you the resources to embrace more fully another ethnicity.

Embrace one another just as Christ has embraced you for the glory of God.

Having stated the proposition of the passage in 15:8–13, Paul described how Christ's service for one race is different from his service for another. Paul believes the one Christ serves different ethnicities differently.

II. Christ's Service for Jew and for the Gentile (15:8-13)

Paul knew that what he had exhorted his churches to do was extremely difficult work. He presented a biblical and theological foundation for the near herculean task. The gist is that Christ served the Messianic Jew in a way that was different than he did with the Gentile. An understanding of Christ work within the two different ethnicities brought the recognition of God's unique work within them. But this difference was also complemented by the understanding that Christ served them both.

Let's go to the text again, Romans 15:8–12.

[servant to the Jew]

> **8** For I tell you that Christ has become a servant of the circumcised on behalf of the truth of God in order that he might confirm the promises given to the patriarchs,

[servant to the Gentile]

> **9** and in order that the Gentiles might glorify God for his mercy. As it is written,
> "Therefore I will confess you among the Gentiles,
> and sing praises to your name";
> **10** and again he says,
> "Rejoice, O Gentiles, with his people";
> **11** and again,
> "Praise the Lord, all you Gentiles,
> and let all the peoples praise him";
> **12** and again Isaiah says,
> "The root of Jesse shall come,
> the one who rises to rule the Gentiles;
> in him the Gentiles shall hope."

In these five verses, Paul provided the basis for his imperative (embrace!). Paul gives two reasons: (1) The recognition of Christ's service unique to the ethnicity. (2) The recognition that Christ is the servant of both. Difference and sameness.

Recognition of Christ's unique service to each ethnicity is spelled out in the two sections of the text, Christ's service to the circumcised (15:8) and Christ's service to the Gentile. Paul said that Christ became the servant to the circumcised—on behalf of "the truth of God in order that he might confirm the promises given to the patriarchs."

Notice the specificity of the service Christ rendered to the Jew. The service vindicated the truth of God by confirming the promises given to the patriarchs. The patriarchs are Abraham, Isaac, and Jacob. To them, God promised a great name, a multitude of descendants, and a land (Gen 12, 15, 17). Paul believed that these remained valid for Messianic Jews. As he said earlier, "for the gifts and the calling of God are irrevocable" (11:29).

You could sum up the Old Testament by describing it as the story of Israel's failure to realize God's promises because of unbelief. As Israel's Messiah, Jesus served the Jews by confirming God's truth and loyalty to his covenant he made with Israel. This is a unique service Jesus rendered because it was a unique covenant people.

What does he say of the Gentiles? How did Christ serve them? There's an important observation to make that isn't so clear. In verse 8, Paul states, "For I tell you that Christ has become a servant" and afterward launches into how Christ served the Jew. Now in verse 9 he assumes it when beginning his discussion of the Gentile. He expects his readers to remember what he said previously. He stated the line once but uses it twice both for the Jew and for the Gentile. So, at the beginning of verse 9, you need to hear, "Christ has become a servant" before the words "in order that the Gentiles might glorify God for his mercy."

This is crucial to understand. Unlike the service rendered to the Jew, Christ served the Gentile *so they may become worshippers of the one true God* on account of his mercy. While the Jew is not excluded from mercy that is implied in the promises to the patriarchs, here there was no mention of the mercy of God. In this context, God's mercy was not relevant, so it was not important to state. The Gentiles on the other hand became worshippers of God because of Christ's work. Christ's service was to make Gentiles God-worshippers by means of his mercy. Before the coming of Christ the Gentile did not worship the God of Israel. What did Paul mean by his statement?

The Gentile in both Old Testament and New Testament times worshipped other gods. From an Israelite and Jewish perspective, all Gentiles were idolators. To be a Gentile was to worship idols. They always had and they always will. Because of this idolatry Gentiles, on the whole, in both canons, were forbidden to participate in the worship of God; and were shunned.

Idolatry was so prevalent in the ancient world that the Mosaic law legislated a stiff separation from the non-Israelite. Christ's service for the Gentile, then, was to put God in a position to show them mercy. By doing so, he created among the Gentiles a group of God-fearers to glorify God for his mercy for his inclusion of them in salvation.

Paul weaved several Old Testament passages to show that his is not new news. The passages include 2 Samuel 22:50; Psalm 18:49; Deuteronomy 32:43; Psalm 117:1; and Isaiah 11:10. This was what God had always planned to do. The central focus of these quotations is the Davidic Messiah and his role in bringing salvation to Gentiles along with Israel.

So, let's summarize. Romans 15:8–12 described Christ's servant-hood differentiated by ethnicity. Christ's service to the Jew is different than the service to the Gentile. For the former, Christ's service vindicated God's truthfulness and confirmed God's promises made to the patriarchs. The unstated implication was that the Jew continued to live as a Jew. The promises to Abraham, Isaac, and Jacob continued to be their possession and remained secure.

The Jew and the Gentile were different ethnically and that has implications for Christ's work. On the other hand, for the Gentile, God created from them a worshipping people who he had always intended to create and to save. This is not new news; it's old news. Christ served the Gentile by making it possible to be free from idolatry and worship the one true God.

Paul intended Christ-believers to embrace each other across ethnic lines. He was bold to demand the embrace because a recognition of Christ's unique service for the other race moves one's own ethnic story, whether good or ill, from the center, opening up space for healing curiosity around the other's story of how Christ served them. "Tell me how Christ has served your race."

However, we should hold no expectation of embrace where it addresses those whose race has been warred against, of ethnicities that have suffered terribly. In these cases, all that can be done is to invite embrace and wait to be embraced.

III. The God of Gentile Hope (15:13)

Romans 15:13 is a conclusion. It's clear. But a conclusion to what?

> May the God of hope fill you with all joy and peace in believing,
> so that you may abound in hope by the power of the Holy Spirit.

An obvious answer is that it is the conclusion to the present passage. Perhaps less obvious, but yet a quite strong, suggestion is that it is a unit of thought that Paul has developed since the beginning of chapter 14. I have thought that it was most likely a combination of the two. But another option occurred to me. I find it convincing, and I wonder what it might add to the idea that we are to embrace one another across ethnic lines.

I think Romans 15:13 concludes Paul's discussion of the Gentile that he began in 15:9. The section dedicated to the Gentile is more than that of the Jew; one verse to five verses. Paul says more of the Gentile than the Jew. Christ served the Gentiles by making it possible for them to glorify God for his mercy. Paul wished that his Gentile Christ-believers would be filled with joy and peace *in believing*. It is the Gentile who had no hope; it was the Gentile who did not believe. With Christ the Gentiles now abound in hope because the God of hope in his mercy has freed them to worship the one true God and not idols. The Gentile's identity is secured by the Christ's service.

There is always a power dynamic at work in relationships across ethnic lines. Someone is the more privileged, while another less so. You see this at work in this passage as well. The Jew is in a position of power based on their ancient relationship to God. The Gentile is in a much more vulnerable state because of their exclusion. To combat this tendency, Paul establishes the Gentile's position, putting it on the same level. He deconstructs the power dynamic. The Jew and the Gentile can embrace one another because they address each other as equals.

God wishes Jewish and Gentile Christ-believers to embrace each other across ethnic lines. Paul exhorted the Christ-believers in Rome to do so. His exhortation was rooted in Christ's example and in his perspective on the way Christ served each group. The recognition of that service provides a bridge, which can allow embrace to happen. It is Christ's distinct service, but nevertheless Christ's service. Two different acts of service, one servant.

Romans and the Far East

Te-Li Lau

THE FAR EAST IS a vast geographical region that includes East and Southeast Asia, comprising countries such as China, Korea, Japan, Vietnam, Singapore, and Indonesia. One of the more prominent religions or philosophies that underpins the political, religious, and cultural landscape of this region is Confucianism. Confucianism originated in China with Confucius (ca. 551–479 BCE), but eventually "spread throughout the East Asian world of Korea, Japan, and Vietnam to become a pan-Asian phenomenon that over the centuries has shaped and been shaped by this family of distinctive and yet inter-related cultures."[1]

Within Confucian thought, *xiao* (孝, translated as "filial piety" or "filiality") is the foundational element in the quest to become fully human. This is borne out in several early Confucian texts, such as the *Analects* (*Lunyu* 论语), the *Mencius* (*Mengzi* 孟子), and the *Classic of Filial Piety* (*Xiaojing* 孝经).[2] For example, Confucius remarks that "filial piety and respect for elders constitute the root of Goodness" (*Lunyu* 1.2). Similarly, Mencius (ca. 372–289 BCE), the second most important sage after Confucius, remarks, "If everyone would treat their parents as parents and their elders as elders, the world would be at peace" (*Mengzi* 4A11.1). *Xiao* is such a fundamental stratum that Qingping Liu considers

---

1. Ames and Hershock, eds., *Confucianisms for a Changing World Cultural Order*, 5.

2. Unless otherwise stated, English translations (ET) and numbering of these texts come from Slingerland, trans., *Confucius Analects*; Van Norden, trans., *Mengzi*; Rosemont and Ames, trans., *Chinese Classic of Family Reverence*.

it "the supreme principle" and "the ultimate value of human existence within the framework of Confucius' philosophy."[3] *Xiao* is also prevalent in Buddhism, Daoism, and Chinese thought, such that "one cannot understand traditional Chinese culture without understanding the role of filial morality."[4] Indeed, a well-known Chinese proverb declares that "*xiao* is most important virtue" (百善孝为先 *baishan xiao weixian*).

The importance of *xiao* in the Far East Sinosphere suggests that a reading of Romans from the Far East must interact with this thought. This essay thus reads Romans through the lens of *xiao*, while also suggesting how Romans might challenge the Confucian understanding of *xiao*. At the outset, it should be said that such a process is not fanciful, for there are similarities between the Confucian concept of *xiao* and the understanding of *pietas* in ancient Rome, the city to which Paul's letter to the Romans was addressed.[5] Moreover, although both *xiao* and *pietas* has its roots in the family, they eventually also came to function as a political tool.

I proceed in three moves. First, I present an overview of the Confucian understanding of *xiao*. Second, I interrogate Romans using several key elements that are drawn from this overview. Third, I draw out the implications of the previous two sections, suggesting how this exercise may mutually inform our reading of Romans and Confucian *xiao*.

I. A Brief Survey of Confucian Filial Thought

The concept of *xiao* precedes Confucius. In sources from the Western Zhou period (1100?–771 BCE), it was connected to ancestor worship: offering food sacrifices to dead ancestors, preserving their memory, and pursuing their goals. With the subsequent development of Confucian thought in the Spring and Autumn (770–476 BCE) and Warring States period (475–221 BCE), the concept was transformed and reinterpreted. Confucians "de-emphasized one of *xiao*'s early meanings, feeding one's elders, and instead accentuated a derivative meaning of obeying one's parents, and by further extension, obeying one's lord."[6] In this section, I

---

3. Liu, "On Confucius' Principle of Consanguineous Affection."

4. Li, "Shifting Perspectives." Problems with some accounts of filial morality that have been put forth in recent years in the West are examined (Jane English, Jeffrey Blustein, and others).

5. See Kim, "*Pietas* in *pro Sexto Roscio* of Cicero and Confucian 孝 (*Xiao*)."

6. Knapp, "*Ru* Reinterpretation of *Xiao*," 197.

broadly examine the Confucian understanding of *xiao* in five strands: its content, its dispositional component, its focus on ancestor worship, its rationale, and its sociopolitical importance.

1. What is xiao?

The Chinese character *xiao* (孝) pictures an old person 老 (*lao*) support-ed by a young child 子 (*zi*). This etymology gives rise to understanding *xiao* as a cultivated disposition that attends to the welfare and desires of one's parents. The concrete expression of this selfless devotion includes a constellation of ideas, but two are primary.

1. Care

To be filial is to provide for the physical and spiritual needs of one's par-ents. Of the five unfilial traits that Mencius mentions in *Mengzi* 4B30.2, three of them center on the failure to care for one's parents. Confucius also remarks that one should not travel far from home so as to be able to give a ready hand to help one's parents. Moreover, one should not stray from a fixed itinerary as this would cause unnecessary worry for parents (*Lunyu* 4.19).

2. Obedience and Loyalty

Obedience and loyalty to one's parents, especially the father, are central to filial piety.[7] One must follow the ways of one's father. Even after the father has died, one must not make any changes to those ways for at least three years (*Lunyu* 1.11; 4.20; 19.18). The obedience and loyalty that Confu-cianism calls for must be held in tension with the need for moral vigi-lance. The focus of one's obedience is not so much to one's parents as it is to the rites (*Lunyu* 2.5)—the set of religious practices, norms, and social practices that were designed to promote communal bonds not only with others, but also with spiritual beings. Thus, when parents commit mor-ally egregious acts, Confucius allows the upright child to remonstrate

---

7. Despite the importance of obedience, Tu, "Probing the 'Three Bonds' and 'Five Relationships' in Confucian Humanism," 125, cautions that "the proper relationship between [father and son] is mutual affection rather than one-way obedience."

gently with them (*Lunyu* 4.18).[8] Xunzi (ca. 313–238 BCE), the third most important sage, also remarks that the son cannot blindly obey his father. Rather, he should follow the Way (*dao* 道) and act righteously (*yi* 义), obeying the father only when it is appropriate and morally obligatory. He writes, "To be careful about the case in which one obeys another—this is called filial piety" (*Xunzi* 29.55).[9]

2. Dispositional Component

Xiao does not just consist of *what* ones does in caring for and obeying one's parents; it also necessitates the *how*. Confucius says, "Nowadays 'filial' means simply being able to provide one's parents with nourishment. But even dogs and horses are provided with nourishment. If you are not respectful (*jing* 敬), wherein lies the difference?" (*Lunyu* 2.7). Zengzi, a disciple of Confucius, echoes his teacher's sentiment. He notes that honoring one's parents is the highest degree of filial piety, but supporting them is only the lowest (*Jiyi* 2.9).[10] This does not mean that honoring one's parents is diametrically opposed to supporting them. Rather, the obedience and service that we render to our parents must be matched with the appropriate demeanor (*se* 色) that is reflective of one's attitudinal posture and disposition (*Lunyu* 2.8).

True *xiao* cannot be reduced to perfunctory or formal obedience. It flows from a sincere disposition to love and honor one's parents, and it must be accompanied by a reverential attitude and a willing heart. Thus, "a true action of filial piety . . . is not merely a physical behavior of supporting one's parents because actions, if they are not fully supported by the right kind of emotion, attitude, and commitment, cannot be regarded as truly respectable and virtuous."[11]

3. Ancestor Worship

I noted earlier that *xiao* was intimately related to ancestor worship in the Western Zhou period. Although the development of Confucian thought

---

8. See also *Xiaojing* 15: "If confronted by reprehensible behavior on his father's part, a son has no choice but to remonstrate with his father."

9. ET and numbering follow Hutton, trans., *Xunzi*.

10. ET is in James Legge, trans., *Li Ki*, vols. 27–28 of *Chinese Classics*, 28:226.

11. Seok, *Embodied Moral Psychology and Confucian Philosophy*, 101.

shifted the emphasis towards living parents, texts that mention the necessity of worship or veneration towards one's ancestors or dead parents still abound. For example, Confucius advises children to "bury [their dead parents] in accordance with the rites and sacrifice to them in accordance with the rites" (*Lunyu* 2.5). Making sacrifices to one's parents cannot be done cavalierly. Rather, they are to be conducted with reverential awe, "as if the spirits [of the deceased parents] were present" (*Lunyu* 3.12).[12]

The motive of ancestor worship is twofold.[13] First, sacrifices to the dead provide food and other materials that are necessary for the departed ancestors to live in a manner that they were accustomed to while alive. Second, these filial sacrifices secure benefits for the living. The *Odes* (*Shijing* 诗经) affirms that ancestors will confer blessings on their descendants for their unceasing acts of *xiao*.[14]

Ancestor worship binds one generation to one another, allowing future generations to connect with those that have gone before. Through the performance of filial duties, each generation becomes a critical link in a familial chain that began in the past and continues down to the present. Each generation does not exist as an isolated unit, but stands within the stream of familial history. Their actions impact the status of their clan, and they in turn are impacted by whatever honor and shame is attached to the clan. Through the interconnected relationships formed by this familial chain, "Confucians believe that a sense of eternity can be obtained."[15]

4. Rationale for Xiao

What is the rationale for *xiao*? Some texts suggest that it is because children owe their very existence to their parents. For example, the opening chapter of the *Classic of Filial Piety* remarks, "Your physical person with its hair and skin are received from your parents" (*Xiaojing* 1). Philip Ivanhoe however argues that mere gratitude for one's existence is a weak reason for *xiao*, since children never did ask to be born. A more powerful reason is the care and concern that parents bestow towards their

---

12. Although Confucius acknowledged the presence of spirits, the focus of his teaching was not on the afterlife but on self-cultivation and ethical living in the present world. See *Lunyu* 7.21; 11.12

13. Yao, *Introduction to Confucianism*, 200.

14. ET is in James Legge, trans., *Chinese Classics*, 4:477.

15. Yao, *Introduction to Confucianism*, 204.

children. He says, "The true basis for filial piety is the sense of gratitude, reverence, and love that children naturally feel when they are nurtured, supported, and cared for by people who do so out of loving concern for the child's well-being."[16]

P. J. Ivanhoe finds support for his view in the following poem from the *Odes*.

> O my father, who begat me!
> O my mother, who nourished me!
> Ye indulged me, ye fed me,
> Ye held me up, ye supported me,
> Ye looked after me, ye never left me,
> Out and in ye bore me in your arms.
> If I would return your kindness,
> It is like great Heaven, illimitable.[17]

Although the first line recognizes that parents do beget their children, the rest of the poem affirms the love that parents give to their children. They feed, nourish, and support them. More importantly, they guide and instruct their children in the path of moral cultivation.[18] Gratitude for such care and support then becomes the basis for *xiao*.

5. Xiao and Political Loyalty

Confucian texts stress the political importance of *xiao*, noting that loyalty to one's political ruler is the natural extension of filial obedience to one's parents. Confucius states, "A young person who is filial and respectful of his elders rarely becomes the kind of person who is inclined to defy his superiors" (*Lunyu* 1.2). The opening chapter of the *Classic of Filial Piety* similarly affirms that *xiao* "begins in service to your parents [and] continues in service to your lord" (*Xiaojing* 1).[19] These texts suggest that "*xiao* is the entrance door to *zhong*, loyalty to the ruler."[20]

---

16. Ivanhoe, "Filial Piety as a Virtue," 299.

17. ET is from Legge, trans., *Chinese Classics*, 4:352.

18. See Cline, *Families of Virtue*, 40–91.

19. See also *Xiaojing* 14: "The Master said, 'It is only because exemplary persons (*junzi*) serve their parents with [filial piety] that this same feeling can be extended to their lord as loyalty (*zhong*).'"

20. Roetz, *Confucian Ethics of the Axial Age*, 54–55.

The move from *xiao* to political loyalty is not surprising, for the state is commonly portrayed as a family and the emperor as a father to the state. Filiality towards our own parents thus prepares us to be devoted to the father-like figure of the emperor. At the same time, Mencius cautions that the ruler must discharge his parental responsibility and not overburden the people. A wicked ruler who exacts too much tax from the people fails to be a "father and mother of the people" (*Mengzi* 3A3.7).

If filiality towards one's parents leads to loyalty towards one's ruler, which pole has priority if there should be a conflict between these two? Pre-Qin Confucian thought gave *xiao* priority over loyalty. Subsequent thinkers, from the Han to the Ming dynasty, however, reversed the priority such that loyalty to the ruler and the state is the intended goal of filiality. Thus, although *xiao* and loyalty are two virtues, *xiao* serves only as a bridge to loyalty. The reverse is never affirmed.[21]

II. Reading Romans through the Lens of *Xiao*

The traditional frame of Confucian *xiao* does not translate directly to Romans. Apart from the vice list which indicts humanity for failing to obey their parents (Rom 1:30), not much is said about filial relationships between children and their human parents. If we however adjust the frame so that it focuses on the family that God seeks to establish in this world, our investigation will be fruitful. To this end, I examine the fatherhood of God, the necessity of obedience to God the Father, and the relationship between politics and filial obedience.

1. The Fatherhood of God in Romans

The fatherhood of God is a fundamental assumption in Pauline thought, for Paul describes God as Father in the opening salutation of all letters that bear his name. This concept is unpacked in four relationships in Romans.

1. God Is the Father of All Creation

Romans does not explicitly tie God's fatherhood to his creational role. Nonetheless, Romans 11:36 ("For *from* him . . . and *for* him are *all things*")

---

21. See Yin, "Emperor Chengzu and Imperial Filial Piety," 141–53.

echoes 1 Corinthians 8:6, a passage which explicitly affirms that God is the Father *from* whom *all things* come about and *for* whom we exist.[22] Second Temple Jewish literature also affirms that God is the Father and creator of all.[23]

2. *God Is the Father of Israel*

In Romans 9:4, Paul remarks that one of the privileges that Israel enjoys is the "adoption to sonship." Although this phrase is hardly used in the OT and Jewish literature, it effectively summarizes the OT teaching that God is the Father to Israel in a way that he is not to the surrounding nations. God is the Father of Israel not only because he created them (Deut 32:6; Isa 64:8; Mal 2:10), but also because he elected and redeemed them to be his firstborn son (Exod 4:22; Deut 14:1–2; Isa 63:16; Jer 31:9; Hos 11:1; Isa 63:15–16). Thus, although all humanity are children of God because they are created in God's image, Israel's sonship is different, for it is based on God's redemptive work within the framework of the old covenant.

3. *God Is the Father of All Believers*

God is "our Father" (Rom 1:7), the one who elects and redeems those who were once not his people so that they might attain adoption (8:15, 23) and become his children (9:26). The sonship that believers have is similar to that given to Israel; both are based on God's election and redemption. It is however different in that it is bestowed within the framework of the new covenant. One necessary entailment of this sonship is the gift of the Holy Spirit, a gift that allows believers to approach God intimately and address him as "Abba" (8:15).

4. *God Is the Father of Jesus*

The salutation in Romans notes that the gospel of God concerns Jesus, "his Son" (1:3). This preexistent Son became a descendant of David and was appointed the "powerful Son of God" on the basis of his resurrection (1:4). Jesus's sonship is unique from that of all humanity. As

---

22. See also Ephesians 3:14–15; 4:6.

23. Josephus, *Ant.* 1.20, 230; 2.152; Philo, *Decal.* 51, 105; *Legat.* 115, 293; *Mos.* 1.158; 2.48, 238, 256.

the preexistent Son, he has always been Son of God and need not be adopted as Son.

In Jewish literature, the legitimacy of God as Father is based on his creative and redemptive role. In Romans, Paul clearly understands God as the creator (1:18–25). Moreover, his reference to the potter-clay imagery (9:20–21) may link God's creative role to his fatherhood, just as Isaiah 64:8 explicitly does. Paul, however, emphasizes God's love and redemptive work as the basis for his fatherhood. God is the Father who demonstrates his deep love for humanity by redeeming them while they were still sinners (5:8; cf. 5:5; 8:39). He is the Father "who did not spare his own Son, but gave him up for all" (8:32). He sent his Son in the likeness of sinful flesh (8:3), so that through faith Jews and Gentiles might receive the adoption to sonship. In essence, God is the Father who acts through his Son so that he might call Jews and Gentiles into the obedience of faith that is distinctive of his children. He is the one who is creating a new family—a family in which kinship is no longer determined by one's blood but by one's obedience to and faith in God the Father.

2. Filial Obedience

The motif of obedience is important in Romans, for half of the Pauline occurrences of obedience (ὑπακούω and ὑπακοή) are found in this letter. Paul begins his letter with the reminder that his apostleship is to bring about the "obedience of faith" (ὑπακοὴν πίστεως, 1:5). This phrase occurs again in 16:19, thus functioning as bookends for the entire letter. The meaning of the phrase is strongly debated, but Douglas Moo is right in claiming that *obedience* and *faith* mutually interpret one another. Faith and obedience are distinct concepts; nonetheless, "obedience always involves faith, and faith always involves obedience."[24] Paul's apostleship is to call all humanity to obey the gospel and the God of that gospel (15:18). Their obedience does not occur in a vacuum. Rather, their obedience is the necessary response to "God's incongruous gift."[25] It is the filial response to the good news of what God has done in Christ, the good news that God the Father has acted in his Son to bring all humanity back into the family of the one true God.

---

24. Moo, *Letter to the Romans*, 50–51.

25. Barclay, *Paul and the Gift*, 492.

The fatherhood of God demands obedience, respect, and loyalty from those who are his children. This is not surprising since both the ancient Jewish and Greco-Roman worlds required children to honor and obey their parents. The pre-Socratic Greek poet Cleobulus succinctly states: "Revere your father."[26] The Roman virtue of *pietas* demands dutiful reverence towards one's father and kin. Jewish literature is also replete with similar injunctions.[27] If reverence and obedience towards one's human father is necessary, how much more towards the divine Father. Thus, God rebukes Israel when they fail to discharge their filial obligations. He says, "A son honors his father. . . . If I am a father, where is the honor due me?" (Mal 1:6).

Humanity sins and blasphemes God when they fail to obey and revere him. In Romans 1–3, Paul relates the sin of all humanity to this fundamental distortion. Gentiles and Jews stand guilty before God because they do not give him the honor that is due to him; both are unfilial children who do not honor and obey their creator (and by implication, their divine Father). Humanity's failure to honor and obey God follows the pattern of their progenitor—Adam.

Paul presents Adam as the archetype of filial disobedience. He assumes that his readers are familiar with the story of Genesis 1–3. God created Adam in his image, effectively becoming his father.[28] As son, Adam should have heeded the voice of his father. Nevertheless, he disobeyed and sinned. In so doing, Adam became the unfilial son *par excellence*. His singular act of transgression resulted in the condemnation of all people (5:18). His filial disobedience condemned all people to be sinners with the result that they are rebellious, disobedient, and unfilial. In their disobedience, Gentiles engage in idolatry and reject God as their father and creator (1:21, 25). Israel is no different, for they cause God's name to be blasphemed (2:24) as they refuse to behave as filial children (Deut 32:5–6; Isa 1:2–3; Jer 3:4–5). Instead of honoring God as their father, they say to created objects made of stone and wood, "You are my father . . . You gave me birth" (Jer 2:27–29; cf. Hos 11:1–4). They repudiate God as their father and fail to carry out their duty as sons who live in filial obedience to God.

In contrast to the disobedience of Adam, Paul presents Jesus as the filial son *par excellence* who honors his father by obeying him until death

---

26. Stobaeus, *Anthologium* 3.1.172. See also Epictetus 2.10.7.

27. See Deuteronomy 5:16; Exodus 21:17; Leviticus 19:3; Sirarch 3:1–16.

28. For Adam as the son of God, see Luke 3:38; Philo, *Virtues*, 204–5.

on the cross (Rom 5:19; Phil 2:8). The results of each individual's action are also stark. Adam's disobedience resulted in the condemnation and death of all people; Jesus's obedience resulted in justification and life (5:18).[29] Through Adam's disobedience, many were made sinners and slaves to sin; through Christ's obedience, many will be made righteous and sons of God (5:19; 8:14). Christ's obedience therefore reverses the effects of Adam's disobedience. He makes it possible for humanity to share in his sonship by participating in the "obedience of faith" (1:5) and by being adopted as sons of God (8:14). In so doing, Christ fulfills God's desire to restore his people and, by extension, all humanity back to an intimate father-son relationship that is marked by filial obedience (Jer 3:19; Jub 1:24–25).

3. Politics and Filial Obedience

The political structure of ancient Rome shares similarities with Confucian China in that it is colored with the father image. First, political figures in Rome were often given the title of "Father" (*pater*). Sallust notes that Roman senators "were called Fathers (*pater*), either as a result of their age or the similarity of their responsibility."[30] Moreover, the senate conferred the title *pater patriae* "Father of the Fatherland" on Julius and Augustus Caesar. Dio Cassius writes that "the term 'Father' perhaps gives them a certain authority over us all—the authority which fathers once had over their children."[31] Second, political authority is modeled on paternal authority. For example, the relationship between a proconsul and his quaestor is described as a father-son relationship.[32] The proconsul should show the same concern for the quaestor as a father would for his son, and the quaestor should demonstrate a son's *pietas* to his proconsul. Third, the power of the Emperor as *pater patriae* supersedes and overrides that of the *pater familias*. This was seen in the implementation of the *Lex Julia de Maritandis Ordinibus,* which mandated marriage and remarriage

---

29. Although not my preferred reading, understanding πίστις Χριστοῦ (3:22, 26) as a subjective genitive further demonstrates that Christ's faithful obedience secures the possibility of righteousness for believers. See Wright, "Letter to the Romans," 10:470.

30. Sallust, *Bell. Cat.* 6.6.

31. Dio Cassius, 53.18.3.

32. See Cicero, *Div. Caec.* 61; *Red. sen.* 35.

for men and women of a certain age, thereby limiting the power of the *pater familias* to obstruct their children's marriage.

In Romans 13:1, Paul exhorts his readers to submit (ὑποτάσσω) to the governing authorities. Paul does not call his readers to obey, but to submit. In so doing, Paul relativizes and subverts the power of the governing authorities. Roman Emperors may style themselves *divi filius* ("divine son"), but the true and powerful Son of God is King Jesus (1:4). Moreover, Paul reminds his readers that the power possessed by governing authorities is not absolute but derivative, for existing authorities are established and instituted by God. Furthermore, submission recognizes one's subordinate position within a divinely ordered set of relationships or hierarchy. Since God stands at the apex of any hierarchy, submission to any human person or governing authority is conditioned on the submission that one ultimately owes to God. The emperor may be the father of the country, but God is the Father of the cosmos. If the authority of the *pater patriae* supersedes that of the *pater familias* by virtue of the fact that the domain of the country is larger than that of the household, the authority of God likewise supersedes that of the emperor by virtue of the fact that God's domain exceeds the emperor's. Thus, the call for believers to recognize the authority of the father of the country is relativized and conditioned on the prior necessity to honor and obey God. The fatherhood of God confronts and subverts the fatherhood of Caesar.

III. Implications

In this section, I briefly suggest how reading Confucius and Paul together might mutually inform each other. Specifically, I suggest how Confucian *xiao* might present a reading of Romans that accentuates certain aspects that may have been underappreciated; and I also note how Romans might challenge the Confucian understanding of *xiao* that is prevalent in the Far East.

1. Reading Romans from the Far East

Confucian *xiao* sensitizes us to the importance of family, honor, and obedience in Romans. If God is the creator of all things, then humanity needs to honor and obey him. Paul, however, contends that humanity refuses to do so. Although they know God to be the Father that created them, they disobey, dishonor, and refuse to show gratitude to him. As obstinate and rebellious children, they exemplify the nature of sin—the repudiation of God as their father. As judgment for their sin, God shames them such that they "fall short of the glory of God" (3:23). They do not measure up to the glorious image of God for which they were created. On the contrary, they share in the shame and disobedience of Adam, the unfilial son.

Despite humanity's sin and disobedience, God demonstrates his love in sending his filial son to be an atoning sacrifice. Christ's obedience unto the cross reverses Adam's disobedience. He provides a way for humanity to share in his sonship through faith—a posture that is diametrically opposite to sin (14:23). For if the nature of sin is to disobey and dishonor the Father, the nature of faith, as demonstrated by Abraham, is to trust and honor him (4:20). God's gracious gift of his Son obligates humanity to respond appropriately, for it is disgraceful not to acknowledge a gift or show gratitude for benefits received. The proper response that God demands is the "obedience of faith." Through this response and posture, believers are reconciled to God as they call him "Abba, Father" (8:15).

Not only does Jesus make humanity's adoption to sonship possible, he is also the definition of all that sonship entails. Christ is the filial son *par excellence*; he models what all children in God's family are to be. Paul therefore exhorts believers to put on Christ such that his character, not least his obedience to the Father, is manifest in their life (13:14). Our imitation of Christ begins in this age, but it will be consummated when we are conformed to the image of God's filial Son (8:29) and attain the eschatological "glory of the children of God" (8:21).

The above reading helps us to contextualize the gospel for the Far East. It presents the gospel as the good news that God the Father acts in his obedient Son Jesus Christ to bring all people back into a right relationship with him as his adopted children. Even though all people were once mired in shame because they were unfilial, they now have hope of sharing in the honor of the "powerful Son of God" through the "obedience of faith" (1:4–5).

2. Preaching to the Far East from Romans

Romans reminds believers in the Far East that God is the ultimate Father that deserves true honor and obedience. Obedience and reverence to divinely established authority within the family and the state is part of the believer's obedience to God. Consequently, such obedience must be subordinated to the allegiance believers owe to their divine father. This confronts believers in the Far East, who may be influenced by Confucian *xiao*, in two ways:

1. Romans Challenges the Practice of Ancestor Worship

A perennial problem that believers in the Far East face is the practice of ancestor worship. *Xiao* demands that children not only revere, but also perform rituals and offer sacrifices to their dead ancestors. Romans, however, unequivocally argues that humanity cannot worship creatures or created things. Rather, they must worship God alone (1:25). Believers in such situations need wisdom to distinguish between ancestor worship and ancestor respect. Cultural elements that are not deemed idolatrous can be maintained. On the other hand, cultural expressions of ancestor worship that are idolatrous in nature should be abandoned.[33]

2. Romans Challenges Uncritical Loyalty to Political Leaders

The tension between *xiao* and political loyalty in Confucian thought has been exploited by autocratic and imperialistic regimes throughout history in East Asia. The Japanese government in the 1930s used earlier Confucian slogans, such as the "unity of *xiao* and loyalty" (忠孝一本), to legitimize the ruler-subject relation in support of a nationalistic and militaristic agenda.[34] In other countries, personality cults portray the supreme leader as a benevolent father in order to evoke the Confucian mechanism of obedience and loyalty.[35]

Romans reminds believers in the Far East that they cannot give uncritical loyalty or obedience to their political leaders. The ultimate authority of God requires believers to assess the policies and demands of their governments against the word of God. Indeed, they can be said to submit to the government even as they, because of their higher allegiance to God, actively disobey and resist what the government demands.

---

33. For a helpful analysis of this issue, see Ferris, "Examination of Some Themes in the Confucian Classics."

34. See O'Dwyer, *Confucianism's Prospects*, 131–62.

35. For example, see Steinmüller, "'Father Mao' and the Country-Family."

Effective ministers of God's word need to be competent exegetes not only of the biblical text, but also of the culture in which they are ministering. By sensitively bringing Paul into conversation with Confucian thought, we allow him to continue to bring the message of Romans beyond Spain (15:28) to the Far East.

Sermon

Reaching the Hope through Suffering

JINWOOK OH

THE SPREAD OF CHRISTIANITY in East Asian countries with varying degrees of success has always been a topic of research for many theologians and missionaries. The fact that Christianity was able to gain a foothold in East Asia is remarkable in its own way, as Christian doctrines rather seem incompatible with traditional East Asian philosophies. The concepts of faith, sin, salvation, and grace found in the book of Romans and Christianity, in general, are quite alien to East Asian cultures. Given the vast differences of worldview and approach to human life, how do the themes of Romans apply to East Asia?

Before diving into the question, it is important to briefly go over the central tenets of the East Asian philosophies. In a nutshell, East Asian philosophies, most notably represented by Confucianism, Daoism, and Buddhism, largely overlap with naturalism, which asserts that the universe operates solely by natural laws and forces. Unlike Christianity, in which the faith in the divine Creator is a prerequisite for salvation, Eastern philosophies largely reject both transcendental figures and reliance on them. Rather, the universe itself is self-reliant, productive, and creative; every element within it is interconnected and transforming, creating causal relationships amongst themselves. Mankind's significance is considerably reduced, and its death is treated as a mere transitional phase towards another form of existence in the grand scheme of the universe. Because

death is another stage of metamorphosis, people who have delved deeply
into Eastern philosophies often do not fear death. Therefore, there is no
need for salvation nor interference from the divine, as one's action in this
life solely determines the results.

In Eastern philosophies, especially in Confucianism and Buddhism,
one can affect and create his or her afterlife through good deeds and self-
discipline. This causal relation becomes the foundation of the Eastern
belief system and has resulted in discipline-based moral codes. However,
we Christians believe and confess that we, all humans, are in slavery to
sin, death, and evil, and are in desperate need of divine grace for salvation and a restoring relationship with God. The love of God the Father
was most clearly revealed in the self-giving love of Jesus Christ the Son
and continues to permeate the lives of believers through the Holy Spirit.
Therefore, in Romans, the apostle Paul defines Christians as "those justified by faith" (Rom 5:1).

Now, back to our initial question of the themes of Romans from an
East Asian perspective. Were the definitions of faith, sin, salvation, and
grace somehow compromised or changed? The answer is no. How? In
Eastern belief, there is no loving Creator or God who has given his only
Son to die on the cross for the vulnerability and brokenness of humanity.
We believe that the God of love, who has always existed, continuously
expresses his sincere interest in mankind's lives and souls, and actively
interferes in history. God has shown himself through his creation regardless of our acknowledgment. The Hebrew word for the "world" and time-
space continuum is "Olam—עוֹלָם." It shares the same root word with the
Hebrew word "Nelm—נֶעְלָם," which means hidden or mysterious, possibly suggesting that God has allowed us to find the trace of divine power
and work in this world. Paul states this clearly in Romans 1:19–20: "For
what can be known about God is plain to them, because God has shown
it to them. Ever since the creation of the world his eternal power and
divine nature, invisible though they are, have been understood and seen
through the things he has made. So they are without excuse."

Then, what is the ultimate purpose of life for us Christians? It is to
live a life that is "sharing the glory of God." Such life is what Paul describes
in 1 Corinthians 10:24: "do not seek your own advantage, but the other's."
Paul says that we can see whether or not a person is living for the glory
of God through one's pursuit of the other's good. After meeting Jesus on
the road to Damascus, Paul traveled around the Mediterranean sharing
the gospel. He was persecuted heavily everywhere he went: in Damascus

and Jerusalem, he was met with suspicion from Christians. In Antioch and Iconium, he was almost stoned to death. In Philippi, he was jailed. Despite all the hardships he faced, he proudly remarks, "we also boast in our sufferings" (Rom 5:3). In Romans 8:17, the apostle Paul argues that the ultimate goal of Christians is to "suffer with God so that we may also be glorified with God." Therefore, the suffering we go through with Christ is not the end itself but part of a larger story that ends with hope.

In any culture or society, suffering has often been understood as a sign of a god's displeasure with mankind. However, Paul emphasizes that we Christians can rejoice in sufferings we face for following Christ as Jesus himself has become a testament to God's glory by carrying and dying for our sins on the cross. Paul goes even further by boasting of his suffering because he understands that suffering is the passageway to endurance and eventually the character of Christ. Then the character of Christ opens our eyes beyond our surroundings to the hope that God provides (Rom 5:2–4).

However, Buddhism offers a very different solution to dealing with our suffering. In the famous parable of the poisoned arrow, Buddha is asked by one of his disciples about the nature of the cosmos and the meaning of life and death. Buddha replies, "Whether the world is finite or infinite, limited or unlimited, the problem of your liberation remains the same. You should rather focus on the state of your being, which is struck by the poisoned arrow called 'life' itself. Your priority should be to get out of Samsara—the endless cycle of life—and this life filled with sufferings, not bothering yourself with questions regarding things beyond your understanding."[1] Buddha's teaching directs us towards a pragmatic approach in life: to rid ourselves of metaphysical concerns and to achieve enlightenment through self-discipline. On the other hand, it urges us to accept the suffering as it is, as consequences of our previous existence with no purpose attached to it. Life, according to Buddhism, is suffering, and only by ridding ourselves of desire can we end it and reach enlightenment.

One day, I went to a beautiful Buddhist temple in Korea where one of the monks drew good luck pictures for the tourist. When the monk saw me in my wheelchair, he sighed and said, "I hope you will be free from your disabilities in your next life." It was a genuine well-wishing remark, but it also revealed the fundamental Buddhist teachings: my

---

1. http://seonbonsa.org/home/bbs/board.php?bo_table=05_1&wr_id=435.

physical disability is a consequence of my previous existence, and my good deeds in present life would grant me a more favorable outcome in the next. In the Gospel of John, however, Jesus gives us a completely different interpretation of the same phenomenon. When the disciples ask Jesus about the potential link between disabilities and sin, Jesus answers that disabilities exist so that God's works might be revealed through them (John 9:1–3). The message of hope, love, and empowerment that this verse has on people with disabilities is beyond description.

In Eastern philosophies, the sufferings in this life are our own doing and assignments to be resolved by ourselves. However, in Paul's message, sufferings are something that Christians must voluntarily go through. In this wretched, broken, and distorted world where justice and equality for the oppressed and minorities are nowhere to be found, Christians must call out the wrongs of this world and challenge the evils found around us. Hardships and pain will certainly follow, but it is the road that Christ tells us to follow. Moreover, Paul says that to bear the burden and sharing the sufferings of our neighbors who hunger and thirst for righteousness is the way to share God's glory. Therefore, the sufferings we go through for following the cross is not a result of our shameful past, as Eastern philosophies claim, but a glorious path leading us to hope.

That is our hope. We no longer worry about the judgments that others pass on us, nor are we forced to act due to external pressure. This is the true liberty of souls, which is freely given if we offer our hearts to Christ. We don't earn it or work for it as it is the gift from God, when we are attached to the true source of life who is Jesus. Paul, with regards to this wonderful mystery, remarks that it is only possible because "God's love has been poured into our hearts through the Holy Spirit that has been given to us" (Rom 5:5). Try to remember when Jesus calmed the storms by rebuking the winds and waves. The winds and waves of this world, whether they be material or spiritual, try to devour our body and spirit as a whole. They constantly remind us to live for ourselves and achieve salvation on our own. Ask for Jesus to come into your hearts and grant his character in you, for only God can calm the storm in ourselves. This is our hope, and it will never disappoint us.

When Your Suffering Becomes Ours

A Song of Arirang by St. Paul (Rom 8:22-25)

SUNG UK LIM

SEVERAL YEARS AGO, I was struck by an artwork that a Korean comfort woman painted. It depicts the fruits about to be picked by greedy, rough, and ostensibly male hands. It comes as a surprise that the fruits are engraved with the images of two young Korean girls dressed in *Hanbok*, a traditional Korean attire.

Without doubt, the comfort woman's painting signifies the heartfelt agony of nature and women, both of whom are relentlessly exposed to the exploitation of the Man in the shadow of patriarchal colonialism. Historically speaking, I would rather alert you to the devastation of both the natural environment and the Korean population, in particular, Korean young women under Japanese colonial rule.

At different but related levels, Paul in Romans 8:22 addresses the groaning of the creation, evoking the imagery of pain during labor. Worse, the combined imagery of the pain of creation, not to speak of nature, and women have conventionally been presented as pessimistic, with special reference to the book of Genesis. At first glance, Genesis 1:28 and 3:16 seems to justify the rule of the Man over nature and women.

Drawing on this imagery, Claude Lévi-Strauss, a French structural anthropologist, would go so far as to uncover binary oppositions of (hu)-man(ity) and nature, and furthermore, between men and women on the symbolic dimension. Central to this is an ideology of androcentrism, an exercise to put the male standpoint at the center. The issue at stake is that men tend to alienate themselves from the female experience.

At this point, I myself cannot help acknowledging my male perspective, which is mostly concealed but operative in intimate relationships with my wife. A decade ago, my wife, pregnant with her second child, had to make probably the most taxing decision ever as to whether or not to have a Caesarean delivery a couple of months earlier than her due date. An OB-GYN warned us of a symptom of placental infection because my wife was occasionally bleeding in late pregnancy. Afraid of pre-term birth, I initially expressed an idea of waiting for delivery until the due date. My wife agreed on my idea because the OB-GYN had already informed us that the baby had the serious problems of growth retardation in the womb. Mercifully, the baby was born healthy on the expected date of delivery. As you may probably imagine, my wife, even in these times, blames me for taking lesser care of her health condition than the baby. Looking back on that dire situation, I still feel deep remorse for my formerly androcentric stance. What a miserable husband I was, who could not afford to notice the unspeakable anxiety of his wife as a mother!

In this connection, let me introduce a Buddhist key concept of dependent arising (*pratītyasamutpāda* in Sanskrit). Dependent arising means that a *dharma*, or phenomenon, is caused by another *dharma*. This means that a phenomenon exists only due to the reality of other phenomena, like an infinite web of cause and effect. To put it simply, everything depends on everything else. Please do not forget the very fact that a life of one's own is ceaselessly connected with those of others.

The notion of dependent arising lends insight into an intrinsic aspect of suffering. The principle is crystal clear: if one suffers, the other also suffers. If men oppress women, then women will suffer. If women suffer from men's oppression, then men will suffer from women's suffering too. The same thing is true of the relationship between man and nature. If humans repress nature, then nature will suffer. If nature suffers from human oppression, then humans will suffer from nature's suffering again. Take, for example, global warming, as a boomerang effect of human destruction of nature. Dependent arising means that the suffering of one's own is mutually interdependent upon those of others.

By the same token, Paul brings to the fore the co-suffering of all beings on earth. Linguistically speaking, it is of premium importance to note that Paul in Romans 8:22 uses the Greek preposition συν, which means "together," twice in the form of composite verbs (cf. συστενάζειν; συνωδίνειν). Interestingly enough, most of the English translations, nevertheless, pass over the *togetherness* of suffering. Paul's original intent patently alludes to the shared suffering of the whole creation. A more correct rendering of Romans 8:22 in English would go as follows: "We know that the whole creation is co-groaning and co-suffering in labor pains until now." In the following verse, Romans 8:23, Paul goes even so far as to aver that human beings themselves groan (στενάζομεν) along with the creation. For Paul, we (ἡμεῖς), human beings, suffer in unison with the creation beyond the gender binary. As a matter of fact, we all, across the distinction between men, women, and nature, live through shared suffering in a web of relationships. The reason is quite simple: all the lives in the world are seamlessly interconnected with each other, influencing and being influenced by others.

From this it follows that the others' suffering affects the self in the end. Consequently, if one desires to cease to suffer, one must take more responsibility for the others' suffering. It is only when the self recognizes the others' suffering like his/her own in order that the self may break out of chains of suffering.

Unexpectedly, however, intervening in others' suffering, wittingly or unwittingly, may give rise to subsequent problems. Here is my personal story. Around the time when I had a chance to present a paper on the comfort women in an international academic meeting, a couple of my female colleagues approached me, alerting me to the hazard of men appropriating female issues such as sexual violence. For a moment, I was at a loss for words because it was not my intent at all to take over the conversation regarding these issues. Rather, the issue at hand concerns both men and women. It is not their issue alone, but our issue as well.

Let me share with you another story of mine that occurred to me much earlier than that event. When I was a private, the lowest-ranked soldier, in the Korean army, I was exposed to a type of sexual assault by a sergeant one night. Out of instinct, I resisted that sudden violence, escaping from the urgent situation. In due course, it turned out that the same sergeant had raped another soldier about a year before then. Based on this experience, I am certain that there is no exception for sexual violence, regardless of gender.

Elisabeth Schüssler Fiorenza gives fresh insight into the social structure of oppression and domination beyond the gender binary under the aegis of what she terms kyriarchy. Schüssler Fiorenza defines kyriarchy as an intersectional augmentation of patriarchy interlocking with other oppressive systems such as sexism, racism, ableism, colonialism, and the like. In the kyriarchal society, those oppressed, including both men and women, or wo/men in an abridged form, remain vulnerable to exploitation, sexual or otherwise, by those privileged. This being the case, we have good reason to say that the suffering of others can be our own in such a kyriarchal system.

Now the time has come for us to reconsider the significance of solidarity for the sake of "the redemption of our bodies" (τὴν ἀπολύτρωσιν τοῦ σώματος ἡμῶν) (Rom 8:23). Remember that redemption cannot be entirely effective unless it is a collective one. To put an end to suffering, we have no choice but to take on more responsibility for the others in a mode of mutual support.

In this vein, Paul addresses a collective redemption rather than an individual redemption, being well aware of the necessity to bond tightly with others. If it is true that we suffer together, we cannot solve suffering until we collaborate with each other.

Look around the world today. Currently, the whole world is in chaos, suffering together from the lack of justice and human dignity. Korea is struggling from the pain of division, being anxious about the probability of a nuclear war on the Korean peninsula. Hong Kong is still desperately crying for political rights and civil liberties. Even worse, innocent citizens on the street in Myanmar, also formerly known as Burma, are being killed by security forces at protests for a return to democracy. Minority groups in the United States, especially African and Asian Americans, are in deepest distress with racism, losing their precious lives daily. These examples are sufficient to state that the entire world is suffering immensely together for various reasons, hoping for a recovery of the global community supporting each other.

We can live through suffering together with a view to restoring a global community in which we have the willingness to rejoice and mourn in unity (Rom 12:15). Let me conclude my sermon with arguably the most popular Korean traditional folk song, called *Arirang*. Literarily, *Arirang* is a song of sorrow or suffering in a collective mode.

Interestingly, the song of *Arirang* has a plural version. Each region has its own version of Arirang. This means that *Arirang* is a collective song sung by so many different people based on their own life experiences. *Arirang*, song of suffering, may ring true to all the ears of all people in the world. It's because life is constantly replete with painful experiences and traumatic memories sufficient to crush our hearts. In this sense, *Arirang* must be a collective song in memory of our shared pains at the local, national, and international levels. Given a variety of pains we have in common within and across difference of cultures, we global citizens can all sing a song of *Arirang* on a global scale, being well aware that one's own suffering is narrowly or broadly interconnected with others'. Nevertheless, *Arirang* does not simply end by recalling our heart-felt pains, but rather hints at a glimmer of hope that life circumstances will be ultimately changed in positive ways. In this line of reasoning, Romans 8:22–25 would be called a Christian version of *Arirang* yet to be remembered and sung altogether with the hopes that the beloved one will come back sooner than later. Crucially, *Arirang* is a song of loss and recovery in solidarity. Once suffering is shared, its pains can be reduced at least or solved at most. It's a lesson from the power of such a collective song of Paul's *Arirang* in Romans 8:22–25.

Let us finish today's worship by singing altogether a song of *Arirang* describing a series of events such as sorrow, parting, reunion, and recovery of love:

> *Arirang, Arirang, Arariyo.*
> You are going over the hill of *Arirang*.
> My beloved one, you are leaving me behind.
> Your feet will be hurt before a long distance move.
> Just as there are many stars in the blue sky,
> there are also many dreams in our heart.
> There, over there, is the *Baekdu* Mountain,
> where, even in the middle of winter season, flowers bloom.

Bibliography

Agosto, Efrain. "Hermeneutics." In *Hispanic American Religious Cultures,* edited by Miguel A. De La Torre, 2:647–56. Santa Barbara, CA: ABC-CLIO, 2009.

———. "Islands, Borders, and Migration: Reading Paul in Light of the Crisis in Puerto Rico." In *Latinxs, the Bible, and Migration,* edited by Efraín Agosto and Jacqueline M. Hidalgo, 149–70. The Bible and Cultural Studies. Cham, Switzerland: Palgrave Macmillan, 2018.

Aldred, Catherine. "Let Me Tell You a Story: Rejuvenating Biblical Narrative through Indigenous Language Translations." *Journal of North American Institute for Indigenous Theological Studies* 9 (2011) 17–30.

Aldred, Ray. "An Indigenous Reinterpretation of Repentance." North Park Symposium on the theological interpretation of Scripture, North Park Seminary, Chicago, September 24–26, 2015.

Ames, Roger T., and Peter D. Hershock, eds. *Confucianisms for a Changing World Cultural Order.* Honolulu: University of Hawaii Press, 2018.

Aponte, Edwin David, and Miguel A. de la Torre. *Introducing Latinx Theologies.* Maryknoll, NY: Orbis, 2020.

Barclay, John M. G. *Paul and the Gift.* Grand Rapids: Eerdmans, 2015.

Barreto, Eric D. "Puerto Ricans." In *Hispanic American Religious Cultures,* edited by Miguel de la Torre, 1:469–77. Santa Barbara, CA.: ABC-CLIO, 2009.

Barth, Karl. *The Epistle to the Romans.* 6th ed. Translated by Edwyn Hoskyns. Oxford: Oxford University Press, 1968.

Bauer, Walter, Frederick W. Danker, W. F. Arndt, and F. W. Gingrich (BDAG). *A Greek-English Lexicon of the New Testament and Other Early Christian Literature.* 3rd ed. Chicago: University of Chicago Press, 2000.

Bertone, John. "The Experience of Glossolalia and the Spirit's Empathy: Romans 8:26 Revisited." *Pneuma* 25, no. 1 (March 1, 2003) 54–65.

Berwanger, Eugene H. "Negrophobia in Northern Proslavery and Antislavery Thought." *Phylon* 33, no. 3 (Fall 1972) 266–75.

Betz, Hans D. *Galatians: A Commentary on Paul's Letter to the Churches in Galatia.* Philadelphia: Fortress, 1977.

Black Elk, Joseph Epes Brown, and Michael F. Steltenkamp. *The Sacred Pipe: Black Elk's Account of the Seven Rites of the Oglala Sioux.* New York: MJF, 1996.

Blount, Brian, Cain Hope Felder, Clarice Martin, and Emerson Powery, eds. *True to Our Native Land: An African American New Testament Commentary.* Minneapolis: Fortress, 2007.

Boulter, James. "An Uncertain Future: The Outlook for Iowa Communities and Flooding as Our Climate Changes." www.iowapolicyproject.org, https://www.iowapolicyproject.org/2019docs/190905-Flood-Climate.pdf.

Bowens, Lisa M. *African American Readings of Paul: Reception, Resistance, and Transformation*. Grand Rapids: Eerdmans, 2020.

————. "Liberating Paul: African Americans' Use of Paul in Resistance and Protest." In *Practicing with Paul: Reflections on Paul and the Practices of Ministry in Honor of Susan G. Eastman*, edited by Presian Burroughs. Eugene, OR: Cascade, 2018.

Boyarin, Daniel. *A Radical Jew: Paul and the Politics of Identity*. Berkeley: University of California Press, 1994.

————. *Judaism: The Genealogy of a Modern Notion*. New Brunswick, NJ: Rutgers University Press, 2018.

Brainerd, David, Jonathan Edwards, and Philip Eugene Howard. *The Life and Diary of David Brainerd*. Chicago: Moody, 1949.

Braxton, Brad. *No Longer Slaves: Galatians and African American Experience*. Collegeville, MN: Liturgical, 2002.

Brenner, Athalya, and Carole Fontaine, eds. *A Feminist Companion to Reading the Bible: Approaches, Methods and Strategies*. Sheffield: Sheffield Academic, 1997.

Bruce, F. F. *The Epistle of Paul to the Romans: An Introduction and Commentary*. The Tyndale New Testament Commentaries. Grand Rapids: Eerdmans, 1983.

————. *The Epistle to the Galatians: A Commentary on the Greek Text*. Exeter: Paternoster, 1982.

Brueggemann, Walter. *The Land : Place as Gift, Promise, and Challenge in Biblical Faith*. Overtures to Biblical Theology. Philadelphia: Fortress, 1977.

Burke, Trevor. *Adopted into God's Family: Exploring a Pauline Metaphor*. Downers Grove, IL: InterVarsity, 2006.

Callahan, Allen Dwight. *The Talking Book: African Americans and the Bible*. New Haven: Yale University Press, 2006.

The Center for Puerto Rican Studies at Hunter College. "Puerto Ricans in the United States at 2019." https://centropr.hunter.cuny.edu/research/data-center/infographics/puerto-ricans-united-states-2019.

Chang, Robert S. "Toward an Asian American Legal Scholarship: Critical Race Theory, Post-Structuralism, and Narrative Space." *California Law Review* 81 (1993) 1241–1323.

Cicero. *Cicero*. Translated by G. L. Hendrickson et al. Loeb Classical Library. Cambridge: Harvard University Press, 1912–1972.

Cline, Erin M. *Families of Virtue: Confucian and Western Views on Childhood Development*. New York: Columbia University Press, 2015.

Coakley, Sarah. *Power and Submissions: Spirituality, Philosophy, and Gender*. Challenges in Contemporary Theology. Oxford: Wiley-Blackwell, 2002.

Cohen, Shaye J.D. "'Those Who Say They Are Jews and Are Not': How Do You Know a Jew in Antiquity When You See One?" In *The Beginning of Jewishness: Boundaries, Varieties, and Uncertainties*, 25–68. Berkeley: University of California Press, 1999.

————. *From the Maccabees to the Mishnah*. Philadelphia: Westminster, 1989.

Concannon, Cavan. *"When You Were Gentiles": Specters of Ethnicity in Roman Corinth and Paul's Corinthian Correspondence*. New Haven: Yale University Press, 2014.

Copher, Charles B. *Black Biblical Studies: An Anthology of Charles B. Copher; Biblical and Theological Issues on the Black Presence in the Bible.* Chicago: Black Light Fellowship, 1993.

Corley, Kathleen. "Women's Inheritance Rights in Antiquity and Paul's Metaphor of Adoption." In *A Feminist Companion to Paul,* edited by Amy-Jill Levine, 98–121. Cleveland: Pilgrim, 2004.

Cranfield, C. E. B. *The Epistle to the Romans, Volume 2.* Edinburgh: T & T Clark, 1979.

Daniels, David D. "Transcending the Exclusionary Ecclesial Practices of Racial Hierarchies of Authority: An Early Pentecostal Trajectory." In *Ecclesiology and Exclusion: Boundaries of Being and Belonging in Postmodern Times,* edited by Dennis Doyle, Timothy Furry, and Pascal Bazzell, 137–51. Maryknoll, NY: Orbis, 2012.

Deissmann, Gustav Adolf. *Light from the Ancient East.* Translated by L. R. Strachan. Grand Rapids: Baker, 1964.

Dio Cassius. *Roman History.* Translated by E. Cary. Loeb Classical Library. Cambridge: Harvard University Press, 1914–1927.

Dobson, J. F. *The Greek Orators.* London: Methuen and Company, 1919.

Duany, Jorge. *Puerto Rico: What Everyone Needs to Know.* New York: Oxford University Press, 2017.

Dunn, James D. G. *Romans 1–8.* Word Bible Commentary. Dallas: Word, 1988.

Ehrensperger, Kathy. "New Perspectives on Paul: New Perspectives on Romans in Feminist Theology?" In *Gender, Tradition, and Romans: Shared Ground, Uncertain Borders,* edited by Cristina Grenholm and Daniel Patte, 98–121. New York: T & T Clark, 2005.

Eisenbaum, Pamela. "Paul, Polemics, and the Problem of Essentialism." *Biblical Interpretation* 13 (2005) 224–38.

———. *Paul Was Not a Christian: The Original Message of a Misunderstood Apostle.* New York: Harper Collins, 2009.

Elaw, Zilpha. *Memoirs of the Life, Religious Experience, Ministerial Travels and Labours of Mrs. Zilpha Elaw, an American Female of Colour: Together with Some Account of the Great Religious Revivals in America [Written By Herself].* London: Published by the authoress, 1846. Reprinted in *Sisters of the Spirit: Three Black Women's Autobiographies of the Nineteenth Century,* edited by William L. Andrews, 49–160. Bloomington: Indiana University Press, 1986.

Elliott, Neil. *The Arrogance of Nations: Reading Romans in the Shadow of Empire.* Minneapolis: Fortress, 2008.

Erdoes, Richard, and Alfonso Ortiz. *American Indian Myths and Legends.* New York: Pantheon, 1984.

Esler, Philip. *Conflict and Identity in Romans: The Social Setting of Paul's Letter.* Minneapolis: Fortress, 2003.

Felder, Cain Hope, ed. *Stony the Road We Trod: African American Biblical Interpretation.* 30th anniversary expanded ed. Minneapolis: Fortress, 2021.

Ferris, Yeoun Sook. "An Examination of Some Themes in the Confucian Classics with Respect to Missiological Implications for the Issue of Ancestral Rites." PhD diss., Trinity International University, 1998.

Fiedler, P. "*Asebēs, ktl.*" *Exegetical Dictionary of the New Testament,* vol. 1, edited by H. Balz and G. Schneider, 168–69. Grand Rapids: Eerdmans, 1990.

Fiorenza, Elisabeth Schüssler. "Paul and the Politics of Interpretation." In *Paul and Politics: Ekklesia, Israel, Imperium, Interpretation,* edited by Richard Horsley, 40–57. Harrisburg, PA: Trinity, 2000.

Fitzmyer, Joseph. *Romans: A New Translation with Introduction and Commentary.* Anchor Bible. New York: Doubleday, 1993.

Foerster, W. "*Asebēs, ktl.*" *Theological Dictionary of the New Testament,* vol. 7, edited by G. Kittel, 185–91. Grand Rapids: Eerdmans, 1964.

Fredriksen, Paula. "Why Should a 'Law-Free' Mission Mean a 'Law-Free' Apostle?" *Journal of Biblical Literature* 134 (2015) 637–50.

Frei, Hans W. *The Eclipse of Biblical Narrative: A Study in Eighteenth and Nineteenth Century Hermeneutics.* New Haven: Yale University Press, 1974.

Gaventa, Beverly Roberts. *Our Mother Saint Paul.* Louisville: Westminster John Knox, 2007.

———. "Reading for the Subject: The Paradox of Power in Romans 14:1–15:6." *Journal of Theological Interpretation* 5 (2011) 1–12.

———. *When in Romans: An Invitation to Linger with the Gospel according to Paul.* Grand Rapids: Baker Academic, 2016.

Gench, Frances Taylor. *Encountering God in Tyrannical Texts: Reflections on Paul, Women, and the Authority of Scripture.* Louisville: Westminster John Knox, 2015.

Gennep, Arnold van. *The Rites of Passage.* 2nd ed. Chicago: University of Chicago Press, 2019.

Georgi, Dieter. *Theocracy in Paul's Praxis and Theology.* Minneapolis: Fortress, 1991.

González, Justo L. *Santa Biblia: The Bible through Hispanic Eyes.* Nashville: Abingdon, 1996.

González, Justo L., and Pablo A. Jiménez, eds. *Púlpito: An Introduction to Hispanic Preaching.* Nashville: Abingdon, 2005.

Grabbe, Lester L. *An Introduction to Second Temple Judaism: History and Religion of the Jews in the Time of Nehemiah, the Maccabees, Hillel, and Jesus.* London: T & T Clark, 2010.

Griffin, Paul. "CDP Carbon Majors Report 2017." cdp.net. https://www.cdp.net/en/articles/media/new-report-shows-just-100-companies-are-source-of-over-70-of-emissions.

Haynes, Lemuel. "Liberty Further Extended: Or Free Thoughts on the Illegality of Slave-keeping; Wherein Those Arguments That Are Useed in its Vindication Are Plainly Confuted. Together with an Humble Address to Such as Are Concearned in the Practice." In *Black Preacher to White America: The Collected Writings of Lemuel Haynes, 1774-1833,* edited by Richard Newman, 17–30. Brooklyn: Carlson, 1990.

Hays, Richard. "'Have We Found Abraham to Be Our Forefather according to the Flesh?' A Reconsideration of Rom. 4:1." *Novum Testamentum* 27 (1995) 76–98.

Hidalgo, Jacqueline M. *Latina/o/x Studies and Biblical Studies.* Brill Research Perspectives in Biblical Interpretation. Leiden: Brill, 2018.

Hoklotubbe, Chris. "A Native American Interpretation of Romans 8:18–23." *Oxford Biblical Studies Online,* edited by Michael Coogan. www.oxfordbiblicalstudies.com.

———. "Native American Interpretation of the Bible." *Oxford Biblical Studies Online,* edited by Michael Coogan. www.oxfordreference.com.

Hutton, Eric L., trans. *Xunzi: The Complete Text.* Princeton: Princeton University Press, 2014.

Irenaeus, Saint, Bishop of Lyona. *On the Apostolic Preaching.* Popular Patristics Series 17. Edited and translated by John Behr. Crestwood, NY: St Vladimir's Seminary Press, 1997.

Irfan, Umair, Eliza Barclay, and Kavya Sukumar. "Weather 2050." Vox.com. https://www.vox.com/a/weather-climate-change-us-cities-global-warming.

Isasi-Díaz, Ada María. *Mujerista Theology: A Theology for the Twenty-First Century.* Maryknoll, NY: Orbis, 1996.

Ivanhoe, P. J. "Filial Piety as a Virtue." In *Working Virtue: Virtue Ethics and Contemporary Moral Problems,* edited by Rebecca L. Walker and P. J. Ivanhoe, 297–312. Oxford: Clarendon, 2007.

Jefferson, Thomas. *Notes on the State of Virginia.* Philadelphia: Pritchard & Hall, 1787.

Jewett, Robert. *Romans: A Commentary.* Hermeneia. Minneapolis: Fortress, 2007.

Johnson Hodge, Caroline. *If Sons, Then Heirs: A Study of Kinship and Ethnicity in the Letters of Paul.* Oxford: Oxford University Press, 2007.

Josephus. *Josephus.* Translated by H. St. J. Thackeray, R. Marcus, and L. H. Feldman. Loeb Classical Library. Cambridge: Harvard University Press, 1956–1965.

Kahl, Brigitte. *Galatians Re-Imagined: Reading with the Eyes of the Vanquished.* Minneapolis: Fortress, 2010.

Kim, Kihoon. "*Pietas* in *pro Sexto Roscio* of Cicero and Confucian 孝 (*Xiao*)." In *Confucius and Cicero: Old Ideas for a New World, New Ideas for an Old World,* edited by Jaewon Ahn and Andrea Balbo, 155–69. Berlin: de Gruyter, 2020.

King, Martin Luther, Jr. *Strength to Love.* Minneapolis: Fortress, 2010.

Knapp, Keith N. "The *Ru* Reinterpretation of *Xiao*." *Early China* 20 (1995) 195–222.

Koperski, Veronica. "Women in Romans: Text in Context." In *The Letter to the Romans,* edited by Udo Schnelle, 441–51. Leuven: Peeters, 2009.

Lampe, Peter. *From Paul to Valentinus: Christians at Rome in the First Two Centuries.* Translated by M. Steinhauser. Minneapolis: Fortress, 2003.

Legge, James, trans. *The Chinese Classics.* 5 vols. Oxford: Clarendon, 1893.

———. *Li Ki,* vol. 27–28 of *The Sacred Books of the East.* Oxford: Clarendon, 1885.

Levenson, Jon D. *Inheriting Abraham: The Legacy of the Patriarch in Judaism, Christianity, and Islam.* Princeton: Princeton University Press, 2012.

Li, Chenyang. "Shifting Perspectives: Filial Morality Revisited." *Philosophy East and West* 47.2 (1997) 211–32.

Lindbeck, George A. *The Nature of Doctrine: Religion and Theology in a Post-Liberal Age.* Philadelphia: Westminster, 1984.

Liu, Qingping. "On Confucius' Principle of Consanguineous Affection: A Reading of the Dialogue about the Three-Year Mourning in the *Lunyu*." *Asian Philosophy* 16.3 (2006) 173–88.

Lozada, Francisco, Jr. *Toward a Latino/a Biblical Interpretation.* Atlanta: SBL, 2017.

Lozada, Francisco, Jr., and Fernando F. Segovia, eds. *Latino/a Theology and the Bible: Ethnic-Racial Reflections on Interpretation.* Lanham, MD: Lexington, 2021.

MacDonald, Mark. "Reclaiming Our Culture." Private video, 2021.

MacLam, Helen. "Introduction: Black Puritan on the Northern Frontier; The Vermont Ministry of Lemuel Haynes." In *Black Preacher to White America: The Collected Writings of Lemuel Haynes, 1774–1833,* edited by Richard Newman, xix–xxxviii. Brooklyn: Carlson, 1990.

Martin, Dale. "Social-Scientific Criticism." In *To Each Its Own Meaning: Biblical Criticisms and Their Application,* edited by Steven McKenzie and Stephen Haynes, 125–41. Louisville: Westminster John Knox, 1993.

Maté, Gabor. *In the Realm of Hungry Ghosts : Close Encounters with Addiction.* Berkeley: North Atlantic, 2010.

Mathew, Susan. *Women in the Greetings of Romans 16.1–16: A Study of Mutuality and Women's Ministry in the Letter to the Romans.* LNTS 471. London: Bloomsbury, 2013.

McCaulley, Esau. *Reading While Black: African American Biblical Interpretation as an Exercise in Hope.* Downers Grove, IL: InterVarsity, 2020.

McGinn, Sheila. "Feminist Approaches to Paul's Letter to the Romans." In *Celebrating Romans: Template for Pauline Theology,* edited by Sheila McGinn, 165–76. Grand Rapids: Eerdmans, 2004.

McKnight, Scot, and Joseph B. Modica, eds. *Preaching Romans: Four Perspectives.* Grand Rapids: Eerdmans, 2019.

McLeod, Neal. *Cree Narrative Memory: From Treaties to Contemporary Times.* Saskatoon, SK: Purich, 2007.

Meeks, Wayne. "The Image of the Androgyne: Some Uses of a Symbol in Earliest Christianity." *History of Religions* 13 (1973–74) 165–208.

Milken Institute of Public Health, George Washington University. *Project Report: Ascertainment of the Estimated Excess Mortality from Hurricane María in Puerto Rico in Collaboration with the University of Puerto Rico Graduate School of Public Health.* https://publichealth.gwu.edu/sites/default/files/downloads/projects/PRstudy/Acertainment%20of%20the%20Estimated%20Excess%20Mortality%20from%20Hurricane%20Maria%20in%20Puerto%20Rico.pdf.

Miller, J. R. "Compact, Contract, Covenant: The Evolution of Indian Treaty-Making." In *New Histories for Old: Changing Perspectives on Canada's Native Pasts,* edited by Theodore Binnema and Susan Neylan, 66–91. Vancouver, BC: UBC Press, 2007.

Moo, Douglas J. *The Letter to the Romans.* 2nd ed. NICNT. Grand Rapids: Eerdmans, 2018.

Morris, Alexander. *The Treaties of Canada with the Indians of Manitoba and the North-West Territories : Including the Negotiations on Which They Were Based, and Other Information Relating Thereto.* Toronto: Belfords, Clarke, 1880.

Mwaura, Philomena Njeri. "Feminist Biblical Interpretation and the Hermeneutics of Liberation: An African Woman's Perspective." In *Feminist Interpretation of the Bible and the Hermeneutics of Liberation,* edited by Silvia Schroer and Sophia Bietenhard, 77–85. Sheffield: Sheffield Academic, 2003.

Nanos, Mark D. *The Mystery of Romans: The Jewish Context of Paul's Letter.* Minneapolis: Fortress, 1996.

———. "Paul's Non-Jews Do Not Become 'Jews,' But Do They Become 'Jewish'?: Reading Romans 2:25–29 within Judaism, Alongside Josephus." *JJMJS* 1 (2014) 26–53.

———. *Reading Paul within Judaism: Collected Essays of Mark D. Nanos, Vol. 1.* Eugene, OR: Wipf & Stock, 2017.

———. "Romans 11 and Christian-Jewish Relations: Exegetical Options for Revisiting the Translation and Interpretation of This Central Text." *CTR* 9.2 (Spring 2012) 2–6.

Nanos, Mark D., and Magnus Zetterholm, eds. *Paul within Judaism: Restoring the First-Century Context of the Apostle.* Minneapolis: Fortress, 2015.

Newbigin, Lesslie. *The Gospel in a Pluralistic Society.* London: SPCK, 1989.

Noe-Bustamante, Luis, et al. "U.S. Hispanic Population Surpassed 60 Million in 2019, but Growth Has Slowed." *Pew Research Center,* July 10, 2020. pewrsr.ch/300Rezf.

O'Dwyer, Shaun. *Confucianism's Prospects: A Reassessment.* Albany, NY: SUNY Press, 2019.

Okim*asis, Jean L., Solomon Ratt, and University of Regina. *Cree, Language of the Plains = N*Ehiyaw*Ewin, Paskw*Awi-P*Ikiskw*Ewin.* University of Regina Publications 4. Regina: Canadian Plains Research Center, University of Regina, 1999.

Ottmann, Jacqueline. "First Nations Leadership and Spirituality within the Royal Commission on Aboriginal Peoples: A Saskatchewan Perspective." Master of Education Masters, University of Saskatchewan, 2002.

Philo. *Philo.* Translated by F. H. Colson et al. Loeb Classical Library. Cambridge: Harvard University Press, 1929–1953.

Pierce, Yolanda. *Hell without Fires: Slavery, Christianity, and the Antebellum Spiritual Narrative.* Gainesville, FL: University Press of Florida, 2005.

Polaski, Sandra Hack. *A Feminist Introduction to Paul.* St. Louis: Chalice, 2005.

Powery, Emerson. "African American Criticism." *Hearing the New Testament: Strategies for Interpretation,* edited by Joel Green, 326–49. Grand Rapids: Eerdmans, 2010.

Powery, Emerson, and Rodney Sadler. *The Genesis of Liberation: Biblical Interpretation in the Antebellum Narratives of the Enslaved.* Louisville: Westminster John Knox, 2016.

Priest, Josiah. *Slavery as It Relates to the Negro or African Race.* Albany, NY: C. Van Benthuysen & Co., 1843.

"Reconciliation as the Mission of God: Faithful Christian Witness in a World of Destructive Conflicts and Divisions." Lausanne Occasional Paper No. 51, produced by the Issue Group on this topic at the 2004 Forum for World Evangelization hosted by the Lausanne Committee for World Evangelization, Pattaya, Thailand, September 29–October 5, 2004. https://lausanne.org/wp-content/uploads/2007/06/LOP51_IG22.pdf.

Rehman, Luzia Sutter. "To Turn the Groaning into Labor: Romans 8.22–23." In *A Feminist Companion to Paul,* edited by Amy-Jill Levine, 74–84. Cleveland, OH: Pilgrim, 2004.

Ricoeur, Paul. *Time and Narrative.* Vol. 1. Chicago: University of Chicago Press, 1984.

———. "Rhetoric—Poetics—Hermeneutics." In *Rhetoric and Hermeneutics in Our Time,* translated by Joel Weinsheimer and edited by Walter Jost and Michael J. Hyde, 60–72. New Haven: Yale University Press, 1997.

Rodriguez, Rafael. *If You Call Yourself a Jew: Reappraising Paul's Letter to the Romans.* Eugene, OR: Wipf & Stock, 2014.

Roetz, Heiner. *Confucian Ethics of the Axial Age: A Reconstruction Under the Aspect of the Breakthrough Toward Postconventional Thinking.* Albany, NY: SUNY Press, 1993.

Rosemont, Henry, Jr., and Roger T. Ames, trans. *The Chinese Classic of Family Reverence: A Philosophical Translation of the Xiaojing.* Honolulu: University of Hawaii Press, 2009.

Rudolph, David. "To the Jew First: Paul's Vision for the Priority of Israel in the Life of the Church." *Kesher: A Journal of Messianic Judaism* 37 (2020) 11–25.

Ruether, Rosemary Radford. *Sexism and God Talk: Towards a Feminist Theology.* London: SCM, 1983.

Saillant, John. "Origins of African American Biblical Hermeneutics in Eighteenth-Century Black Opposition to the Slave Trade and Slavery." In *African Americans and the Bible: Sacred Texts and Social Textures,* edited by Vincent Wimbush, 236–50. New York: Continuum, 2000.

Sallust. *Sallust.* Translated by J. C. Rolfe. Loeb Classical Library. Cambridge: Harvard University Press, 1921.

Sanders, E. P. *Paul and Palestinian Judaism: A Comparison of Patterns of Religion.* Minneapolis: Fortress, 1977.

Schottroff, Luise. *Let the Oppressed Go Free: Feminist Perspectives on the New Testament.* Louisville: Westminster John Knox, 1993.

Schroer, Silvia. "'We Will Know Each Other by Our Fruits': Feminist Exegesis and the Hermeneutics of Liberation." In *Feminist Interpretation of the Bible and the Hermeneutics of Liberation,* edited by Silvia Schroer and Sophia Bietenhard, 1–17. Sheffield: Sheffield Academic, 2003.

Segovia, Fernando F. *Decolonizing Biblical Studies: A View from the Margins.* Maryknoll, NY: Orbis, 2000.

Sengupta, Somini. "This Is Inequity at the Boiling Point." *The New York Times,* August 6, 2020. https://www.nytimes.com/interactive/2020/08/06/climate/climate-change-inequality-heat.html?campaign_id=9.

Seok, Bongrae. *Embodied Moral Psychology and Confucian Philosophy.* Lanham, MD: Rowman & Littlefield, 2013.

Slingerland, Edward G., trans. *Confucius Analects: With Selection from Traditional Commentaries.* Indianapolis: Hackett, 2003.

Smith, Mitzi. "'Unbossed and Unbought': Zilpha Elaw and Old Elizabeth and a Political Discourse of Origins." *Black Theology: An International Journal* 9.3 (2011) 287–311.

Soulen, R. Kendall. *The God of Israel and Christian Theology.* Minneapolis: Fortress, 1998.

———. "Supersessionism." In *Dictionary of Jewish-Christian Relations,* edited by Edward Kessler and Neil Wenborn, 350–51. Cambridge: Cambridge University Press, 2008.

Steinmüller, Hans. "'Father Mao' and the Country-Family: Mixed Feelings for Fathers, Officials, and Leaders in China." *Social Analysis* 59.4 (2015) 83–100.

Stendahl, Krister. "The Apostle Paul and the Introspective Conscience of the West." *Harvard Theological Review* 76 (1963).

Stobaeus. *Anthologium.* 5 vols. Edited by Curt Wachsmuth and Otto Hense. Berlin: Weidmann, 1884–1912.

Stowers, Stanley. *A Rereading of Romans: Justice, Jews, and Gentiles.* New Haven: Yale University Press, 1994.

Szakolczai, Arpad. "Liminality and Experience: Structuring Transitory Situations and Transformative Events." *International Political Anthropology* 2.1 (2009) 141–72.

———. *Reflexive Historical Sociology.* London: Routledge, 2000.

Tamez, Elsa. *The Amnesty of Grace: Justification by Faith from a Latin American Perspective.* Translated by Sharon H. Ringe. Eugene, OR: Wipf and Stock, 1991.

Thimmes, Pamela. "'She Will Be Called an Adulteress . . .': Marriage and Adultery Analogies in Romans 7:1–4." In *Celebrating Romans: Template for Pauline Theology,* edited by Sheila McGinn, 190–203. Grand Rapids: Eerdmans, 2004.

Thomassen, Bjørn. "Thinking with Liminality: To the Boundaries of an Anthropological Concept." In *Breaking Boundaries: Varieties of Liminality,* edited by A. Horvath, B. Thomassen, and H. Wydra, 39–58. New York: Berghahn, 2018.

Thorsteinsson, Runar M. *Paul's Interlocutor in Romans 2: Function and Identity in the Context of Ancient Epistolography.* Stockholm, Sweden: Almqvist & Wiksell International, 2003.

Tinker, George E. "Tink." "Christology: Who Do You Say That I Am?" In *A Native American Theology,* edited by Clara Sue Kidwell, Homer Noley, and George E. "Tink" Tinker, 62–84. Maryknoll, NY: Orbis, 2001.

Tozer, A. W. *That Incredible Christian.* Carol Stream, IL: Tyndale, 1977.

Trible, Phyllis. "Feminist Hermeneutics and Biblical Studies." *Christian Century* 99.4 (February 1982) 116–18.

Tu, Wei-Ming. "Probing the 'Three Bonds' and 'Five Relationships' in Confucian Humanism." In *Confucianism and the Family*, edited by Walter H. Slote and George A. De Vos, 121–36. Albany, NY: SUNY Press, 1998.

Tucker, J. Brian. *Reading Romans after Supersessionism: The Continuation of a Jewish Communal Identity.* Eugene, OR: Cascade, 2018.

Turner, Victor. "Betwixt and Between: The Liminal Period in *Rites de Passage.*" In *The Forest of Symbols.* New York: Cornell University Press, 1967.

———. *Process, Performance and Pilgrimage: A Study in Comparative Symbology.* Ranchi Anthropology Series 1. New Delhi: Concept, 1979.

United States Census Bureau. "65 And Older Population Grows Rapidly as Baby Boomers Age." June 25, 2020. www.census.gov/newsroom/press-releases/2020/65-older-population-grows.html.

———. QuickFacts chart. https://www.census.gov/quickfacts/PR.

United States EPA. "What Climate Changes Means for Iowa." https://19january2017snapshot.epa.gov/sites/production/files/2016-19/documents/climate-change-ia.pdf.

Valentín, Benjamín. *Mapping Public Theology: Beyond Culture, Identity, and Difference.* Harrisburg, PA: Trinity, 2002.

Van Norden, Bryan W., trans. *Mengzi: With Selections from Traditional Commentaries.* Indianapolis: Hackett, 2008.

Vollmer, Thomas. "A Theocentric Reading of Romans 8, 18–30." In *The Letter to the Romans,* edited by Udo Schnelle. Leuven: Peeters, 2009.

Wan, Sze-kar. "Asian American Method." In *Paul and Critical Approaches,* edited by J. Marchal, 175–90. Minneapolis: Fortress, 2012.

———. *Romans: Empire and Resistance.* New Testament Guide. London: T & T Clark, 2021.

———. "'To the Jew First and also to the Greek': Reading Romans as Ethnic Construction." In *Prejudice and Christian Beginnings: Investigating Race, Gender, and Ethnicity in Early Christianity,* edited by E. Schüssler Fiorenza and L. Nasrallah, 139–41. Minneapolis: Augsburg/Fortress, 2009.

———. "Wrestling with the 'Body of Christ' in an Age of Tribalism: Towards an Asian American Hermeneutics of Dissent." *The Bible and Critical Theory* 16:1 (2020) 92–116.

Waugh, Earle H., and Wayne Chief Roan. "On Concepts and 'the Best Place:': Comparative First Nations, Chinese and Western Traditions on Comprehending Reality." *Religious Studies and Theology* 25.1 (2006) 7–36.

Weems, Renita J. *Just a Sister Away: A Womanist Vision of Women's Relationships in the Bible.* San Diego: LuraMedia, 1988.

Westfall, Cynthia Long. *Paul and Gender: Reclaiming the Apostle's Vision for Men and Women in Christ.* Grand Rapids: Baker, 2016.

Wesley, John. *The Works of John Wesley Volume 1: Sermons I (1–33).* Nashville: Abingdon, 1984.

Wiefel, Wolfgang. "Jewish Community in Ancient Rome and the Origins of Roman Christianity." In *The Romans Debate,* edited by K. P. Donfried, 85–101. Rev. and expanded ed. Peabody, MA: Hendrickson, 1991.

Woodley, Randy S. *Shalom and the Community of Creation: An Indigenous Vision.* Grand Rapids: Eerdmans, 2012.

Wright, N. T. "The Letter to the Romans," in *New Interpreter's Bible.* Nashville: Abingdon, 1994.

———. *Paul and the Faithfulness of God: Book I Parts I and II.* Minneapolis: Fortress, 2013.

Yao, Xinzhong. *An Introduction to Confucianism.* New York: Cambridge University Press, 2000.

Yee, Gale. "'She Stood in Tears Amid the Alien Corn': Ruth, the Perpetual Foreigner and Model Minority." In *They Were All Together in One Place? Toward Minority Biblical Criticism,* edited by R. C. Bailey, T.-s. Benny Liew, and F. Segovia, 119–40. Semeia Studies 57. Atlanta: Society of Biblical Literature, 2009.

Yin, Lee Cheuk. "Emperor Chengzu and Imperial Filial Piety." In *Filial Piety in Chinese Thought and History,* edited by Alan K. L. Chan and Sor-hoon Tan, 141–53. London: Routledge Curzon, 2004.

Subject Index

Abraham, God's covenant with, 58–60, 128n12

Acts, book of, Paul's life story in, 86

Adam, 161–62, 164

Aeneid (Virgil), 50

African American Readings of Paul (Bowens), 117

African Americans. *See also* Black/ Brown communities; racism

    anti-Black ideologies, 38

    the Black church, 66

    centrality of Scripture to, 26

    diversity of scriptural interpretations, 37n36

    ongoing victimization and enslavement, 21–25, 28, 33

    Pentecostal church, 40

    trauma experienced by, 36, 38, 45–47

Agosto, Efrain, 20–25

Agosto, Joel, 23

Aldred, Catherine, 78–79

Aldred, Raymond C., xiv

ancestor worship, 155–56

androcentrism, 102, 171–72

Anishinabek and Cree people, 81

apocalypticism, xvi, 57, 108n18, 130–31, 139

Aquila (ministry partner), 33, 98

Arirang (Korean folk song), 174–75

Aristotle, 109

Asian American Christians

    countering racialized status quo, 69, 74

    and the model minority trope, 68

    parallels to Gentile converts in Romans, 48–49, 63

    permanent liminality of, 49, 61

    role in promoting Christian unity, 65, 67

Asian Americans

    complex ethnic categories within, 67

    discrimination against, 48–49, 49n3, 67

    expectations and stereotypes, 67–68, 72

    identity of, and understanding the past, 72–74

    responses to oppression, 61

atheos, Paul's usage of, 61, 61n36

Augustine, 75

Augustus, 105n12

baptism, 20, 23, 25, 55, 57, 57n21, 115

Barth, Karl, 25

Baxoje and Meskwaki nations, 91–92

Being Black in America (NPR), 46

Bertone, John, 110

the Bible. *See also* Hebrew Scripture; New Testament; Paul;, Romans, epistle to the, *and citations in the Scripture Index*

    androcentrism in, 102

    birthing imagery in, 110

    an evangelical focus on sin, 86

    reading from diverse perspectives, xiv–xv, 77–78, 147

    reclaiming the voices of women in, 102–3, 109n19

Scripture Index

Printed in Great Britain
by Amazon